MAKING
OUR LIVES
OUR OWN

By the Same Author

Facing Shame: Families in Recovery (with Merle Fossum)

MAKING
OUR LIVES
OUR OWN

*A Woman's Guide
to the Six Challenges
of Personal Change*

Marilyn J. Mason

HarperSanFrancisco
A Division of HarperCollins*Publishers*

FIRST EDITION

Library of Congress Cataloging-in-Publication Data ·

Mason, Marilyn J.
    Making our lives our own : a woman's guide to the six challenges
of personal change / Marilyn J. Mason. — 1st ed.
      p.   cm.
    Includes bibliographical references and index.
    ISBN 0-06-250592-0 (alk. paper)
    1. Women — Psychology.   2. Life change events.   I. Title.
  HQ1206.M3457   1991
305.42 — dc20   90-55297
                                                  CIP

91 92 93 94 95 HAD 10 9 8 7 6 5 4 3 2 1

This edition is printed on acid-free paper that meets the American National Standards Institute Z39.48 Standard.

To my grandmother, mother, daughter, and sisters—
and to all my other teachers along the path
who have challenged and told.

I'm ceded—I've stopped being Theirs—
The name They dropped upon my face
With water, in the country church
Is finished using, now,
And They can put it with my Dolls,
My childhood, and the string of spools,
I've finished threading—too—

Baptized, before, without the choice,
But this time, consciously, of Grace—
Unto supremest name—
Called to my Full—The Crescent dropped—
Existence's whole Arc, filled up.
With one small Diadem.

My second Rank—too small the first—
Crowned—Crowing—on my Father's breast—
A half unconscious Queen—
But this time—Adequate—Erect,
With Will to choose, or to reject,
And I choose, just a Crown—

EMILY DICKINSON
"I'm Ceded—I've Stopped Being Theirs"

CONTENTS

ACKNOWLEDGMENTS

I have felt privileged to write this book; this work is filled with so much from so many, it is impossible to acknowledge all the contributions.

I especially appreciate the friendship of my feminist colleagues: Constance Ahrons read and gave me honest feedback and Rachel Hare-Mustin challenged my ideas, continuing to push my thinking. Marianne Walters has been supportive throughout.

The support of my friendship family has been constant. I am grateful for all the conversations and explorations and listening with Connie Hilliard, Iris Butler, Norma Rowe, Sally and Jack Flax, Ethelyn and Howard Cohen, Pauline Boss, and Eleftherios and Jane Papageorgiou. My special thanks to Connie Hilliard who, with friends Craig and Jane Nakken provided a rich ritual in the memorable book-naming gathering. Norma Rowe and Ethelyn Cohen supported me by reading those first chapters and staying with me along the way.

I thank my work family at Family Therapy Institute in St. Paul, Minnesota, who were so enthusiastic; their flexibility and generosity made it possible for me to take the necessary time to write.

I thank women of another generation—Muriel Whitaker, who co-led the first "Becoming Women" group with me, and my mentor and philosopher friend Jacqueline Van de Putte, who was with me as a woman who made her life her own. Her voice echoes vividly through several stories even though she died seven years ago.

Special support came from family. My daughter, Jeanine, was with me throughout, trying on ideas, giving feedback, and always listening. To my son Jerry, and daughter-in-law Lorrie, I am grateful for enthusiastic support. My sisters, brothers, and their spouses have always believed in me. I am grateful for my mother's active voice, especially when she said, "That will not do!" Her spirit, as well as my father's, is in this. My sister Sue not only shared sisterhood with me and our sister Phyllis; with our thirteen-month age difference, our relationship was my first true peer relationship. From her I learned about the mutuality and loving support of true sisterhood.

Thanks to Rene Schwartz, who once again gave invaluable, insightful feedback on early chapters of the book. I am grateful to Dick Leider who was especially helpful with the chapter on spirituality; he truly knows about dialogue.

I am still impressed with Kathleen Michels, who read the earlier chapters of the book. Her editing craft is so well honed that, when added to her wisdom and sense of humor, it made getting feedback a rich and deepening experience. I appreciate her sensitive yet direct criticism, her constancy and competency.

I am indebted to Marilyn Peterson who supported the work since its inception and read each chapter, often more than once. I am deeply grateful for the exquisite, careful reading as well as the time to share stories that the writing process awakened. She was masterful in balancing friendship and honest criticism, a unique challenge.

Pat Benson not only encouraged me at the beginning, but gave me the fine epigraph poem of Emily Dickinson and led me to Tom Grady at HarperSanFrancisco. I understand it is not tasteful to gush over editors. Tom Grady at Harper could not have been better at his job with his patience and his support. His strong feminist consciousness never faltered; I felt believed in. Barbara Moulton, Robin Seaman, and Kevin Bentley of HarperSanFrancisco have rounded out a fully supportive publishing group.

My deepest appreciation goes to my clients and workshop participants who, over these past eighteen years, allowed themselves to be known so that collectively we could share our knowing with other women. My gratitude runs deep.

INTRODUCTION

This book grew out of the experiences of women. It began with a question—a question asked so often in my office—"Why don't I feel grown up?" This and other honest questions naturally led to tentativeness, but it was the underlying theme that was disconcerting. Women put themselves down stating that if they were grown up, they *would* know and wouldn't have these questions. Obviously this very statement is frought with the assumption that there is some steady-state place we reach called "grown up" and that once a woman is "grown up" she will have all the answers. At that time I responded by affirming the cultural mythology of "separate but equal" spheres for men and women that resulted in a reality of inequality and oppression. I recognized I did not have any solid answers. Also, I learned that many of my clients' questions were my own questions. The fact that I was forty-one years old before I had my own bedroom but was in my seventh life-style (the first one I had freely chosen) confused me.

I read; I talked with friends and colleagues. I led women's groups focused on "Becoming Women." I read more; I dialogued more. I learned, as other women had, that there was no model of adult development for women. Like other women, I looked outside of myself for direction. I decided to pursue the question from the perspective of women's experiences. I developed a workshop in the early 1980s entitled "Making Our Lives Our Own" at the University of Minnesota Medical School and then offered it in the community. The audiences were women of all ages from late twenties to late seventies. They were educators, career women, mothers working at home and in community, psychologists, physicians, social workers, psychotherapists, family therapists, church leaders, community workers, and leaders of girls' organizations (such as the Girl Scouts).

The workshop theme was an exploratory model of adult development for women— in answer to "What does it mean to be grown up?"

This question led me to the adult development literature. As had been true in the rest of psychology, adult development meant *male* development; the early research came from men's lives.[1] In fact, one of the statements I read about women's psychology said, ". . . children of both sexes sooner or later 'know' the penis to be missing in one sex, leaving in its place a woundlike aperture . . ."[2] Indeed, what has been missing has not been the penis, but the recognition of an honest reality that includes women!

I saw that the absence of gender was glaring in all the linear male-based models of development.[3] Other psychologists expanded on the writing of the "father of stage theory," Erik Erikson, describing adulthood as the development of self and work. Their writing made a strong statement about the value and place of women. In the focus on "self" and "work," "self" meant male self and "work" meant work outside the home. Women's "work" in the home had no place. In the life cycle material I found portrayals of men "distant" in relationships, in need of a "special woman" and without intimate friendships.[4] I wondered what their wives would have said had they been interviewed.

I saw repeatedly how the experience of women was described as the "struggle with separateness and individuation"—hence a failure to develop! We were taught that women were "dependent" and men "independent." Male identity was rooted in separation and work, leaving men distant from others. To be deemed "successful" a women had to become more like men. I could now see how women naturally felt deficient and naturally asked, "Why don't I feel grown up?"

Until the work of feminist scholars we were locked into the male experience of "separate," "autonomous," "self-reliant," and "individuated." Success was "paid for." Today we know that economic development does not equal human development. We have all seen that this sense of independence and self-reliance can be the ruination of our world when carried to extreme. It is also the trait that fosters competition, hyperindividualism, and aggressiveness. It has become the "god" of corporate America and has been widely linked to depression—especially when not accompanied by commitment to the common good.

Today we recognize that this model of adult development is riddled with misinformation and scientific inaccuracy. Erik Erikson asked an essential question in 1968: "Do we and can we really know what will happen to science or any other field if and when women are truly represented in it—not by a few glorious exceptions, but in the rank and file of the scientific elite?"[5] We are indeed learning what will happen when women are represented in the scientific elite. Because of the many women who have been widening the path to include the experiences of women, we now are moving toward a more honest mapping of growth in adulthood. I looked for what women had offered.

In reviewing the developing field of women's psychology, women's names surfaced. Bernice Neugarten at the University of Chicago had established the Chicago School of Human Development two decades ago, studying the psychology of adulthood. She stated that life events, not age, determine our grownupness, arguing for integrating the biological, psychological, and social perspectives of development.[6] We have known this intuitively but have heard little of it said aloud. And since her work was not popularized, it seemed to be whispered when compared to Erikson's and Levinson's.

I found another "missing person" in the life-stages literature, the almost unheard of Else Frenkel-Brunswik. After writing biographies of four hundred famous personalities she identified five clearly defined phases in the life cycle that people all move through. She wrote about the external events in their histories *as well as* their subjective experiences of them and published her stage theory in 1936 at the University of California, Berkeley.[7] This was thirteen years before Erikson published his stage theory.

In identifying those outstanding women who through the years have been shaping the evolving women's psychology, I saw that women turned to the lives of women for their knowledge. And in response to the argument about the "lack of empirical knowledge," they recognized that life experience *is* empirical knowledge. Simone de Beauvoir addressed the issue in describing the "second sex" back in 1953.[8] In the early days of the resurgence of feminism in the 1960s we heard Betty Friedan, Phyllis Chesler, Jessie Bernard, Nancy Chodorow, Kate Millett, and Carolyn Heilbrun. Then came Jean Baker Miller, Dorothy Dinnerstein, Robin Morgan, and Gloria Steinem. The list went on.

I saw different methodology and this methodology became my compass—it was going deep inside our own experiences. Writers Lillian Rubin and Maggie Scarf contributed greatly by translating the academic work for the public world of women through their books and magazine articles; *Ms.* magazine had arrived.[9]

And on the heels of these women came the feminist scholars from the field of psychotherapy and family therapy who added remarkable contributions. Rachel Hare-Mustin broke the silence in the family therapy field in 1978 when she presented a "feminist approach to family therapy."[10] Four women—Marianne Walters, Betty Carter, Peggy Papp, and Olga Silverstein—addressed the missing context of women in family therapy, formed the Women's Project in Family Therapy, and challenged us all theoretically and clinically.[11] Other women—Monica McGoldrick, Virginia Goldner, Deborah Luepnitz, and Harriet Goldhor Lerner—continued to focus on the previously invisible category of gender and the inequalities in therapy.

All of this work supported my going where I needed to be, deep within myself, trusting my own thoughts. Carol Gilligan's *In a Different Voice* presented a breakthrough in acknowledging the differences in how women make moral decisions. Gilligan examined Lawrence Kohlberg's pioneering study of moral development and saw that perhaps the main reason women appear to be so different (at "lower" stages of moral development according to Kohlberg) was because Kohlberg's research was based on eighty-four males! In her research, Gilligan found that women's way of making decisions is based on an ethic of caring about others rather than a sense of justice.[12] Again I noted, *of course* women ask the question, "Why don't I feel grown up?" This perspective contributed to our awareness of the complexity of women's development. The impact on me was profound.

I saw that other women were exploring women in relationships, expanding the theories of women's development, moving us away from deficiency models. The "self-in-relation" has been continued through the Stone Center at Wellesley with pioneering names of Jean Baker Miller, Nancy Goldberger, Janet Surrey, Judith Jordan, Alexandra Kaplan, Blythe Clinchy, and Irene Stiver, who explore the developing relational self. Through their research on empathy, connection, roles, mutuality, and mother-infant relationships, they are reframing many of our psychological terms and clinical approaches.[13] Rather than look at autonomy as a a marker for adulthood or "grownupness," we now look at attachment and care, similarities *and* differences leading to interdependence.

This has naturally led us to another confounding challenge today. How do we separate women's relational patterns from the cultural context of how women have survived? How do we acknowledge what is innate and what is learned coping behavior in a culture that oppresses women? There is no solid agreement today. Feminist theorist and clinician Rachel Hare-Mustin cautions us not to focus too intently on difference, often a mask for inequality, but to concentrate on similarities.[14] She states that we must be careful to recognize that our "pleasing" also comes out of subordination, of being "one down" in a white male system. We do recognize that any model of women's development is incomplete if it does not demand social change; the personal is political.[15] We can never be context free, but we can continue this as a live issue.

In looking at women's issues in therapy, I saw that abuse (emotional, physical, and sexual) of girls and women had also been ignored in women's psychology. I saw high percentages of women facing buried childhood shame and pain and living with childhood perceptions from growing up in alcoholic or otherwise dysfunctional families, perceptions that still ruled their adult relationships.[16] As more women sought psychological health, they joined together in supporting and empowering one another and gave birth to the fastest growing social movement in America today.[17] A spirituality-oriented program based on the Twelve Steps of Alcoholics Anonymous was the foundation for many groups. I think the success of a Twelve-Step program is so widespread because it is nonhierarchical, with mutual sharing and anonymity. I saw women find their voices and inner strength as they entered recovery programs, therapy, and other self-help groups.

Obviously I could not write this book without stepping on the minefield of my personal history; I found myself haunted by voices from the past during my writing. First, I had to overcome my mother's legacy of omitting the personal pronoun "I" in writing (we don't want to draw attention to ourselves) while simultaneously brushing aside the nagging male "voice" that demands the supremacy of facts over intuition. Both voices cast me outside myself continually; I had to keep returning to myself. I did not find my "voice" until Chapter 3; and then once having found it, I would continue to lose it repeatedly. The textbook language, academese, kept creeping in. I had to continually go to a deeper place.

We are in an evolutionary process, constantly turning the soil of women's adult growth. This is the time of turning concepts over, challenging meaning, context, and language. Women's spirituality books abound. We face challenging questions today about being women. But today we are probing the questions as *women* studying the lives of women *from* the experiences of women.

I recognize that the women's stories here do not reflect the cultural diversity of race and class issues that so deeply affect women's lives. I do believe, though, that the challenges here are the challenges facing all women in our country. The stories themselves, with few exceptions, are composites, heavily disguised for the protection of the women they belong to.

This book is a synthesis of women's psychology, sociology, feminist theory, adult development, and above all women's experiences. Most of the ideas here are not new, but they do represent women's psychological and social changes. This work is not definitive. The challenge to me in writing this book and the challenge to readers is to make known our deep "invisible" that we share in a world that still tries to keep us down. I take responsibility for what appears here in this step toward "making our lives our own."

CHAPTER 1

I'M AN ADULT WOMAN:
Why Don't I Feel Grown Up?

One is not born a woman; one becomes one.
SIMONE DE BEAUVOIR

*It always comes back to the same necessity: go deep
enough and there is a bedrock of truth, however hard.*
MAY SARTON

Feeling confused, Jean entered therapy saying, "I am living a life of contradictions." After a twenty-year marriage, she was divorced and, at age forty-two, felt that her whole life, her identity, was invalid. She was living a single life-style while parenting three children. She was a high-school teacher and a student in a university graduate school program. She was reexperiencing dating and all of its adolescent feelings at the same time her children were starting to date. She was asking her gynecologist about birth control while focusing on her children's sex education. At times, she felt like an awkward girl of sixteen; at other times, she felt like a wise woman of eighty. "The inner and outer clearly do not match," she reported to me.

When I asked her what brought her to see me, she exclaimed through her tears, "I have already been through these stages! What am I doing here again?" She remarked that her sense of being a grown-up felt invalid. In reflecting on her early years, she commented, "You know, at that time I *did* feel that the decisions I made were solid, lifelong decisions." Indeed, she *had* felt grown up then—by her and others' definitions. She said she had done whatever was expected; she had even given up her full scholarship and left college to save money. After all, her husband needed the education; she didn't. She recalled making homemaking a challenge and meeting her esteem needs through decorating, cooking, and involvement in community organizations. Jean had developed a self-image that pleased others; by their standards, she had "done it right." Outwardly successful, she had a wilderness within.

Until the time of her divorce, Jean did not realize that she had joined the great majority of American women in defining her criteria for being a grown-up based on her roles in life rather than on the process of life as she lived it. She had conducted herself in ways that proved her loyalty to our society's expectations of woman as wife, woman as mother, and woman as lover. Now, looking back through her delusions, she realized that even though she certainly had *known* this, she now *felt* its repercussions and felt inadequate, shameful, and alone in her pain. She joined the choir of women's voices: "I'm not where I should be. I haven't done it right." Jean was surviving the shattering awakening of her role-wrapped "sleeping" self.

Most women do not stroll into maturity; like Jean, they are thrust toward it by a shattering, awakening crisis. What Jean has in common with thousands of other women is that she has experienced the sudden, unexpected, devastating consequences of an event that has the potential to become a turning point in her life, an opportunity for growth.

LIFE CRISES

We all know that life brings crisis. Each of us eventually learns that life is not fair and that we are often powerless over what it brings to us — the sudden loss of a job or income; physical, emotional, or sexual abuse; betrayal by a lover; chronic illness; physical disability; the untimely death of a loved one; the awareness of an addiction in the family (ours or another's); the death of a relationship; our parents' traumatic divorce. The list is endless. Many women learn to live with each crisis that comes along, run right over it and on to the next one, filled with anxieties and stress. In our culture women have often been trained or socialized to feel responsible or even guilty for everything that happens to them; the painful experiences of their lives start to feel "normal" and lose their ability to trigger a turning point. Often we have been stuck and didn't know it. Some crises take us to feeling like we're "coming unglued." "Coming unglued" to get unstuck is often through an awakening crisis.

THE AWAKENING CRISIS—THE WAKE-UP CALL

An awakening crisis signals a dramatic shift in consciousness with a definite turning point. This awakening can feel shattering, for it takes us to a different level of reality. Suddenly we find ourselves sitting in the ground glass of our delusions. This shattering triggers a total shift in our constructed reality—how we position ourselves in the world, how and what we perceive, and to whom and to what we listen. We have a different lens for viewing life. This is why so many refer to it as the "wake-up call."

The word "crisis" comes from a Greek word meaning the "turning point of a disease . . . vital or decisive stage."[1] The Chinese define "crisis" using two characters: *wei*, meaning "danger" (a face-to-face encounter with a powerful animal), and *chi*, meaning "opportunity" (the blueprint of the universe).[2] When we combine both East and West, we can see how crisis contributes to our "awakening" and is often seen as a "gift."

The "gift" in the crisis is the opportunity to awaken our feelings, clear the lens through which we see reality, and go deeper in our understanding of who we are. Wake-up calls often trigger past crises that have been buried deep within us, held in delusion, denial, or repression that insulated us for many years. Some are held subliminally, just below the level of consciousness; others are buried deep in a young girl's denial system, that ancient protector against overwhelming emotion and trauma. For many of us, there *had* been crises and upsets previously, but we ignored them or were protected from feeling them because we perhaps weren't ready. When we are ready to meet the crisis, we are ready to meet more of ourselves.

This is not to imply that we can face crises with blind excitement—"Oh, good, I wonder what the gift is!" A crisis can tear at our souls. We will feel betrayed; we will experience devastation and humility. We will learn about powerlessness. It isn't until the postcrisis period that we can acknowledge what we have learned about ourselves, about life. Life *does* intrude and, as author-analyst Florida Scott-Maxwell strongly states, "Life does not accommodate you, it shatters you. It is meant to, and it couldn't do it better."[3]

Whether the triggering event comes from the past or from the present, the crisis presents an opportunity for an integration of our historical "feeling self," an integration of the child we left behind, into the adult self. If we can work through this crisis "awake," our growth is enhanced, giving us better coping responses for future life events. If we do not allow ourselves to face our pain, we pass our buried feelings on to the next generation and guarantee the repetition of psychic numbing.

Often, this awakening crisis forces another crisis—a crisis of awareness. This crisis is not an event outside ourselves; it is an *internal* crisis—the crisis of feeling directionless.

When Jean was forced by her financial crisis to move out of her suburban home into the inner city, she certainly experienced the crisis of a major life change. She found herself in poverty. Jean also discovered that much of her belief and meaning system was built on loyalty to her family's rules, patterns, and values. In breaking through her denial and facing deep pain for the first time, she was able to see her part in her marriage and, more important, the fact that she was repeating her mother's and her aunt's marriages. Now she felt herself to be without a compass, to be separated from the body of meaning in which she had been anchored. She said she felt her identity waffling; nothing seemed to make sense anymore. In therapy, she took a leap of faith and broke her loyalty to her family by examining her family of origin, confronting some painful "facts," and allowing years of buried pain to come to the surface. "I feel lost," she exclaimed. "And not only do I not know who I am anymore; I don't know where I'm going."

WHY WE DON'T FEEL GROWN UP

Jean's story is the story of many women who, after experiencing a "wake-up call," feel lost, overwhelmed, and certainly not "grown up."

10

I am writing this book because I hope it can be a guide for the many women like Jean who have lived on "automatic pilot" through the years, feeling grown up on the outside, in their roles, and uncertain and self-doubting on the inside. Countless women report intense disappointment when their sense of *feeling* fully grown up does not accompany their thirtieth, fortieth, or fiftieth birthday.

We need to examine *why* we don't feel grown up—we need to look at the belief systems that are fed by social, political, historical, and psychological forces and that have kept us in this predicament, confounding and perplexing our adult developing process. We tell ourselves, "I don't feel grown up because . . ."

- "What right do I have? I'm just a woman" (the "women are less" syndrome).
- "I can't disagree with anyone; I might disappoint them" (the "good-girl" socialization).
- "At my age I should . . ." (the ageism bias).
- "Despite my efforts, my family has not changed" (the "adult child" syndrome).
- "I'm not where I should be in life" (the lack of model of women's adult growth).

We are stuck in the beliefs that keep us from feeling grown up because no one has ever laid out an adult model of women's growth based on women's lives; as women we *have never had* a map to guide our adult growing process. "You're never too old to grow up" says the adage. I explored a model that describes how women move through the adult growing process. I observed six challenges that women moved through in transforming their "awakening" changes into growth. Before we can continue with these specific challenges, we need to understand the root system.

THE ROOTS OF WOMEN'S BELIEF SYSTEMS

The "reasons" described above can be considered the five major roots that have inhibited our natural growth for generations. Four of these roots are not new and have been widely discussed; the fifth only recently came to light.

Root One:
The "Women-Are-Less-Than-Men" Syndrome

In our culture, women are the "second sex" economically, politically, educationally, socially, physically, and religiously.[4] All of us have been raised in a white, male system, with its obvious power imbalances, that devalues us.[5] Economically, our status remains the same as it was in the preindustrial age, where working in the home had no exchange value in the marketplace.[6] A working mother (i.e., a woman working outside the home) still faces an average of 35 hours a week of housework and has the least childcare help of any mothers in the world.[7] Politically, we have yet to see a Congress in which 50 percent of the representatives are women. Educationally, women have not been encouraged to seek higher levels of study and we remain a fraction of tenured faculty in university and college systems. Socially, women are still referred to as "girls," a constant reminder that we are viewed as childlike and immature. Physically, women have to "look up to" men in a culture where we have all learned that "bigger" is "better." Only in recent decades have women legitimately entered the sports world. In religious settings, women clearly play the subordinate role.

Learning and growing, we discovered that these truths were the product of a male-focused belief system by which women are socialized to accept and accommodate to a lesser role in a patriarchal society. Feeding this belief system are cultural myths that glorify our lesser role. Of course while we women are becoming more aware, we are continually amazed at the degree to which we unconsciously accept the dominant male beliefs about "women as less."

Connie wept as she recalled her mother's message to her: "I was happy the day you became a surgeon; I was happier the day you married one." Several women in the group gasped as they heard her story. We then talked about how much more deeply ingrained these messages are in our mothers than in us and how important it is not to "blame the victim" by "mother bashing." Still, uprooting our belief system will take time, unlearning, and reeducation for a shift in consciousness. Women, like their mothers before them, have long carried the strong beliefs of the culture. Elizabeth reminded me of her graduation party after earning her doctorate; she and her husband had both completed school together. Her mother thanked Elizabeth's husband for what he had done for her daughter and gave him a handsome briefcase. She gave her daughter a woman's handbag. All these sad examples clearly illustrate the messages that keep women from feeling grown up. Most women have been true to a belief system that perpetuates cultural myths in which women are "good" and "lovable" only if subordinate to men.

Root Two: Good-Girl Socialization

We have been socialized into the "good-girl syndrome," a natural outgrowth of the "women are less" syndrome; that is, we have learned to become what family therapists Claudia Bepko and Jo-Ann Krestan refer to as "too good for her own good."[8] "Good girls," socialized to take care of others and defer their needs, follow all the rules.

A few years ago a group of us gathered in a friend's home; we had been supporting one another in making serious life changes—going to work, divorcing, choosing new life-styles. Many times we had laughingly referred to the "good-girl syndrome" that frequently seemed to get in our way. Unknown to us, our host friend had purchased some large corduroy pillows from a local discount store. Stitched to each pillow was the ever-present tag that warned: "Do not remove . . . under penalty of law." The ritual began . . . Each of us broke our loyalty to our "good girl" by boldly tearing the tag off a pillow. Not one woman in this group of educators, psychologists, and administrators had ever torn a tag from a pillow, cushion, or mattress. Unaware that this message was intended for manufacturers and retailers, *not* consumers, we simply had done what we were told.

This ritual is a constant reminder to me of the multitudes of bright and capable women who are imprisoned by our socialization messages. Most of us carry indelible moments of knowing in our "awakening memoirs." The "high price of nice" is often not humorous, though.

A friend of mine, Iris, recently recounted a friend's statement, "She never gave her mother a difficult day in her whole life — and her mother has the *nerve* to brag about it!" Statements such as this reflect women's gradual changes.

Root Three: Rampant Ageism

I recall my confusion during an incident in a drugstore. Having recently returned from a backpack trip and feeling very "fit," I had stooped down to examine some boxes of notecards on the bottom shelf. Sitting there on my haunches, I heard a young clerk ask, "May I help you up?" For a moment I was stunned; I snapped, "You certainly may not!" Obviously, she was offering kindness to the gray-haired woman below her. Yet I felt a flush of indignation before I saw any humor in this no-win situation. I didn't like to hear "You don't look your age" comments any more than I liked being seen as a woman too old to take care of herself. How many women still feel flattered when told "Why, you certainly don't *look* your age!" On the one hand, it's a compliment. On the other hand, the statement reflects that looking good is looking younger. The implicit message is, "You look good because you don't *show* your aging." This message and others like it only add to women's self-doubt about their inside-outside conflict.

Women who link maturity with chronological age often get trapped here. Many middle-aged women say, "Of course, I want to *be* mature, but I want to *look* young." While entering a phase of life where they might fully enjoy some of the abundance they have created, they continue to strive for "youthfulness" at a time when their bodies show signs of age-related changes. Women spend many millions of dollars on cosmetics and beauty aids. Recognizing the value placed on youth in our culture, many women fear growing old. In time we do learn that we are "only young once but we can be immature forever"— that our maturity has nothing to do with our age in adulthood.

Women also face ageism in the work arena; many companies do not want to employ "older" women because they fear paying too much in health benefits. Still another aspect of ageism that powerfully affects women is the increasing number of ex-husbands who marry younger women and often start a second family. To face a life of near poverty *and* a life alone is rightly terrifying to the many women who were socialized into the ageist, "lesser-than" track.

One final aspect related to ageism is vivid in the "empty-nest syndrome." Research data as well as women's stories dispute the "womanhood equals motherhood" myth. Women typically report relief when children leave home.[9] The emptiness some often face stems from not being needed anymore when their entire life has been shaped toward that end and the recognition that there is a person inside the mother role who now has the time to do something for herself but does not know who that self is or what she wants.

Root Four:
The Historical Self or "Adult Child" Syndrome

This root came to me by surprise. A representative from a national magazine had called to schedule an interview with a couple in therapy and asked what "problem" to focus on. When I suggested an alcoholic marriage, the representative replied that the magazine had recently covered the subject and wanted something different. I searched through my client files and was shocked to learn that approximately 90 percent of my clients were working on problems resulting from growing up in addicted or emotionally dysfunctional families. By "emotionally dysfunctional" families I am referring to those families who experienced painful events or trauma in their history. In addition I include families with losses both natural or "unnatural." It is *not* the events themselves that create dysfunction—it is the decision to hide the truth in an attempt to "protect" the next generation from the pain.

In these families, parents have denied themselves and their children their natural feelings about the painful happening. Thus, children from these families often survive by shutting down their affect and denying their own shame, pain, hurt, loneliness, and fear.

Some adult children are the other extreme. As children they became emotional sponges and learned to express feelings for anyone close to them, especially those who were shut down. When adult women face their historical selves, they often use the term "adult child" to refer to the childhood history that was denied. They often return to childhood experiences to examine the internalized mental representations that became such an active part of their adult psychic life. Author Lillian Rubin writes, "The adult responds to the archaic memory of those early feelings even though they're very far from consciousness."[10]

The term "adult child" was coined by the ACoA (Adult Children of Alcoholics) movement, in which adults reared in alcoholic families come together to learn about what they missed developmentally while surviving in their emotional chaos. Others who grew up with similar family patterns, but without drugs or alcohol, found that the Twelve-Step group validated their realities and so attended ACoA meetings for support. Out of this phenomenon came the ACA (Adult Children Anonymous) movement for the millions from families damaged by mental illness, chronic illness, sexual abuse, or other painful events. ACA groups provide a place for mutual sharing; they are anonymous and nonhierarchical and thus offer a safe place for adult children to begin healing. Given the twenty-nine million Americans from alcoholic families plus the millions who grew up in other types of dysfunctional families, it is easy to see why ACoA plus ACA is the fastest-growing social movement in America today. At some level, we adult children know that we cannot heal alone. Based on the Twelve Steps of Alcoholics Anonymous, these two groups bring promise and hope to the many millions of adult children.

Recently I have found that many of the women who attend workshops on healing shame grew up in families where the source of the family pain was in their *grandparents'* families — in other words, many women are "adult children" of "adult children." This has made it confounding for those women who have looked back to their parents' families and searched in vain for some buried tragedies. A painful experience that is buried and becomes a block to grief is termed a "source experience."[11] Adult children find their own source experiences but also discover that they unconsciously inherited coping behaviors from their parents who had not faced their source experiences. As children, these women intuitively sensed their parents' buried childhood pain and unconsciously attended to their parents' neediness by taking responsibility to protect them from further pain. When this dimension is added to the already strong socialization messages for women to take care of others, it is not surprising how women have lived their lives to meet the needs of others.

As children, these women had to shut down to survive. In their attempt to cope, they learned to normalize clearly inappropriate patterns of behavior and, unaware, carried their denial into their adult relationships. What appeared to be their acceptance was really their denial. Realizing how being raised in these families affects growth and development, I knew that many of us had grown up with impaired models of "normal adulthood." Clinically I saw individuals and families who were arrested in their affective, or feeling, development and struggled with intimacy. I saw women who were struggling to know themselves turn to others to learn "how to be." Most had role models who were even more "stuck" than they were. Loyally passed down from one generation to the next, the pattern of dysfunction was the most powerful shaper of their learning. Compounding the impairment are the deeply embedded messages from churches, schools, and other institutions that women deserve to live with disrespect and shame. It is no wonder that the cognitive restructuring and emotional healing of the recovery process can take years for many women.

The term "codependent" originally grew out of the disease model of alcoholism; it referred to the coping behaviors of spouses or family members of an alcoholic or drug-dependent person. This early definition implied equality between males and females in keeping the symptoms alive and ignored the power differential inherent in gender. "Codependent" is now used to describe the adult child who learned to become overresponsible for the feelings and behaviors of others — to the exclusion of his or her own needs. Harriet Goldhor Lerner reminds us that "For women, being codependent means simply that we have learned what the culture has taught."[12] Family therapist and author Marianne Walters states that this can be just one more way to blame women for their caring.[13] It is important to be careful in our use of this word. We do not want to trivialize the painful experiences of those in addicted or severely impaired families; nor do we want to pathologize women in yet one more way.

Root Five: The Lack of a Model of Adult Growth for Women

As I have already stated, women have not had an honest model that illustrates how we grow up. Through the years we have accepted a single, linear model of adult growth based on models developed by men based on men's lives. The implication here is that by the time you are a certain age, you will be in a certain stage of your psychological growth with specific tasks to accomplish.[14]

The linear model did serve as a guide to corporate success, with men expected to have an established career by age thirty-five and to retire at age sixty-five. This model incorporated the view that we move through life in identifiable stages in which the timing of life events is predictable; thus, at any given age, a man supposedly *knows* where he should be. Unfortunately, this model not only ignores the life experiences of most women but also has not worked well for men.

So on this confounding note, I began to examine and demythify the foundation we had all accepted. While the linear model can be very true for a few people, life is not a straight line just because we move through it. No fixed-stage model or timing-of-events model can adequately describe the complexity of women's adult growth.[15] As psychologist Mary Baird Carlsen points out, adult development is a contradictory term.[16] "Adult" is a definition of one who is "fully grown and mature," implying a static state of being, while the word "development" implies an unfolding process. This paradox only adds to our confusion about what it means to feel grown up.

Another confusing factor is that most studies of human development are based on the notion that our growth is marked by how separate and "individuated" we can be. Until recently, these themes of separateness, stages, adult development, and male development have held fast in all major writing and teaching and in counseling programs about adult growth. The experience of women and our struggles with separateness and individuation are seen as a failure to develop! We are seen as deficient rather than acknowledged for our sense of connection, relatedness, and ability to see relationships in context. Women are devalued because of their differentness. To be deemed "successful" in our society, a woman has to become more like a man.

The addition of this fifth root to an already unnatural root system almost guarantees that our taproots are blocked from growing down into our depth. As we examine these five roots, we can understand Jean more clearly and why she felt so confused about where she was in life.

As she worked in therapy, Jean began to see that her story was a natural outgrowth of this root system. She had grown up quite unaware of the power imbalances imposed by the white male hierarchy and how it influenced her. In leaving her marriage, she realized that she had grown up in what today would be called an alcoholic family and had married into one. In her guilt, she had never considered the courage it took for her to leave a marriage of many years. She struggled with her issues — her fear of intimacy, her desire to please and be liked by everyone, her staying busy to avoid feeling. In addition to living with the "newness" of starting over, she lived with the anxiety of aging and its effects on relationships and employability. She said she felt lost at sea, like a small bobber floating about in big waves. She said to me, "I know there's a shore, but I don't know where it is." She knew at some level that she lacked a compass for her course. At some point in our sessions, Jean concluded that the decisions she had made long ago *had* been valid — but only in terms of a set of assumptions she later discovered were erroneous. Jean said she now knew that she had based her decisions on the prevailing cultural myths that mandated how women should "act" to be accepted. Added to this was her limited perspective, limited because a part of her had to shut down to survive the pain of living in her alcoholic and abusive family; she was now "growing up" this part of herself.

In a newspaper interview about being grown up, one eleven-year-old girl stated, "People become grown up when they stop liking people for their outsides and start liking them for their insides."[17] This simple but profound statement is the challenge. We each must start to know and accept ourselves in order to accept a woman-grounded model of growth. I believe women must go within *and* look to our own experiences. This dynamic, ongoing process is our natural compass. I told Jean that there can be creative growth from these changes, but first we had to examine a different foundation for women's growth—a foundation based on *women's* lives. I reminded Jean that when we have some guidelines to think differently about how we grow and mature, we can turn our life changes into creative, growth-enhancing challenges and experience feeling grown up. Jean agreed that she had become aware of many things through her crisis but knew that awareness is not enough. We both knew that women's ways of growing have been untold.

THE UNTOLD WAY:
THE "GROWN" WITHIN THE GROWN-UP

The way of women has always been *known*, but until recent decades, untold. The untold way within involves clarifying what women really mean by the word "grown-up" and then proceeding to create an honest model of women's growth based on women's lives.

The untold way is women's success in growing relationships—in living out our values of care and responsibility for relationships that are so natural to us. These achievements are often minimized by women as well as men because the power brokers in the patriarchal society do not value them.

I showed Jean four models I had developed. The first, Women's Life Circle, illustrates women's natural circle of growth; the second illustrates Women's Cycle of Competence and Care, our honest growth cycle. Women's Tree of Truth is the third model that guides the journey inward. The last model, the Spiral of Women's Vital Life Challenges, illustrates the process of growth by naming the markers that both challenge and deepen our maturity as women.

NATURAL MODEL OF WOMEN'S GROWTH—
WOMEN'S LIFE CIRCLE

An honest model of women's growth requires that we think differently about how we move through life. Having had only one model, the linear, male-based model, to illustrate our life line, we have been loyal to the injunction "Act your age." Legally, a person is considered to be an adult at age eighteen or twenty-one. However, dictionary definitions reflect our ambiguity about the words "adult" and "grown-up." Typically, "adult" is linked to the chronological age of eighteen, whereas "grown-up" refers to a person who has completed development. These words imply that we reach some fixed state, a static position in life.

While the chronological, linear model may fit the biological aspects of life (e.g., childbirth and menopause) and role events (e.g., launching a career and marriage), after age twenty, it does not account for the life experiences of women.[18] Nor does it include the *growing process* by which women move toward maturity through these experiences. Surely no woman plans to be widowed at thirty-five, unemployed at forty, attending college at fifty, becoming a corporate vice president at thirty-eight, dating at forty-five, or entering the work force at fifty-four! These events have no place in the traditional, linear, chronological model of human development.

A woman's life is a relational life. By going within, we find that our true sense of feeling grown up is our sense of maturity. In choosing this word, I am very aware of its diverse meanings. For many women, the word "mature" is not the opposite of "immature." Quite comfortable with using the word "immature" to describe unformed or half-grown thoughts and behaviors, many women shun the word "mature" because they equate it with dead, old, and boring. Some women, especially mid-life women, see maturity as the depth or wisdom we exercise in our decisions as we interact with life and as the self-acceptance that comes from a known self who feels well-seasoned in what she knows. Women's sense of feeling grown up includes not only what she has *done* but who she has *become* in her relationships, that is, her sense of *connectedness.*

We are the sum of all our relationship interactions in life. Guiding us is an "ethic of care," the term used by psychologist Carol Gilligan, who writes about women's moral development that is expressed "in a different voice."[19] Yet this ethic of moral maturity is missing in traditional models of adult development. What does make the difference?

Are women *different* from men because of our tendency, existing at the unconscious level, toward continuity in relationships? Or are women really more *like* men, the products of oppression and patriarchy?[20]

Whether this sense of gender is born out of subordination or is innate, women do care and nurture. Indeed, the very base of our sense of feeling mature comes from our sense of connectedness *and* our sense of competence. By "competent" I mean our capability, what we can *do*, with or without pay; by "connection" I mean our feeling of being connected with intimate others and *being* with our world. Our caring shapes our sense of connection and is an ethic that is a political necessity for the preservation of our world.[21]

From Life Line to Life Circle

If women are to have a true model of growth, we must shift from a linear, chronological model of the life cycle to a circular model. The frame of my model of women's growth is the life line—the chronological time line from birth to death. Traditionally referred to as the life cycle, the life line has typically been represented as a straight line, indicating that we move right through life in some orderly manner.

To illustrate the full circle of life, I bent the life line to form the Life Circle (Fig. 1). The Life Circle encompasses the predictable events in life, which include biological events such as puberty and menopause as well as socialization events such as school, paid work, leaving home, and retirement. Just as important but missing from other life-cycle models are the unpredictable events in life, such as paired relationships, a single life-style, marriage, divorce, remarriage, loss of close relationships, job loss, infertility, disabling accidents, chronic illness, and untimely death of loved ones. These stressful events have a profound effect on our growth. Because of their unpredictability, they cannot be contained within any one line but are scattered throughout our lives, as shown in Figure 1. These are the events that often engender our adult crises, and with hope, rather than floundering we can transform them from change into growth.

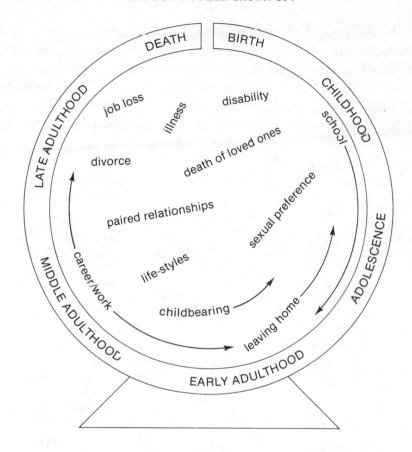

Figure 1
Women's Life Circle

WOMEN'S CYCLE OF COMPETENCE AND CARE

While visiting a Third World country, Sally boarded a bus to go to the next village. An elderly native woman sat down next to her and softly asked, "And what do you grow?" Sally warmed at the common threads in their lives that united them across cultures. Women the world over grow ideas, plants, children, relationships, and community. Historically, across all cultures, women have been the growers, the gatherers.

Yet we have not had a model that included our "growing" competencies. Who women are in relationship is what is missing from the

23

male-based models of adult development. No wonder so many women feel inadequate and isolated. Invisible, unpaid, and unmarketable, our personal and interpersonal competencies—our "being"—have never been considered as "tasks" or accomplishments. We must begin to take our strengths seriously and not put them down or minimize them. Clearly, an honest model of women's growth cannot be an either-or model. It must include both doing and being, both competence and care (Fig. 2).

We grow through our competency experiences; in this regard, my model is not unlike the male-based developmental models of doing,

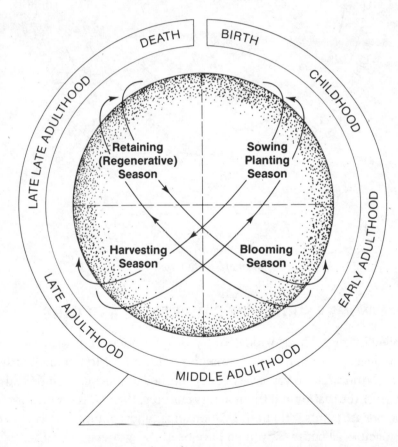

Figure 2
Women's Cycle of Competence and Care

but it is different in terms of how that competency makes us internally strong. When I refer to "competence" here, I do not mean the idea of "superwoman" as a setup for women to "do it all."[22] I am referring to women's capabilities and seasoning. The ancient root of the word "competence" meant "to seek together."[23]

Often women who "discover" some new talent find that seeds were planted early in life and had been slowly growing through the years. So often women's "new discoveries" are harvests from the past, nurtured through developing competency through the years.

But while we're looking at the life circle, let's acknowledge the growing bed within it. We all understand nature's cycle of the growing seasons, but "season" has another meaning, "to make more usable as by aging."[24] To show how experienced or "seasoned" we are in different qualities of our growth, I divided the core of the life circle into four seasons: sowing, blooming, harvesting, and retaining.[25]

In the *sowing season,* we plant seeds, often scattering them, sometimes planting them in distinct rows. These seeds are first attempts, thoughts, risks big and small, learning stages. In the *blooming season,* we begin to see healthy sprouts and buds that evolve toward full blossoming. In this season we focus closely; we water and fertilize and weed and transplant for solid growth. As we weed, we leave the weeds at the base of our plants to nourish them. In the *harvesting season,* the fruit ripens and we reap the rewards of our planting. All cultures engage in harvest rituals to celebrate the gift of abundance. In the *retaining season,* what goes on is going on inside. In this regenerative process, we hold seeds for future plantings in our still pods. "Every seed destroys its container else there would be no fruition," says Florida Scott-Maxwell.[26] So the cycle continues.

Yet our past is also within us, so experientially we live simultaneously in all seasons. No growing season is ever totally empty. As some of our qualities grow fully into the retaining season, new starts occur in the sowing season, and others are in full bloom or ready for harvest. The "new" beginnings women constantly experience could often more honestly be called "*renewing.*"

In my "Making Our Lives Our Own" seminars, I ask women to reflect on how "seasoned" they are in each of the following aspects of life. Next, I ask them to place each word into the appropriate "season" of the model.

Physical exercise

Financial know-how

Work/career

Community service

Grieving

Connectedness-self

Play

Health care

Emotional expression

Home repair

Responsibility

Family-of-origin connections

Affectional expression

Homemaking skills

Creative expression

Spirituality

Religiosity

Parenting

Intellectual growth

Education

Intimacy

Friendship-men

Friendship-women

Political action

Social action

When we have finished, I ask women to "claim it" by sharing their awarenesses with the group. On completing this exercise, women find that they are "green" in some areas but fully "seasoned" in others. The women in my seminars are quick to acknowledge that their seasoning has nothing to do with age. By acknowledging their fullness of growth, women feel comfortable in assessing where their new growth is occurring and where they might want to do some fertilizing or pruning. As we continue to grow, we can periodically assess our progress by our internal standards.

We all have innate strengths, parts of our self so well developed that no further "work" is necessary, except, of course, the "work" we need to do to claim our "seasoned" strengths. We need to recognize what is within us, for we not only are blind to many of our growing strengths that are so obvious to others but blind to how we grow.

In our blindness there is darkness. When we think of growing in the model, we tend to think of sunshine and water as life-sustaining elements. Yet we grow in darkness as well; we need the moon as we need the sun. The ancients knew the importance of the moon cycles.[27] In some areas of the world, planting cycles are still based on moon and/or menstrual cycles. "The ever-changing moon is the image of transformation of those parts of ourselves which usually live in the dark. Protected from the enlightened mind, the very essence of life is gently distilled from concrete experience," writes author Marion Woodman.[28] So our growth is the product of the energy of both the sun and the moon, both the conscious and the unconscious. As we move through our life cycle, we bring the accumulated past into our present. And we grieve; our tears provide essential natural "rains" for our healing and growing.

Jean told me she had always had a positive attitude about life and usually faced it quite directly. Yet, near holiday time, usually after Thanksgiving, she felt vulnerable and highly emotional, her tears often near the surface. She had learned to live with this feeling, attributing most of it to her sentimentality about Christmas. Then, several days before our session, she had stopped in a card shop to buy special Christmas cards for her family. There she saw the flaglike markers projecting out from the sea of cards; like family guideposts they read, "Father," "Mother," "Grandmother, "Grandfather," "Brother," "Husband." Jean felt overwhelmed. With tears streaming down her cheeks, she had to pass six markers before she found a relationship category where there was life. All six relationships had died, most of them in December. Even her divorce date was in December! As she talked with friends and then with me, she realized what all her "sentimentality" was about; she was grieving all the relationship losses in her history. Jean said it felt like a real relief not to struggle with it any longer.

Jean had not realized that her grieving was cyclical; she had certainly been aware of the losses in her adult life, but she had not considered the ongoing connectedness of her grieving. When she understood what was happening, she found it easy to surrender to her grief, realizing that her sense of attachment was known to her through her sense of grief.

Jean said, "I used to think that grief was an event rather than a process; this makes more sense. I can't believe how my beliefs are changing." We began to explore more of Jean's "I used to thinks."

Jean could see that her inner knowing was deepening. She commented that she was tapping what she thought she had really always known—at some level. I told her that we women had to go underground to find our connectedness to our authentic self and our truth.

WOMEN'S TREE OF TRUTH:
FROM CULTURAL MYTH TO UNIVERSAL KNOWING

A friend of mine named Iris and I often tease each other about how stubbornly we clung to our "I used to think" truths—"Two will become one," "If I am patient, he will soon realize . . . ," "When I'm married, I'll feel grown up." Myths are the foundation of every culture's belief system and social values; the truth of any myth is based on the beliefs of its hearers. Our myths underwrite a male-dominated, capitalistic, consumer culture and grip us tenaciously because, as philosopher

Suzanne Langer writes, in each myth there is a piece of reality.[29] Jean said she had begun to see that her beliefs were indeed changing as she began to unravel her cultural myths.

Lacking our own female-based model of growth, women have naturally relied on cultural myths and their resultant belief system to define their sense of self. Clearly, however, women in search of a self, in search of their own truth, must take their truth from the lives of women. We must be aware of how our cultural myths shape our reality—and then demythify our belief system.

I assured Jean that although some of her concerns could be called psychological, most of her struggles grew out of what she had *learned* about being a woman. I reminded her that her social learning was contaminated and fed by toxic cultural myths. I continued, "To delve down into our authentic knowing, we must examine what we have been taking in through all of our senses all these years. Only after we examine and debunk the myths," I reminded her, "can we go underground to find the bedrock of truth."

A natural metaphor for women's growth is a tree (Fig. 3). Imagine yourself as a tree whose trunk, branches, and leaves are fed and supported by a tangle of roots in the topsoil. The large, bracing roots extend down into another layer, the subsoil, and one major root, the taproot, goes deepest—into the bedrock. To find our truth, we must follow our taproot underground to its source. In other words, we must delve down through the topsoil of cultural myth and social learning and the subsoil of our personal history, the unconscious, and fairy tales to reach the bedrock that holds our hidden history and spirituality. Only then can we come to understand how we are where we are today.

The Topsoil:
Cultural Myths and Social Learning

In our everyday world the media—magazines, newspapers, television, movies, music, and advertising—inundate us with our cultural myths. The messages in these myths tell us that if we are thin, white,

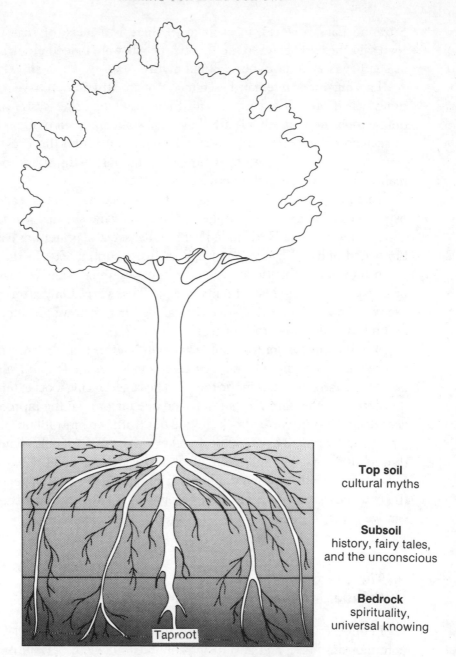

Top soil
cultural myths

Subsoil
history, fairy tales,
and the unconscious

Bedrock
spirituality,
universal knowing

Taproot

Figure 3
Women's Tree of Truth: From Cultural Myth to Universal Knowing

rich, and young, the world is ours. The messages also promise we can command respect through accumulating things. The cultural myths suggest strongly that we develop an *image* rather than character, and the "in" image will guarantee love and happiness. The media also tell us we should feel good all the time. Because of this constant barrage, we take them in, whether we are conscious of doing so or not. Unconsciously, we are true to many of them. As women we have been defined by our families, churches, schools, and other institutions, and the media has shaped us.

All the social stimuli we take in through culture's myriad media shape our attitudes. While an increasing number of us have focused on self-help psychology, we have long ignored our social learning. We struggle through our growing years with little awareness of its impact.

Let's look at four pervasive cultural myths and see how they have shaped us. While I don't believe these cultural myths, I think it is essential to name them.

Myth One: Beautiful Women Get What They Want. Women who conform to the cultural stereotype of beauty do receive higher grades, are more popular, and often have higher incomes. We spend ten *billion* dollars a year on the diet industry, including books, health spas, and diet groups. Yet attractive women are more unhappy in midlife—often because they have relied solely on their physical attractiveness to guarantee their happiness. Loss of youth becomes equated with the loss of beauty.

Myth Two: Men Will Protect and Take Care of Women. Most women look to men to defend them physically and to provide economic security; in short, we believe we can be safely dependent on men. We invest heavily to keep this myth alive. Women continue to take a second place and stay "lesser than" to guarantee their "protector's" place. Because men are out in "man's world," women excuse them from their responsibility to be present in their homes and relationships.

Myth Three: Women Are Solely Responsible for Relationships. Trapped by this myth, women are the receptacles of and the connectors for family caring. We are to take charge of the intimacy in all relationships. "Good" equals "selfless" in the world of women. Jo-Ann Krestan and Claudia Bepko state it clearly in their book title *Too Good for Her Own Good*.[30] Women buy family gifts, write family letters, make social arrangements, and maintain contact with family members, childcare givers, aging parents, neighbors, school teachers, and clergy. Our investments in relationships are reflected in the great number of self-help books, therapy sessions, and family magazines we buy.

Myth Four: A Good (and Normal) Woman Is Found and Married. This myth asserts that women only have significance when they are in paired heterosexual relationships. This myth is so powerful that many women who discover later in life that they are lesbian recognize how they thought enacting the myth would change their sexual preference. Today's women go to extremes to be paired. In self-hate, millions of women mutilate and abuse themselves. At least ten million women are bulimic (binging and purging), and countless others subject themselves to cosmetic surgery and liposuction. The reality is that we have to learn how to love the self and grow a relationship with the self before we can have a good relationship with someone else.

The Subsoil: Personal History, the Unconscious, and Fairy Tales

The next layer, the subsoil, contains our personal history, our unconscious, our fairy tales. While this soil level of our truth is less contaminated, it is not pure. It is saturated with compost, the decomposed growth of the cultural myths, that has filtered down through the topsoil to the subsoil.

The subsoil contains our personal history, but that history is a combination of our family history and our cultural history. Women's cultural history is interpreted by men and told in male language. This history (his-story) has not been healthy for women and has often stunted women's growth by limiting our options and life-style choices.

We not only have to consciously look back to our past personal history but we need to acknowledge the unconscious in each of us that stores the universal cultural archetypes, the original models of women's collective history.[31] These archetypes are ideal models of woman-hood. The unconscious passes these archetypes on from generation to generation. In contrast to the conscious mind, the unconscious divulges its information to us as *it* chooses. We cannot call it forth at will; it has its own life and can surface through discovery or through crisis.

Unconscious learning can be joyful or painful. Jean learned about her unconscious in therapy after her divorce. When Jean's denial broke in group therapy, she learned that she had repeated her mother's and grandmother's pattern—by marrying a man who later abused alcohol and identified himself as an alcoholic. Unconsciously, she had re-peated her family's "learned" pattern of taking on the role of the over-responsible, in-charge partner, a role that felt very natural to her. Jean was both surprised and unsurprised when she learned that her daugh-ter and sons had never seen their father (Jean's husband) drunk. Jean too had only seen *her* father drunk two times.[32] Jean now saw the possiblities of the unconscious "repeat after me" pattern for her chil-dren. The family unconscious held injunctions for family members.

Yet the family unconscious isn't all of it! Throughout our child-hood, our cultural values are passed on through the symbolic; through the symbolic, the metaphorical, they insidiously enter the uncon-scious. Fairy tales are examples of one of our powerful symbolic shapers; they pervade our daily lives. Deeply embedded in our uncon-scious, fairy tales are reflected in our idioms, poetry, music, dance, art, literature, religious stories, and films.

Sue, a divorced woman, told her story of a backpack trip into a deep canyon in Baja, California. As she was placing her sleeping bag on the ground, a small toad sat down in the middle of it. As she went to brush him aside, her son called out, "Be careful, Mom, it might be the prince." At one level, his humorous remark shows the prevalence of fairy tales in our everyday life. At another level, his message can be interpreted as a son's wish for his now-single mother to find another "prince."

We hear our messages in our daughters' stories. In one of my semi-nars, I asked the women about the messages they had received from their parents about being a woman. Janice narrowed her eyes for a moment in thought and then stated slowly, "The message from my mother was, 'You can do anything.'" "But," she added, "that was countered by my father's message, 'Be my princess.'" She said she felt both loyal to and torn by these disparate messages. Women who "awaken" feel surprised and then shocked when they discover how deeply ingrained these tales are and how literally they had taken these metaphorical stories that enjoin girls — and women — in our culture to "be pretty, be helpful, be passive, and do as they are told." Fairy tales influence us so profoundly, we need to examine them closely.

The Brothers Grimm fairy tales are perhaps the most well known and stereotypic of women's cultural myths. However, not many people know that nearly one-third of the original Grimm collection came from a never-married old woman, nurse Alte Maria, of Niederzwehren, Germany, who told stories in the feminine tradition, the oral tradition.[33] Many of these stories were written into tales about little girls who are "stuck" and then get "unstuck," often with the help of a fairy godmother or a prince. Often, the prince has to survive a heroic struggle to "rescue" the princess. The princess has only to sleep to become a woman. Here again is the cultural myth that women need men to save them.

With a feminist lens focused on our fairy tales, we see distressing findings. First, we see that themes of abandonment, child abuse, and negligence prevail in the world of "enchantment," allowing parents to deny their responsibility. Indeed, "well over 100 [of the Grimm tales] are about children who experience some form of mistreatment."[34] The notion of women as victims is constantly reinforced in traditional fairy tales, with child and adolescent heroines held responsible for the behavior of adults.

The Bedrock: Hidden History and Spirituality

As women become more aware, they find their natural connection to the bedrock. The bedrock anchors our taproot, our universal connection with our archetypes, with our past, and with all women. This is the domain of spirituality. By spiritual I mean our connectedness with all that is in the universe, our connection with the creative, life-giving forces. Here we no longer *believe*; we *know*—this is our true knowing, our intuition. It is the home of the sacred where our creation myths are not contaminated. Timeless, it is the home of our spiritual connectedness with all of life. It embraces the hidden stories of matriarchies and goddesses and links us to our universal truth. This is the primitive truth of time eternal, of women of all time whose spirits live on despite their invisibility in a male-dominated world. This is the home of our true voice, the voice of the wise woman within, the Great Mother we can connect with and listen to for direction. This sacred level holds the universal myths; it cannot be contaminated. This is the center of spirituality that so many women have been searching and longing for. Mary K. Richards writes, "There is a creative spirit in you desiring to be free, and you may as well get out of its way for it will give you no peace until you do."[35] The energy of this creative spirit comes from the bedrock. It is the place where we meet our serenity. And when we do touch this place we know we are united with all women of all time; we know universal sisterhood. We feel passionate when we connect with our bedrock; we see that our taproot has been choked by strong, gnarled roots in the topsoil and subsoil. These roots are diseased and contaminate our soil. We must turn and detoxify this soil and clear the diseased roots away to make room for the natural growth of our taproot. When we clear the way for our taproot, we are freed up to return to our real self. We need to go through the topsoil and the subsoil and the root system of cultural myths to get to the bedrock.

So this, then, is our guide to women's lives. It is our journey inward that will bring us to our destination. We cannot stand directionless. Now it is time to identify our markers for the "inventure"[36] that awaits us. We need these markers to identify the growth challenges that await us. These challenges are in the form of a spiral.

THE SPIRAL OF WOMEN'S
VITAL LIFE CHALLENGES

To illustrate women's pattern of growth, I use an upward-moving spiral (see Fig. 4). In choosing the ancient symbol of the spiral, I recognized that it runs counter to logical, linear thinking. I was also aware of the part of me that had difficulty with following my truth; my training demands that I not be "intellectually sloppy." The habit of deductive thinking gnawed at my intuition and inner knowing as I spoke and wrote about the spiral. I knew that some listeners and readers might have problems accepting a nonlinear model and would find their analytical, critical voices. Yet for others the spiral is a natural symbol. Author-lecturer Jill Purce describes the spiral of growth:

> ... Situations recur with almost boring familiarity until we have mastered them in the light of the previous time round. The more we do this, the steeper the gradient, which is the measure of our growth. The spiral we travel round life is the means we have to compare ourselves with ourselves, and discover how much we have changed since we were last in the city, met our brother, or celebrated Christmas. Time itself is cyclic, and by the spiral of its returning seasons we review the progress and growth of our own understanding.[37]

The upward-moving spiral represents the natural movement of nature—"winds move in spirals, ocean currents travel in spirals, sunflower seeds grow in spirals, our galaxy itself is a spiral."[38] The spiral's loops broaden as they continue to rise, depicting the slower movement as we grow farther from our base.

My model fits well with the models of family life-cycle growth showing the oscillations at different times in adult life—the coming together that occurs with deaths and births and the individual focus that occurs with new relationships and job changes.[39] Psychologist Bernice Neugarten says we are less alike at sixty-five than we were at eighteen because of the increasing dividing and subdividing of personal variables in our interaction with life experiences.[40] In listening to the stories of women in therapy, I identified six major challenges for women. Placed on the spiral in Figure 4, the vital life challenges, based on women's experiences, are:

1. Leaving home
2. Facing shame
3. Forging an identity

4. Integrating our sexuality
5. Finding our voices
6. Meeting our creative spirit

These life challenges are dynamic *process* challenges—the challenges we will meet time and time again as we evolve toward maturity. At times, our challenges touch one another; at other times, they are apart. Nevertheless, they are connected and they are continuous. These challenges do not occur in stages. Stages imply hierarchy, with

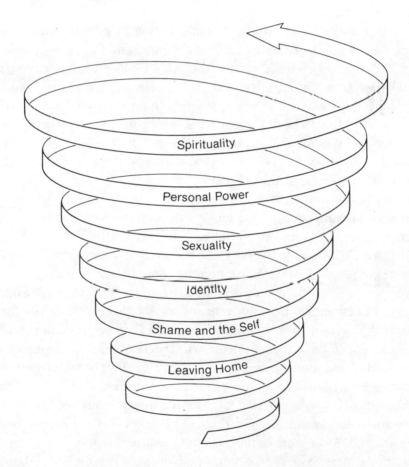

Figure 4
The Spiral of Women's Vital Life Challenges

one period higher or more important than the other. We will meet our challenges at another place in our history and thus can count on the learning and wisdom we have accumulated within to help us face them. These challenges *are* interrelated. They force us to dip down into the past, recycle our history, and add to our maturity. For example, at the time of her divorce, Jean had to look back at her family of origin to gain insights about why she had chosen the husband she did. She reexamined other losses and grief and had to redefine her sexuality. She also had to express her authentic voice and throughout deepened her spirituality.

This dipping into the past to build a stronger present brings any number of growth issues to the surface, but in no fixed progression. In fact, one generation's benchmarks may be the next generation's maladaptation. The life crises that Gail Sheehy wrote about no longer fit for today's adults.[41] If you're still searching for your "real" work, you are unlikely to have a career crisis. And you can't experience the empty-nest syndrome if you've been living in a closeted lesbian relationship for years. And how would you know about the seven-year itch if you're still single at thirty-five?[42]

As we move through our life challenges, we are moving toward a balance of competence, care, and connectedness. Our depth comes from repeatedly facing our challenges. To illustrate this, I now add the Spiral of Challenges to the life circle for an honest and natural model of women's growth. (Fig. 5) We become more of who we are; that is, we become more mature. To become mature, we need to separate our sense of connection from our sense of self-sacrifice; they are not the same.[43] We need to resign from being stuck in moral dichotomies and take a stand by being intentional, by choosing. Women can be connected and available to others and, at the same time, hold on to their separateness. Our maturity grows out of the creative life force or energy flow *between* people; it includes the unconscious, the intuitive, the invisible—in short, the spiritual. This process is the core of our ethical self. As women we must come to realize that it is through our connectedness to *all* of life, born out of our interaction with others, that we experience true growth.

I reminded Jean that, as therapy progressed, we would be talking about each of the vital challenges that could guide her toward moving through the cultural myths toward her bedrock of truth. I also assured her that it would not always be easy, and that just to prove it we would start with her family of origin.

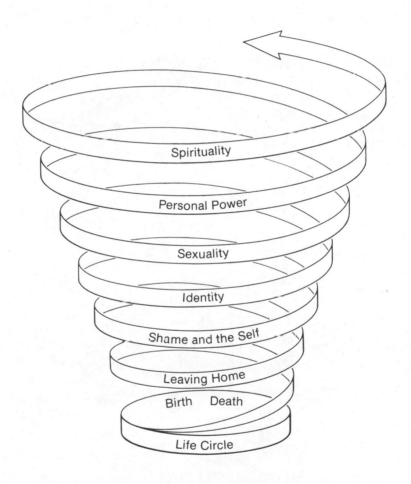

Figure 5
A Natural Model of Women's Growth:
The Life Circle and Life Challenges

CHAPTER 2

MOVING OUT IS NOT LEAVING HOME:
The Challenge of Leaving Home

To look backward for a while is to refresh the eye,
to restore it, and to render it the more fit
for its prime function of looking forward.
MARGARET FAIRLESS BARBER

Moving out of our home can take hours; leaving home can take a life-time. Several rituals give permission for young adults to leave home the first time—going away to college, taking a full-time job in or out of town, moving into an apartment alone or with a partner or friend. Not so long ago marriage was the major ritual for leaving home, but today, with women and men marrying later in life, it is not as common in that regard. A cultural mandate to leave our family home between ages eighteen and twenty-two spurs us on. Many of us look on our moving-out ritual as one of our first truly adult acts. It is our first step in separating from our families; we leave our childhood roles behind us as we move up to physically establish ourselves in the adult world. We move out feeling like we are individuals, but in truth we are what family therapist Carl Whitaker calls "family fragments."[1]

Our physical separation can be swift, but eventually we realize that our moving out did not mean we had left home psychologically. In fact, most of us never even consider that we *should* leave home emotionally. Our history is in us. If we're lucky, we eventually realize that we are being held captive by a powerful cable of many invisible threads. These threads are the unconscious loyalties that emotionally bind us to our families. For those who have grown up in dysfunctional families, these invisible interfamilial bonds carry deeply ingrained messages that continue to operate in the patterns of our adult relationships. I remember thinking the time would come when all the threads in this cable would be neatly severed, like cutting through a telephone cable. But even the deaths of our parents and siblings fail to sever the bonds; we carry the relationships within us.

As children, my sister and I wrote secret messages on paper using lemon juice for ink. When the juice dried, there was no sign of a message. When we held a flame under the paper, the invisible became visible! Finding all the unknown invisible bonds in family relationships and translating their messages is not so easy. I now know that I can have another surprise when a deeply stored memory chooses to become vivid. Leaving home psychologically is a lifelong process.

The likelihood of "surprise" lessens when we go home again to examine our family history from an adult perspective; therefore going home is an essential challenge. Our childhood perceptions are the birthplace of our *process*, that is, how we learned to be in the world, to see ourselves, and to be in relationships. These perceptions are stored in our slidetray of memories. My colleague Kathleen Michels says these perceptions are the images projected on the screen of the mind. They shape our interpretations of our life experiences and the meaning system we live with as adults. Family therapist Rene Schwartz states it clearly:

> As long as we are content to stay within the confines of the memories, recollections and conclusions about our family formed out of our childhood experiences, we are destined to continue to enact our childhood position of no-choice reactor to the forces — conscious and unconscious — in our families.[2]

Our fidelity to our families is a major unconscious binding force. There are two types of family fidelity. The first is the natural conscious relationship we have developed; it includes all our feelings for our family members. We understand and can appreciate, or merely tolerate, the family group into which we were born. We are loyal to it for giving us life, taking care of us, and guiding us through our young years. The second is "invisible loyalty," which is not overt, not consciously known, and therefore not understood.[3] This loyalty is highly functional in families; it protects the family's tolerance for pain by means of taught and learned *unstated* rules that have implicit injunctions about what we can see, hear, feel, and comment on.[4] These rules determine what is allowed and what is not. More importantly they let us know who decides, who is the authority. We see these rules played out in who can get angry with whom, who can be close to whom, who can talk back, who can sit where—all at an unspoken level. We automatically enact this deeply submerged programming in our roles, relationship patterns, and life decisions. Some of these rules are life-enhancing; many are not.

Jean and Bob saw a family therapist before they decided to divorce. Very early in the initial interview the therapist turned to Jean and provocatively said, "You had a crumby father." Jean immediately burst into heavy sobs; his statement had come down on her like a blow from an ax.

The therapist had been testing what he intuited; her response showed that he had touched a nerve in Jean's vulnerable relationship system. Almost immediately Jean pulled herself up in her chair and angrily retorted, "He was not! We all loved Dad! He was a wonderful dad; how dare you talk about him like that! And how would you know?"

Jean's reactivity was a clue to what therapists would call her negatively fused relationship with her father. Many women are bound in relationships with their fathers and mothers. While the therapist was not as sensitive as he could have been, he did make the initial puncture in Jean's myth about her father. This was the beginning of Jean's awakening to the fact that her divorce would be a double divorce—when she divorced Bob, she would also be divorcing her father.

Jean had been loyal to the family "rule" that no one ever spoke badly about father; he was to keep his throne, his halo. Obviously Jean still saw her father through the eyes of a child and along with her sisters had a great investment in keeping a mythic father. Jean said later, "Well, yes, I always knew I was Dad's favorite. I guess everyone in the family knew that. And since my sister was Mom's favorite, it all kind of balanced out. That is, except for my older sister, Diane. She acted like she never minded." Jean acknowledged that she had felt special, not exploited. When her father had told her that she looked like his mother ("a fine, fine woman"), Jean had felt pleased about her identification with the grandmother who had been so special to her father.

Jean, like many of us growing up in a male-dominated world, learned early in life to please her father. Reinforced for pleasing "daddy," it became quite natural for her to work at pleasing all men. Pleasing also had positive rewards; Jean felt special. She naturally set out to become a good student to fulfill her legacy from her unknown grandmother. Did this ever feel manipulative to Jean? Never! This all gave her a place in the family, a confidence in being "special" and successful at school. It was many years later that she realized her exploitation by and her negative emotional fusion with her father. The pain he did not share became the pain she carried. The song title "But My Heart Belongs to Daddy" has been an especially literal theme for many women who grew up in dysfunctional families. At first Jean didn't understand the high price she had paid for her negative fusion with her father.[5] She had many questions.

Hearing Jean reminded me of my relationship with my own father. I recalled the day I had my final oral examination for my doctoral dissertation. When I left the university and got into my car to drive home to the celebration evening awaiting, I heard myself saying out loud, "I'm done, Dad!" "Now where on earth did that come from?" I asked myself. "Hadn't I been doing this for me?" As I drove, I reflected on the roots of it all. I recalled my father giving me my grandmother's valedictorian address, saying "I just thought you might like this." No, there were no explicit, direct statements about achieving, but the injunction was clearly received and followed. Once again I was reminded of how my own issues often meet my clients' issues. Jean asked a question.

HOW DOES NEGATIVE FUSION HAPPEN?

Negative fused relationships grow out of parents' unmet emotional needs. Parents whose emotional needs were not met in their childhoods enter their adult relationships with a great deal of buried pain. How many unmet needs in a marriage are due to loneliness caused by gender socialization? When spouses can't depend on one another, they begin to depend on their children. Fearful of mutual surrender and with deficient models of adult love relationships, they turn "safely" down to a child to fill their unmet emotional needs. Often this is not at a conscious level. When parents have buried their hurt and painful feelings, little children, so naturally intuitive and caring, focus upward to their parents to protect them from further pain. Whether it is the emotional focusing down of the parent or the focusing up of the child, an invisible lasso is formed, an energy connection that is powerful and tenacious.[6] Often "intrafamily marriages" form.

Nancy said she felt clearly that her husband, Doug, loved their daughter, Lisa, more than he loved her. "In fact, he seems to have a more romantic relationship with Lisa than with me!" As Nancy listened to Doug in therapy, she learned about the "intimate" relationship he had had with his mother. She also was able to find her own part in this family formation. Nancy had been her dad's favorite and had experienced a lot of sexual affection in their relationship. While his affection was expressed in appropriate behaviors—hugging and holding—Nancy had always felt an energy from his touch, an energy she later saw as sexual energy. Both Doug and Nancy were still fused in their relationships with their parents. Doug had been trying to distance himself from Nancy (the pattern he lived out with his mother) and Nancy pursued Doug to take care of his unexpressed emotions (her pattern with her father). As Nancy looked back she saw how she had been drawn into her parent's intimacy vacuum, creating a triangle. Her depressed mother spent much of her day in her room alone reading. Nancy had blamed her mother for her father's apparent loneliness and unexpressed pain and became his "little partner." Little Nancy was naturally caring, and like all children her age sought approval. She was also intuitive and, sensing something was wrong, set out to take care of his needs. This lay at an unconscious level; no one ever commented on it out loud. Her partnership with her father later led to her attending community functions, family functions, and dances with her father, often in the role of his adult partner.

Nancy the girl was blind to the fact that she was the victim of *vertical love.* Vertical love develops when a parent attempts to satisfy his or her neediness by crossing the generational line between parent and child. This line, or boundary, between parents and children is the line that must remain strong and clearly defined in order for children to grow up with the security and protection required to develop their own growing selves. Nancy's father, because of the lonely isolation in his marriage, had turned to Nancy to fill his emptiness. So rather than receiving the one-way flow of love a child needs, Nancy was taking care of her father's needs and the line between them became blurred. Nancy later learned that her growing-up process had been profoundly arrested because her father invaded her emotional boundary as he crossed over the generational line; she carried this relationship into adulthood and her marriage. At a time when Nancy's emotional self was developing, her father had torn open the boundary screen needed to keep her self separate from his self, a screen so essential to a child's development. Nancy's father fought his wife through Nancy. Loyal to her father, Nancy expressed his anger toward her mother. She grew up believing she could truly read his mind and anticipate his needs.

This blurred boundary became an invisible destructive root in the foundation of her marriage to Doug. As Nancy looked back, she vividly remembered one troubling scene from her wedding day. That day was the first day she had ever seen her father cry! Deeply etched in her memory but not consciously felt was the message that she was not to leave her father; his tears were a reminder. Confused, Nancy had cried throughout her wedding. In therapy Nancy was complaining aloud about the very dynamic in which she had played such a vital part—the dynamic that also kept her distanced from her mother. Until this time Nancy had not seen that she was victimized by her father's love lasso just as her daughter was caught in Doug's lasso.

Doug had also experienced with his father what Nancy had with her mother, a "missing parent"—that is, a psychologically absent parent. Doug's dad had done what most men of his time had; he spent sixty to seventy hours a week at the office. The son of an alcoholic immigrant family, he had set out to save the family image and had been successful in garnering status and money for his family. When Doug's dad was home on weekends and holidays, he was still "not home" psychologically. When he did take a break from his reading, he seldom showed any interest in his son or wife.

Doug's mother, in her traditional role, worked at home taking care of their four children, chauffeuring them to school activities and lessons, and involving herself in community and school activities. Doug's father "married" his work, investing all his energy there and enjoying it fully. His mother was alone and lonely in her marriage. There were two marriages, his and hers.[7] Doug was the last child at home and said he felt sad that his mother had such a busy yet empty life. He remembered his mother sitting up and waiting for him to come home from his dates and then asking him for details. Doug said he had often noticed a wine bottle on the table when he came home. His mother was not drunk, but she had been drinking. And he never said anything about it. He said he could clearly recall thinking how natural it was for her to have a "little nip" in the evening to help her sleep.

Doug's invisible loyalty prevented him from seeing his mother's use of alcohol to medicate her pain. Feeling uncomfortable, he had shut down his feelings at about age sixteen in an attempt to distance himself from his mother. In so doing, he took after his dad's model of psychological absence. Doug had not realized that he had been denied his rightful position as a child when he was usurped across the generational line to fill his parents' marital void. He too was a victim of vertical love.

Both Doug and Nancy came to see that their family *bonds* were, in reality, family *binds*. Tied vertically to their parents' marriages, each of them was still victim of "emotional incest." This dynamic resulted in Doug and Nancy's inability to form a horizontal, mutual relationship. Each had a three-person marriage with the primary loyalty to one of the parents (Fig. 6). With therapy, reading, and an adult children's group, they both freed themselves from their binds and have now "remarried." Over several years, Doug and Nancy worked out of the binds to have the kind of mutual, horizontal, and intimate marriage Gus Napier refers to in his book *The Fragile Bond*.[8]

Nancy had not realized that blaming her mother all these years had kept her "stuck" in her family. She wondered aloud, "Why didn't

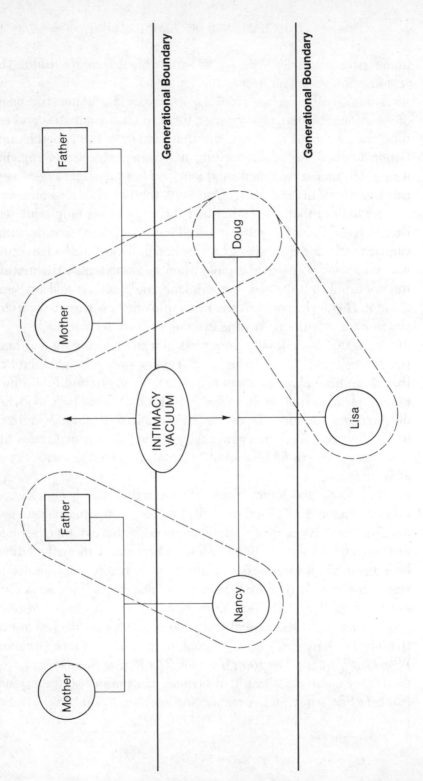

Figure 6 *Vertical Love and "Intrafamily Marriages"*

Mother do something about her depression? And why didn't she speak up to her husband to protect me? Why did Mother refuse to give me the support I needed? Or was it not a refusal but rather an inability because she was following *her* family rules? (And what about Doug's mother's emotional neediness?)" I reminded Nancy that women *often* become the victim of "blame the mother" therapy. We needed to examine two stories—Nancy's story and her mother's story. We had a three-generation session with Nancy, her mother, Joan, and Lisa.

While Nancy and Doug's story illustrates the powerful grip of their relationships with their opposite-sex parent, this same dynamic can be seen with our same-sex parent. What Nancy now saw clearly was the need to "go home" and find the missing pieces. She needed more information before she could focus on forgiving.

Nancy asked her mother to tell her what had happened in her childhood to cause such a major depression. Nancy learned that her mother's siblings had been severely beaten by her father when she was young. Joan feared being beaten if she didn't do things "perfectly." Joan said she also felt confused about her role in her family. She was exempted from some inside chores because of all the outside work she did with her dad but, at the same time, was expected to be the parent to her younger retarded sister.

Nancy's mother had shut down her emotional self and needs at about age eight when she began caring for her sister. She had inherited the "never express anger (or fear or sadness)" rule and was still loyal to it. Her family's unexpressed grief had helped blanket her rage and anger at the family injustices. It had all been converted to depression. Nancy learned that two of her mother's sisters had been heavily medicated for depression and subsequently hospitalized. Joan voiced her fear that her husband, Nancy's dad, might hospitalize her as well.

Nancy's eyes welled up with tears as she listened to her mother's story; this was the beginning of Nancy's compassion for her mother. When Nancy asked her mother if she had ever thought of leaving, her mother replied that she had no income of her own and no place to go. Nancy's mother was imprisoned, as many women have been. In later months Nancy could identify with her mother as a woman and have compassion for her struggle and begin an adult relationship with her mother. For the first time, Nancy understood that she *and* her mother were both trapped in "leaving home" by at least two generations of unresolved and untold family pain.

Nancy was now deeply involved in "leaving home." Her story is a good example of a daughter not knowing the woman in her mother. When Nancy could talk with her mother openly about her past, she could begin to have a woman-to-woman relationship with her mother. Women as mothers have had unrealistic expectations heaped upon them. Marianne Walters states this so clearly, "Mother is not a woman, she is MOTHER."[9] Our culture constantly reinforces the motherhood myth. While our literature probably recounts the most honest inner stories of women as mothers, much of it tells of women blaming themselves, almost denying that there are any other persons or forces responsible for their daughters' inheritance. In *Up the Sandbox* Anne Richardson Roiphe illustrates the depth of self-blame in a mother-daughter relationship:

> Is it something perhaps in the secret sticky protoplasm out of which I molded her—myself now devoted to a replica of myself, to a now slave, now master, caught in a bind; not pleasant, certainly *nowhere* happy, predictably bound for clashing of wills, disappointments, expectations unmet, pride hurt—all that I know will happen between a mother and a daughter, between me and Elizabeth. What do I want from her when she grows up? Whatever it is, I am sure I won't get it. Whatever she will do will be less than what I have planned, because I can't help planning so much, asking so much of her. I always used to share the joke and point the finger at the ambitious stage mother, or the possessive Jewish mother ... And now I think those are visible caricatures of the even more sinister reality, the more ordinary poisonous ooze that flows between parent and child—Elizabeth is marred because she is mine and each waking hour I transmit in a thousand unconscious ways the necessary code for her to absorb my personality, to identify with my sex, and to catch, like a communicable plague, all my inadequacies and mimic them or convert

them to massive ugly splotches on her own still young soul. For example, I have never told her in any kind of words that I am afraid of the dark, and yet she will not let me put out her bedside lamp and I don't insist, because I remember giants and witches, evil blobs of unknown menace, lying directly at the cover's edge when it's dark. I still sometimes feel an unseen presence behind my back, readying itself to leap and force me into some unspeakable violence. Sometimes I think perhaps it's wrong, morally wrong to have children, when I am so uncertain whether or not I am a good person, enough of a person to create another. I so badly want my children to grow strong and be meaningfully rebellious, to take some corner of the earth and claim it for their own.[10]

As I copy these words, I want to shout out to this mother, "Stop! Don't you see what you're doing to yourself?" Then I respond from another place within and tears come as I connect and identify with this woman. While I know another reality today, I grieve for the many years we mothers have felt so damned guilty. I want to ask her if she also intends to take credit for all her daughter's successes. I doubt it. My contemporary indignant voice cannot erase the history in her, or in me. Perhaps the sadness I feel is because too many women today could still write this same paragraph. Sometimes my feminist voice feels like a drop in the bucket of women's history. Actually, it will take several generations to recast the cultural myths.

Finding our true voices is easier when we have faced the going-home challenge, that is when we no longer have to "look in the mirror through the eyes of the child that was me" and can break our loyalty to the past.[11] Meeting the world of our repressed feelings clears us to have access to our true knowing. Jean had fleeting thoughts while in therapy that if she and Bob both looked back to their family histories, perhaps they could have another start. She was disappointed when Bob said he didn't think that was necessary; he wanted to live with their original marital "contract."

Jean remembered asking Bob, "Would you marry me if you met me today?" Bob had replied, "I think that's your question, not mine!"

It *was* her question, and now that she was finding her honest voice, Jean could no longer live with her former marital contract and its well-polished "role voice." Jean grieved in therapy and then wondered, "Will this be it? Can I get on with my life and know that I am done with this?" We told her that she wouldn't like the news—the news that we are never totally done. Yes, the main cord has been severed, but who can be arrogant enough to think that they truly *know* there is no more repressed history? One of the fascinating aspects of aging, I told her, is that as we grow and age, our past also changes, grows, and ripens. Jean said, "Well, in my case it was pretty clear about my 'marriage' to my dad. But now I have another question."

HOW DO WE KNOW IF WE NEED TO "GO HOME"?

There are seldom clearly defined messages about our need to look back at our roots. Typically we only see symptoms that overlap one another. Some of the major symptoms are intrafamily "marriages," depression, blind relationship repetitions, desperate dependencies, stuckness, and unresolved grief.

Intrafamily Marriage

A sign of the need to go home was laid out fully in the "intrafamily marriage" story of Nancy and Doug. On the basis of my clinical practice, I would guess that about 85 percent of divorces among "adult children" couples are an attempt to divorce a parent. Many couples are still enmeshed in their family-of-origin intrafamily marriages. This enmeshment, or emotional overinvolvement, with family members hinders our psychological growth and creates self-loss dependencies.[12] These vertical relationships are typical of dysfunctional families, not just alcoholic families. In my earlier professional years I felt cautious when adults brought their parents into therapy. Not knowing how psychologically sophisticated they were, I wanted to be certain they understood what we were talking about. I learned that parents know to whom they are "married" (emotionally fused or enmeshed), so I now use the word when referring to these vertical relationship binds.

When I asked Karen's father, "Are you ready to 'divorce' Karen?" he said, "Why, no ma'am! Absolutely not! I'll divorce Jan (Karen's sister), but not Karen." Of course Karen knew by this time that it was to be *her* divorce; if her father was going to relinquish his concealed power, he probably would have acted on it much sooner.

This dynamic is not gender-bound. We often see father-son, mother-son, and mother-daughter binds as well. We often tell couples that we believe in divorce and we believe in marriage; we just want to be sure that they divorce the right person. And it is essential that women hear that it is not their fault. Too many self-help books blame women for the emotional intrafamily marriages that were born out of power imbalances and the simple fact that children are often more emotionally available to women than their husbands.

Depression

Another sign pointing to the need to go home is depression. The incidence of depression in women is high; many studies show the number of depressed women to be steadily increasing; we find depression two to three times as frequent among women than men. What is this about? Could it be the constraints on women to bury their own feelings and needs and not express themselves?[13] Is it also because women are carrying storehouses of repressed anger denied them through the years? How many women have obediently followed the social rules, converting their anger into sadness and depression rather than being openly honest and angry? I have noted extremely high rates of depression linked to women with years of buried anxiety and terror of childhood sexual abuse that has been blanketed by anger and rage turned inward. Their buried childhood rage and anger have naturally come with them into their adult relationships. We have known scores of women who have been controlled by medication, typically prescribed by a male physician, with little or no inquiry into past abuse and the inability to express anger.

Another cause of depression can also be lack of fulfillment. We do know that a major factor in depression of women is the lack of satisfying employment. Too many women have been told that if they are depressed, they are "not doing their work." This simply is not true.

Many women have spent years doing their "going home" work and are still depressed; these women experience clinical depression, a biochemical depression that therapy alone cannot cure. Often women with clinical depression find they have a new beginning when they take medication for the depression. Maria was severely depressed. Through her tears she unfolded her story for the first time. She was a victim of buried secrets and the accompanying pain. She revealed slowly her father's sexual abuse. Her voice choked when she said, "But I know that I should have stopped him or told Mother. I even let it go on for several years!" She also disclosed that her father, on his deathbed, had told her that "some things are best not known." Maria had deeply concealed her rage and grief, which then had been converted to helplessness, depression, and tears. As Maria continued to get support in her women's group and work through her victimization, she began to raise the shade of denial and find her rage and terror. She eventually got to the place where she could go to her father's grave and face his spirit and, much later, forgive him.

Many professionals explain away depression in women using the cultural myth that the depression is probably due to menopause or the empty-nest syndrome. Again, physicians prescribe medications. While statistics tell us that 78 percent of non-Jewish and 86 percent of Jewish women experience depression at mid-life, especially if they are "overprotective" mothers, we have to examine our assumptions about what this means.[14] First we must recognize that mothering is what is allowed women to give them meaning in life; the culture has made women responsible for children. The "overprotective" mother is the mother who has tried to excel in her prescribed role. Second, we also need to acknowledge that many middle-class women who have gained their esteem through their role as mother find themselves at mid-life with no map. They feel the loss of the only active role from which they derived a sense of self. This intense sense of loss often results in denied grieving, which is converted to depression. Some studies have shown that women at mid-life are *relieved* to have freedom and many are excited about new possibilities.[15] Yet how many investigators have asked depressed women if they stuffed their feelings during childhood and then took their unfinished business into adulthood, often emptily playing out their "good mother" roles. When the mother role is no longer active, many women face a depression that may have lingered since childhood. I wonder how many women who are described as depressed could be defined as women who have shut down their feelings to protect others or as women who have become the emotional sponges for their families' unresolved grief and pain. I often describe this shutdown visually, that our range of feelings is like an accordion that can fully expand and contract. When sensitive children shut down their own feelings to protect parents, their feelings contract like a closed accordion. These restricted feelings freeze women in depression. Many women who awaken recognize their feelings are from the past. Thus they are ready to "go home." This "going home" can be psychological or literal, often both.

Blind Repetition

A third symptom of the need to go home is the blind repetition of inherited patterns that no longer work for us. When we are unaware of our unspoken family rules and secrets, we are vulnerable to loyally living out the story lines from our family's unconscious plots. And while we usually feel we are making our own decisions, we often are stuck in repetitive patterns that block our growth and feel self-loathing because we have "done it again."

Roxanne felt torn apart when she told her best friend about her affair. She said she thought she truly loved her neighbor, Dan, but didn't know what to do about her life—her marriage, her children, her place in the community. Her friend suggested she see a professional.

After Roxanne talked with her clergywoman, Celia, she agreed to take some "time out" from her relationship with Dan and examine her marriage and her family of origin. Roxanne was shocked when Celia suggested she talk with other women in her family about affairs. "Do you mean I should literally ask them out loud?" Roxanne gasped. Celia nodded, saying "Yes, let's look at women's relationships with men on your family tree. You're entitled to your history." Soon Roxanne discovered that her mother had also had an affair—and at the very same age! And she had never told anyone about it but said she had carried the secret and the shame for too many years. Roxanne's mother said she had also heard a rumor in the small town where she grew up that *her* mother had had an affair with the local newspaper editor. Then Roxanne learned about even more secretive affairs. She also came to realize that the women in her family married successful, workaholic men who provided their families with high status and income but little emotional involvement. She described a pattern in which the women ended their affairs, their husbands never talked about them, and the wives felt imprisoned with mixed feelings of guilt, shame, and gratitude.

Roxanne realized that she was blindly following the unconscious family script, taking her turn. Roxanne decided to get honest about her lonely marriage and entered couples therapy with her husband in an attempt to work toward a new marital contract. Celia reminded her that now, by breaking the pattern, Roxanne was also freeing the next generation from blindly repeating the unconscious family pattern. After Roxanne faced her challenge, she forgave herself and smiled saying, "Well, I guess apples grow on apple trees."

Desperate Dependency

Another sign of the need to go home is "desperate dependency."[16] Women with "desperate dependency" have learned to believe that they simply cannot be without . . . a man, alcohol, sexual contact, and so on. Culturally we have learned that female dependence is integral to femininity (inherited from Freud). Many women have grown up financially dependent on males and dependent on males for status in community. Yet when we examine emotional dependency, we find *males* who are dependent on women. So women who are often "apparently" dependent are truly emotionally independent or inter-dependent with other women to meet their emotional needs.

We have lived with confusion about the word "dependency." Surely we need to be able to rely on others, whether it is for help or for approval.[17] It is not that the word itself is good or bad; it is what it means culturally. Culturally we have told ourselves that independence is desirable, a natural outgrowth of a dominant social myth; yet we see the loneliness and isolation in male "independence." We know that when we look at traits that are dependency-related, we learn that there are no consistent effects that are gender-related.[18] Of course we know that children need to be dependent and as adults we seek *interdependency*.

Desperate dependency refers to the end of the dependency continuum where there is an unhealthy, limiting dependency shaped by a belief system that one is unable to take care of oneself in thoughts, actions, or feelings. All the stereotypic cultural messages about women support this dependency, fueling the unhealthy learned dependencies in women's adult relationships. Often an integral aspect of this desperate dependency is the fear of abandonment and/or rejection. When a child experiences emotional withdrawal as punishment she naturally fears abandonment. Therefore, in desperation to stay connected *in any possible way*, she learns to get her needs met indirectly, pretending to be who others tell her she is. This survival pattern becomes internalized with a strong set of beliefs.[19]

Jackie, "desperately dependent" on men and in alcoholism recovery, came on a women's rock-climbing trip I led on the north shore of Lake Superior in Minnesota. The purpose of the women's wilderness therapy trips was for women to "face their edges" and discover their dormant inner strengths through a high-risk physical experience. Former Outward Bound instructors joined us as our professional climbing staff.

Jackie was working in therapy on her relationships with men; she felt little and inadequate, often helpless, around men. Divorced for several years, she was very focused on finding a man so she could be "complete" and get her needs met. Still referring to herself as "dad's whipping post," she was strongly connected to her father despite his disrespectful attitude toward women (including his now dead wife). He constantly reminded Jackie that she hadn't been smart enough to "hold" the man she had divorced three years ago. Now Jackie and her son were living in her father's home after her husband left her. Jackie felt like a dependent child, the child who feared abandonment if she did not remain who her father needed her to be. She feared her father and was not trusting of anyone at this time.

On the trip, one of Jackie's first lessons was how to literally "let go." Anchored securely to both a tree and a rock near the edge of a steep cliff over the lakeshore, I was Jackie's "belayer"; that is, I literally held her "life line," the belay rope tied onto a harness fastened around her waist. We jokingly referred to this as the "umbilical rope"; the connection between climber and belayer is critical. Jackie had to lower herself down (called rappeling) the steep rock wall with Lake Superior below her. After she faced her terror about letting go, Jackie felt exhilarated and beamed as she stood shakily on a small rock ledge to unhook her double rappel rope. This meant it was time to climb up, relying on the belay rope and me, her belayer, to catch her if she should slip. Jackie suddenly filled with fear; her internalized messages about being inadequate and helpless screamed through her mind. She began to plead with all of us at the top to pull her up; she then got furious and started swearing at us for "doing this to her." She threatened to untie her tightly anchored belay rope and jump off the rock's ledge. At one point she even called out to a passing sailboat. We encouraged her to start climbing, lowered some water down to her in a helmet so she could quench her thirst, and constantly assured her she could do it. It was as emotionally hard on our small group above as it was on Jackie. A part of me wanted to rescue her, but at the same time I knew it would strip her of her dignity. Eventually Jackie realized that as much as we cared for her, this was *her* climb. With mascara streaming down her tear-filled face and with broken fingernails, she began to climb. Slowly, steadily, she made her way up the rockface, seriously concentrating on what was before her. As she neared the top, her expression changed. Her eyes were wide and tear-filled, but wonder filled her face. When she toppled over the edge, exhausted, she sobbed deeply for a long time while we held her. She then raised her head and looked at us with glowing face and shining eyes, saying "I really have to thank you. This was the first day in my forty-two years I couldn't manipulate to get what I wanted. Thank you all for not letting it happen."

That night in our group meeting, Jackie's face beamed with dignity and self-respect as she proudly told her climbing story. Later, back in town, she told us that when she arrived home after her climb, her eleven-year-old son had come out to carry her bag. She said, "No, Son, from now on I carry my own stuff." Within the month Jackie faced the challenge of confronting her father about his abusive language and disrespect for her. Within the year Jackie had enrolled in a college program and had moved out of her father's home.

"Stuckness"

This symptom of the need to go home takes myriad forms. It is easy to see stuckness in relationships, but just as often we can get stuck in our professional lives as well. At age fifty-six, Irene was a successful professional academician and highly respected lecturer. Friends wondered why she had never let herself take her rightful place in her professional world. They attributed this to her choice of a quiet life-style.

Irene had decided to submit the first chapter of a book she had written to a publisher. She knew she wrote well and could convey her ideas clearly and colorfully. But as she began writing the cover letter, she froze in fear at her typewriter; her mind went blank. She thought she was blacking out or having some kind of anxiety attack. She could not focus on a whole sentence; her eyes darted. What was the subject; what was the verb? She felt frightened out of her mind; she had left the dates out of the references. She felt a tremor moving through her body and put the letter aside. She felt better, but totally unsettled. She recognized that her fear was more than a fear of rejection. Irene had "done her work"; she was keenly aware of her past and her family. But where was the source of her terror?

That night a dream answered her question. In her dream she saw herself standing alone and being knocked over the head with a blunt instrument. She felt the terror and fell dead! Irene knew the blow had been struck by her mother's hand, the powerful strong arm that had held her back all these years. She awoke, trembling with her verification. She realized now that she was not hallucinating; what she had been terrified of was something very true in her past, but no longer true today. To have exposed the truth in her family would have cost her her life; she felt a threatening "dark control." But that was no longer true today. In sending off the proposal, she was exposing as an adult what would not have been allowed as a child—her own intelligent thoughts. But she felt the same fear that she had felt as a child. Now she no longer had to honor the fear of her childhood. Although Irene's mother is dead, she is a very real residue of Irene's past. This realization allowed her to get on with her life and not let her mother's jealousy and domination stop her. She did write the book; it was highly acclaimed and she is now writing another. Irene knew that we can never predict how or when we are going to learn what we need to know. By "going home" and dipping down into her family history, she gained another piece of freedom.

Unresolved Grief

This symptom of the need to go home is often not visible. Judith truly faced a "wilderness within" when she signed on for a rock-climbing trip. She did not realize how literal the metaphor would become. She wanted to explore her relationships and knew she had never grieved her father's death when she was twenty-seven. Now, six years later on a wilderness therapy trip, she rappeled over the cliff edge, taking much longer than most other climbers. "I'm afraid of letting go," she said. Finally she rappeled to a safe ledge, where she was to unlock her carabiners (oblong metal rings that hold the rope) from the double rappel rope and begin her climb. She knew she was to climb up the rockface, trusting herself and her belayer. She froze; she cried profusely, releasing deep sobs. A climbing therapist encouraged her from above while her belayer held her securely. After almost a half hour of sobbing while standing tip-toe on the narrow rock ledge and struggling to be free of the double rappel rope, she realized she had to climb.

I told her that it was time for her to put her tears aside and begin climbing. She then struggled up the rock, slipping often but each time her belayer caught her. When she reached the top and her supportive group of women, she fell exhausted on the ground next to her belayer and her therapist. She then related to the small group that as she let go of the solid double rope, she learned that it symbolized her father— she had finally let go and begun her grieving process. She also made another major discovery, saying that the smaller belay rope signified "my mother, who has been quietly belaying me all these years, supporting me by being there to catch me if I fell." She recalled this was the first realization of what it was like to be mothered; she was angry at first. "That little rope? Where the hell is that going to get me?"

Not only did Judith begin her grieving process in facing her loss, but she was also able to discover the supportive role her mother had been playing through the years. She realized her father's strength was "apparent" strength.

An equally lasting consequence of her climb, Judith said, was that it had been the first time anyone ever told her she had the right to be afraid. This, she recalled, was the conversation she had wanted for thirty-two years—that she could still do something even if she was afraid, and people would stick with her if she had trouble.

More of our unconscious becomes conscious through each of our edge-facing experiences. We can never know which life experiences will become our challenges. When we make the decision to no longer live safely but to risk, we become more of ourselves. While rock climbing is a physical and concrete experience, the learning lies in translating our *own* metaphors. We climb the "mountains of the mind" in many ways. We can examine our growth by reflecting on our edge-facing experiences.

Jean became aware of this when she recognized she had the freedom to become angry, yet knew when she was irritated with her mother, she usually told her sister, not her mother. Her sister, Ellen, suggested that she might want to try that with mother. Jean soon had the opportunity.

Jean recalled sitting in her mother's kitchen one day and feeling guilty when she heard her mother ask her about her divorce by asking how the children were doing. Jean's mother had never told Jean how disappointed she was that Jean was the first woman in the family to divorce. Jean said she thought her mother had attempted, in her own way, to be understanding and bury her disappointment and anger. Jean said she suddenly felt a slow burning from deep inside her and her face reddening. She recalled spontaneously blurting out, "I'm so fed up with your indirect messages; why don't you tell me that I disappointed you? I'm sick and tired of being guilted! Do you think I can't feel your disapproval?" At that moment, Jean said, her mother left the table and the room in a huff. She stood crying in the next room. Jean's heart sank. Now I've done it! Then she felt Ellen's arm on hers. Ellen said, "Don't get up; you didn't do anything wrong." Jean said she took a deep breath and sighed, "You know, you're right; I don't think I *did*!" She then walked over to her mother and they had one of their first woman-to-woman conversations. From that day on, Jean said she felt a deeper closeness to her mother. Jean said, "I never knew how trapped I was!"

Jean saw clearly now that her own "prison" was just one of several symptoms women experience in leaving home. She said that she saw how deeply entrenched she had been in her family and that she had a newfound sense of respect for how long it takes to leave home.

Jean said she realized the process was like working herself out of a maze. She then said, "I have another question."

"HOW DO YOU GET THROUGH
THE FAMILY MAZE?"

There *is* a way through the maze, but it does not typically fall into ordered categories. The stories in this chapter reflect the various aspects of our leaving home psychologically. Often, in family therapy sessions when we bring in our parents to "leave home" in person, we learn our parents' history and we know what really happened and what we told ourselves. We can move toward accepting and empathizing with our parents. When separate, we can appreciate our differences and be free to move on. When we're ready, some arousing event typically nudges us back. But we may or may not see the need to "go home" at that time; we may not "get it." But when we do stand still and examine our family's history, we often will find buried feelings, misinterpreted stories, and family myths. We can then identify what we learned to call "normal" and see our families through our adult eyes. Going home can, in the words of Rene Schwartz

> . . . offer opportunity for you to lose some of your cynicism and your naivety which are just opposite sides of the same coin. To move beyond the veil of the legends about one's family is to confront simultaneously the cruelty which exists in all our families (people do get abandoned or shamed) — and the strengths. Out of the grief families do renew life. To see the parts intertwined in one's own family is to be opened in a fuller way.[20]

In this process we also go through a change in our belief system; that is, we turn our childhood memoirs into our adult stories without glorification, without denial, without shame. Our history happened, and it is in us. As soon as we are clear about our family life, and work through our feelings toward our family members, we can voice our truth to some close friends and spouses or partners. Next we can face the challenge of sitting face to face in a supportive setting with our family members or perhaps just our parents. The goal is not to "dump" our negative, blaming feelings but rather to resolve. Don Williamson, family therapist, talks about "peerhood" coming when we can sit eye to eye with our parents and tell our stories and hear theirs.[21] By breaking our family's "no talk" rules, we open ourselves to a mutuality across generations. In answer to the frequent protest "But I don't want to hurt them," we need to remember that we cannot take responsibility for what feelings our parents may bring into the room. Yet honesty without sensitivity is brutality. When we hold others accountable, we become more of our adult selves. We do this for ourselves; we learn to care for ourselves. We can do this only by being honest, respectful, and sensitive. Most parents feel relief when they can release some of their burden and be known and accepted. A colleague, Mimi, said it clearly, "The truth *will* set you free—but it will make you miserable at first!"

What makes us miserable is that in order to leave home we must face our core challenge, the challenge of facing shame.

CHAPTER 3

HOW DO I LOVE ~~THEE~~ ME:
The Challenge of Facing Shame and Finding the Self

A boundary between self and not self is the first one we draw and the last one we erase.

KEN WILBER

An outline is not a boundary.

FLORIDA SCOTT-MAXWELL

Climbing the "mountains of the mind" has been a powerful metaphor for growth. As Rene Daumal says, "For a mountain to play the role of Mt. Analogue, its summit must be inaccessible, but its base accessible to human beings as nature has made them. It must be unique, and it must exist geographically. The door to the invisible must be visible."[1]

The "visible" experience of rock climbing has provided rich feedback about the "invisible," our process in life. In the last chapter's "leaving-home" loop of the spiral, I stated that going home meant meeting our core challenge, facing shame. Shame is at our center, and we cannot find our true selves without facing shame.

While climbing has been a dominant metaphor for me, I have learned much more from *downclimbing* than I ever have from ascending. The climbing metaphor describes well the process of intimacy, but I learned that we are not always ready for that climb. Like others, I wanted to climb the rock and reach the "top." But first I had to downclimb and let myself enter the downward spiral that led to more of myself. That process involved facing shame. My inward journey

65

started in Wyoming at Devil's Tower, a 1300-foot columnar rock monolith that has challenged climbers since the early 1900s. My friends suggested that we spend a weekend climbing the "Tower," and I eagerly agreed even though this was just my second experience. (The first time I had climbed erratically, often klutzily, but I had managed to reach the top of each climb.) My climbing friend/instructor said, "I think you are ready to do the Tower, but it will probably be the hardest day of your life." Little did he know! I couldn't resist the challenge and lay awake the night before excited and fearful.

The next morning I began the ascent with bubbling confidence, recalling my friend Rolf's words, "There's no going back once you commit to the climb." I was committed and, tied in securely, began climbing. Almost immediately I fell. I felt trusting, knowing Rolf would hold the belay rope tightly so I couldn't fall farther. It worked! I returned to the rock, then slid back. Again, I returned to the rock and continued my struggle, thinking, "I'm not a quitter; I can do it." My mouth dry, my body exhausted, my hand bleeding from jamming it into a crack, I climbed with all my energy and force to get to the top of the first pitch. Exhausted, I fell into a heap at the top of the rock section. Then my friend called down, "The next pitch is twice as hard as this one." My heart sank; I had taken almost an hour to climb less than 50 feet. There were four more pitches to climb, and we would be coming down in the dark if I continued at this pace.

I was physically and mentally spent, and my self-doubt was quickly expanding. I felt torn; I was a climber, not a downclimber! I had made a commitment! After moments of silence, holding back the tears, I called up, "I need to be lowered; I have to downclimb." Rolf nodded and gently said, "I think that's best; I'll hold the rope for you." A molten shudder rushed through me. "I'm a failure," I thought, and the tears came. I felt humiliated and immediately began berating myself for attempting the Tower. "A forty-four-year-old woman should know better!" I raged.

As I went down, I felt every negative feeling imaginable—shame, inadequacy, stupidity, helplessness, envy, anger, and rage. Then other feelings trickled in—feelings of being released, of relief, of freedom. I felt grateful and sensible. I knew my decision was right.

By the time I reached the talus, the 300-foot rockpile at the base of the climb, I suddenly felt light. Untied from the rope, I continued to downclimb and felt gratitude and even some peace as my insides quieted down. I paused to look up at what I had attempted; the morning heat continued to rise. Seated on a rock with another person who had not climbed, I began to focus on the rest of the climbing group to cheer them on. By the end of the day I felt renewed and helped prepare a celebration party for the climbers. On their return, I learned the temperature on the rock had reached 110 degrees. I knew then at an even deeper level that I had made the right choice.

My downclimbing is now a part of my story, a part of me. It is indelible so that even now, years later, I have no difficulty remembering it. As I write, I smile at my scarred hand. By facing my shame (even though I didn't call it that back then), I had faced my secret fear of failing. Now I know how essential downclimbing is in learning to climb successfully. By downclimbing into the spiral of shame, I was able to learn what I didn't know about myself. The "invisible" became "visible." The postscript to this story is that I returned to the Tower the following year and climbed it successfully. I felt ready; my head and gut were no longer two separate realms. I felt an inner unity.

How many years have we struggled but failed to get to where we want to be? Stuck, we repeat old patterns and feel discouraged. Stuck, we do not grow. And when we do not grow, we pay the price of what might be called "selficide." Different from suicide, selficide, a term coined by Tom Malone, refers to the living death of the self by standing still.[2] Many of us have felt stuck or paralyzed because of our shame. So before we face the upward climb, perhaps we should examine the process of downclimbing into shame.

SHAME AND THE CORE SELF

Shame is powerful; it lies at the core of the self. It is what we experience, what was done to us, and what we do to others. The shame and self-contempt we inherit from our dysfunctional families is called toxic shame, the implanted toxin stored within us that can kill the self. Jean Paul Sartre called shame "the immediate shudder which runs through me from head to foot without any discursive preparation." He described toxic shame as the internal hemorrhage.[3]

Before writing *Facing Shame* with my colleague and friend Merle Fossum, I included both shame and guilt under the umbrella called guilt. I felt comfortable talking about guilt; it was outside me. Guilt had to do with my violating my values and making mistakes, about my behavior, about what I *did*. I never felt any loss of self when I told my "guilt" stories—my divorce, my parenting mistakes, my political naivete. I could talk openly about discovering my guilt during a period in my life when I was constantly late for meetings with friends. There was a way back, a way to repair. I could forgive myself and move on.

Shame was not that easy to recognize or to name. It took me five years to know that I had been publicly shamed by another professional who had lied and exposed me in front of my colleagues. All I knew then was that I felt paralyzed. My words froze; I felt like I was losing my self. There was no way back. Speechless, I had walked away numb and shuddering internally. I knew this was not guilt. This was inside me; my whole self seemed to meld with my shame. It was about me, who I *am*, not what I did. Puzzled, I tucked it away for years until I began writing about my clients' shame. Only then did I realize that I had been shamed in that experience! And of course this insight was just the beginning. I could not write about clients' shame without facing my own. Shame has been called the "master emotion."[4] In *Facing Shame* Merle Fossum and I define shame:

> Shame is more than loss of face or embarrassment. Shame is an inner sense of being completely diminished or insufficient as a person. It is the self judging the self. A moment of shame may be humiliation so painful or an indignity so profound that one feels one has been robbed of her or his dignity or exposed as basically inadequate, bad, or worthy of rejection. A pervasive sense of shame is the ongoing premise that one is fundamentally bad, inadequate, defective, unworthy, or not fully valid as a human being.[5]

Is there anyone who has never known this experience? No wonder we want to escape it. Shame carries strong injunctions; we can't say we're wrong, we're sorry, we made a mistake. With guilt, the self says, "I *made* a mistake." With shame, the self says, "I *am* a mistake."

I wasn't aware how deeply our shame is implanted within us. Shame is born within relationship. Since women are highly sensitive about relationships and relationships are the primary experience from which shame emerges, women experience higher levels of internalized shame than men.[6] Recent studies of young children show that all infants respond affectively at birth; shame is there at the beginning. Shame is preverbal.[7] And because children fear rejection, it is easy to see how the shamed child becomes the alienated adult. Psychologist David Cook, researcher of shame, has shown that women's *alienation* is always higher than men's.[8] Since women feel like failures when relationships don't work, the close connection between alienation and depression in women is not surprising. Also, women have higher *inferiority* scores than men. Given that we women enter the world as "lesser than," our sense of inferiority only adds to our inherited shame. Moreover, each time we experienced shame and couldn't respond because our family rules didn't allow us to be human, we took the shame in and each event added to our toxic reservoir of shame. As children in shamebound families develop ego-consciousness, they at first experience the rejection by parents and other family members who matter, but in time it becomes the child's rejecting contempt of her *own conscience*. Thus we see in adults the contempt in its fullest force, turned upon the *self*. Some painful shame events are known to us; most are not.

Jean discovered a minefield of shame during her postdivorce period. As she was leaving her marriage, Jean became intensely involved with a friend and experienced passionate love. When Josh broached the subject of marriage, Jean halted. With her children upset and her life in turmoil, she felt overwhelmed. She told Josh she could not even think about marriage; she had to know who she was. In anguishing pain she said, "I must know me before I can get involved again. If we're supposed to be together, we will. I'll have to trust that." Now she grieved another loss. After engaging in a series of short-term relationships, Jean revealed her secret. "I feel ashamed of my loving. I think my love is toxic. I had better stay away from relationships. I cause too much hurt and pain to others. There's something wrong with my loving."

There was nothing wrong with her loving; what was wrong was her delusion that she was totally responsible for the ending of any relationship. Jean was experiencing the shame that most women feel when relationships are broken. Because we are so attuned to the importance of relationships, we tend to suffer more acutely and immediately when relationships end.[9] Later on Jean saw that her trust of her subjective knowing was the beginning of her spiritual awakening. She said this was not a commonsense decision; it seemed to come from a place deep inside.

Our buried and denied collective history makes us vulnerable as adults. We can experience shame anywhere, anytime. Any one outside us, in speech, through body language, in person, or in media (print or film), can trigger our shame. When someone else's words enter the air, we can immediately take them inside us. We think they are about us. We can't even hold them outside long enough to question anything; shame is internal. Knowing our shame at a subconscious level, we learn to protect ourselves with defenses, our survival devices. Denial served a positive function in our early years; it protected us against the pain. Eventually we mask our shame in a provisional self, a false self; we pretend. The mask can range anywhere from supersuccessful, to syrupy sweetness, to raging hostility, to hyperindependence. We play our parts so well that we even begin to believe the mask is true. But deep down we feel fraudulent and don't admit it to anyone. As adults we *appear* to be self-sufficient and highly competent. We develop good social skills. We keep busy to avoid feeling, or we get depressed. We may live a secret life, often struggling with compulsions, not telling anyone about how isolated, inadequate, and insecure we feel. We obsess. We form delusions.

Only when we learn ways to "disinternalize" the shame—to hold it outside of us—can we feel safe and lower our defenses. We need to face shame, not run from it. Facing it sets us free—free to be a person, free to be real and spontaneous: acting, rather than reacting, we can live our values. Facing shame in therapy is like using Drano; all the jammed gunk has to come up before our drains (our spiritual centers) can function properly. But facing shame in ourselves and our family of origin is only a part of the solution. Shame is institutionalized in our churches, schools, workplaces, and communities. We cannot experience in our families that which does not exist in our nation. Shame is in the very air we breathe. As Merle Fossum says, "We live in a shamebound, sexist, racist, ageist, addicted society."[10] We could also add homosexist and classist to the list. We cannot change our culture; but we can change ourselves. And we begin the downclimb.

Some women choose therapy for a supportive environment to work through their downclimb experience. Beverly, an attractive thirty-eight-year-old, came for her first therapy session. After completing treatment for alcoholism, she wanted to look at herself. Beverly revealed that she had felt contemptuous of herself before treatment. She felt guilty about neglecting her daughters, Sandy and Lois. She also wanted to clear the darkness from her relationship with her husband. The daughter of a religious fundamentalist attorney and an alcoholic mother, she and I began to explore her history. When I mentioned the word "shame," she said, "No one ever put a name to it; that's it — and it never goes away!" As we talked, I felt tightly controlled by her eyes. She leaned forward and never let her gaze move from my face. I felt a sense of responsibility to her; her gaze seemed to indicate that she realized someone was offering her the possibility of a way out of her shame.

In later sessions Beverly revealed how angry she was with her husband, Ted, who had also participated in her treatment program. She was furious that their relationship was not changing and it seemed it was "her problem." She said she now felt shut down sexually, even though she had previously had an active sex life with Ted. She said, "I now think I had often felt abused and raped by Ted."

As we discussed shame, Beverly asked how it all started. We talked about *external shame.* I gave her examples of the painful events that become shameful when not talked about — addictions, rape, incest, suicide, disabilities, poverty. She could see how the painful experiences in her family history had never been talked about. In fact, most were kept secret. She soon discovered that her own behavior was linked to her family's secretive behavior. Her father had been sexually inappropriate with her and had called her a whore and kicked her down the stairs. No one mentioned her mother's alcoholism or pill use. And no one talked about her grandmother's abuse or her father's experiences in World War II. There were two guiding rules in her family: "There's nothing going on here. Don't tell anyone."[11]

I explained that when families attempt to protect their children from the pain, the children are recipients of *inherited shame*. Beverly inherited the shame and the unexpressed pain. She learned that she told stories, or myths, to protect the secrets. She also uncovered the many deaths and losses in her history—her mother and father had both lost siblings early in life as well as parents and never discussed them. Beverly said she always felt unlovable and hated how she felt about herself. She recalled feeling shame about not doing something when her mother would sit up late at night, drunk, and flirt with Beverly's boyfriends. Beverly had taken in the unexpressed pain of her parents. Unknowingly she had "normalized" her family's dysfunctional behaviors.

She carried these behavioral patterns into her adult life. Beverly had become blindly loyal to *maintained shame*. She felt rejected when her first husband abandoned her after the birth of their daughter, Sandy, in the first year of their marriage. She had an abortion during this period and felt ashamed about it. Beverly had met her second husband at their workplace while he was still married. She felt ashamed about that. She drank to ease the pain. She had a second daughter, Lois, shortly after she married Ted. Then she felt more shame because she had neglected her daughters when she drank. She was caught in the cycle of shame. Attempting to control her chaotic life, she only increased her compulsive behaviors. Beverly perpetuated shame through her disrespectful behaviors and relationships. A heavy smoker, she went through a period of bulimarexia. In therapy she said, "I lived my whole life to get love."

In the early stages of therapy, Beverly and Ted went to a domestic abuse program to work on their physical abuse—battering—of one another. When she returned to therapy, Beverly now saw she needed to downclimb and face the shame. I explained she didn't do this alone;

it happened in relationship, and that relationships were also the way through. She knew she could not change her behaviors until she changed the rules that governed her interaction with herself and others.

Rules of Shamebound Families

Beverly seemed confused about rules. I told her they were not the spoken rules about what time to be in from weeknight dates or verbal expectations about the dinner hour. Rather, they were implicit, unspoken, growth-stifling rules. Beverly now saw how she learned not to comment on what was going on. She learned that her family rules were rigid. "No one questions or disagrees with Dad, no one comments on Mother's drinking, women don't count" were the first rules that came to her mind. I warned Beverly that breaking rules is very difficult and that when she broke them, she would be punished. She learned this quickly when she brought up the subject of sexual abuse to her mother. Her mother did not speak to her for months. When she wrote a letter to her father, her brother called to tell her to "stop this therapy stuff."

I showed Beverly the eight rules of shame that Merle Fossum revealed in our book *Facing Shame:*

1. *Control.* Be in control of all behavior and interaction.
2. *Perfection.* Always be "right"; do the "right" thing. Be admired. Look good.
3. *Blame.* If the unexpected occurs or you're surprised, blame yourself or someone else. Remember, you're either totally responsible or it's someone else's fault.
4. *Denial.* Deny feelings, especially vulnerable feelings of anxiety, fear, loneliness, sadness, or grief.
5. *Unreliability.* Expect little of people; don't count on constancy in relationships.
6. *Incompleteness.* Be sure you never complete a transaction; keep the anxiety going.

7. *No Talk.* Don't talk openly and directly about what is going on, especially about the disrespectful, shameful, abusive, or compulsive behaviors.
8. *Disqualification.* When disrespectful, shameful, abusive, or compulsive behavior occurs, disqualify, deny, dismiss, or disguise it.[12]

Beverly exclaimed, "Well, I guess I didn't have a chance, did I?" She saw that her loyalty to these rules kept the shame alive in all her relationships—her friendships, affairs, work, family, and marriage. Beverly was understanding the connection between the rules and her family shame.

She said that our definition of family shame in *Facing Shame* made sense:

A shamebound family is a family with a self-sustaining, multi-generational system of interaction with a cast of characters who are (or were in their lifetime) loyal to a set of rules and injunctions demanding control, perfectionism, blame, and denial. The pattern inhibits or defeats the development of authentic intimate relationships, promotes secrets and vague personal boundaries, unconsciously instills shame in the family members, chaos in their lives and binds them to perpetuate the shame in themselves and in their kin. It does so regardless of the good intentions, wishes and love which may also be part of the system.[13]

Now Beverly was ready to break the rules. She felt intense shame when she discovered she was married to someone who was sexually compulsive but acted like the innocent one in her treatment group. In addition she got in touch with her rage about being the only woman in her treatment group and about the verbal shaming abuse heaped on her by her counselor there. Livid about the experience, she worked through the pain. Then she reported the treatment center counselor and testified before a community task force about the maltreatment of women in treatment for chemical dependency.

As she broke the rules, she felt wobbly. She wasn't sure where this would all end; she couldn't be in control of it. She was starting to trust me more and was trusting the women in her recovery group as well. The intensity of her gaze had lessened; she could now sit back while talking with me.

At this point Beverly inquired about the term "codependency." Some friends had told her she sounded "codependent" regarding her increasing fights with her teenage daughters. She said, "Look, I know what I didn't get; I just wanted to do it right for them." We talked about codependency as a term used to describe the overresponsible interactional process of those of us who grew up in shamebound families. Our overconcern with protecting others' feelings plus our desire to be accepted results in our walking away from our true selves to accommodate others. Rather than inner or self-esteem, we collect outer or other-esteem. We can literally become lost in someone else. We can begin to obsess about others' behaviors and try to control them. We can lose touch with our own needs and can either shut down or sponge up the feelings of others. Also, we believe that if we don't continue to believe that others are more important than we are, everything will fall apart (and it truly might). Codependency is the flower of shame; it grew out of the toxin.

Beverly acknowledged that she *was* controlling, she *had* let others' behaviors affect her, and she *had* been involved in self-defeating patterns. I said, "How could it have been any different?" I reminded her that she became controlling because everything around her was out of control; that she manipulated because that was the key to getting something accomplished; and that she thought she was going crazy because having lived with so many lies, she no longer knew what was real. We talked about how the rules of codependency grow out of the rules of shame. When we live in families shattered by schizophrenia, chronic illness, or addictions and can't and then later don't talk about our natural painful feelings, we remain loyal to the shame. I explained that any family with one person who is chronically impaired can create a dysfunctional family system with his or her silence.

Beverly said she felt shame when she was called codependent. I explained that many used this term as a shorthand reminder that we were leaving ourselves and overresponsibly obsessing and worrying over people and situations we have no power to control. I did agree that it probably sounded like we were blaming the victim one more time and went on to remind her that this is not just a psychological issue; this is also a *social* issue. Women are socialized to be caretakers; every woman knows about overresponsibility (or codependency) and how exaggerated caring can make us miserable. Socialized to put others first and be "pleasers," we learn to say yes when we mean no. We protect others from any disappointments. Gloria Steinem has suggested that "most women need to reverse the golden rule and learn how to treat ourselves as well as we treat other people."[14]

What confounds women about codependency is that they are both victims of their socialization *and* held responsible. We certainly don't want to give up our caring. We are socialized to be overresponsible, and growing up in dysfunctional families intensifies this as we try, out of protection of others, to control the addict's or impaired person's behavior. As we clarify the issue of responsibility, we can then experience our own victimization and become freed up to make decisions based on something other than loyalty. Our family's rules become enmeshed with our cultural rules and we live in extreme loyalty to unspoken commandments.

WOMEN'S UNSPOKEN COMMANDMENTS

1. Thou art a giver; thou shalt not exist except as a giver. Thou shalt be abandoned if thou art not a giver.
2. Thou shalt not ask for thyself. Thou are not worthy to receive. Thou shalt feel ashamed for having need.
3. Thou shalt be a perfect "good girl." Thou shalt not acknowledge unpleasant feelings, especially anger. And thou shalt be ashamed of unpleasant feelings.
4. Thou shalt have a one-way boundary between other people's feelings and thine. And thou art responsible for the feelings of others. Thou shalt absorb others' feelings and not be vulnerable with your own.
5. Thou shalt not have failed relationships. Thou art responsible for all relationships.[15]

Beverly sighed, "Wow, I didn't think you knew my family. What do we do about this? I do know about breaking the rules; I've started doing that. What is all this boundary stuff about?"

BOUNDARIES OF THE SELF

Three boundaries affect the way the self grows (Fig. 7). The first boundary is the boundary that surrounds the family, regulating who is in and who is out of the family—physically and emotionally. Some family boundaries are quite rigid and others are quite permeable. One

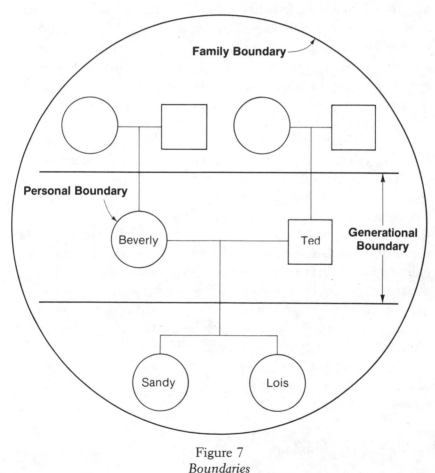

Figure 7
Boundaries

way to identify our family boundaries is by how receptive family members are to relatives and neighbors coming to visit. Ethnicity and lifestyle are major factors in family boundaries.

The second boundary is the horizontal generational line that separates the parents from the children, as I discussed in Chapter 2. The third boundary is the personal or individual boundary that encompasses the self.

When parents have an intimacy vacuum between them, they often cross over the generational line to get their needs met. This is known as a "generational crossover." When parents "triangle" a child into their intimacy vacuum and into their anxiety, they dramatically affect the personal boundary of the child. The triangle is the basic relationship structure and any couple triangles with other family members or even friends when anxiety is high. In the shamebound system, however, the anxiety is constant, and the generational triangling becomes fixed because it occurs during early childhood before the self is developed.

I explained to Beverly that our personal boundary is the protective screen that develops around the self to hold the growing self, our budding ego, intact. It encompasses our most inner space, our sacred space through which we interpret what our senses bring us. A baby has no sense of self and nonself at infancy. As children grow, they form an identity and develop boundaries to separate the self from the rest of the world. These boundaries provide a sense of security for children and protect their innocence. Later our boundaries determine our sense of self-esteem, our self-confidence, our sense of control over our lives, and our personal freedom. With clearly defined boundaries, we know our own thoughts and feelings. Through this screen we interpret and regulate our interactions with our world.

In dysfunctional families, our boundaries become blurred because of the generational crossovers of parents through *boundary invasion* or *boundary neglect*.

Boundary Invasions

Beverly's boundary awareness surfaced in a therapy session with her brother. Fred sat close to Beverly and as they talked, he rubbed his hand on her thigh. Beverly seemed unaware of what I saw as an invasion. I took note of this and we discussed it. As we explored the boundaries in Beverly's family, I learned that her mother listened in on her telephone calls, had long conversations with Beverly's first husband, and would sit up until early morning with him, drinking and flirting. Beverly's mother had also joined her in parties with her friends, becoming "one of the gang."

Beverly could see how natural it was for her to be triangled into her second husband's marriage, since she had been triangled into her parents' marriage, fighting her mother for her father. Later when she learned about her husband's incestuous relationship with his daughter from his first marriage, she felt rage. It seemed that everywhere she turned she saw boundary violations. Beverly remembered being spanked constantly with a wooden stick and her father punching holes in the wall. She recalled how perfect she had tried to be to avoid punishment. She also recalled that during her last visit home, her father had turned to her when they were alone and, staring into her eyes, asked, "Is there anything I can do for you?" Beverly realized it felt sexual. She now realized she had been sexually harassed by Ted, who wanted intercourse several times a day. She worked through the feelings about the shaming boundary violations that occurred during her alcoholism treatment. She especially recalled one of her bitter fights with Ted when he told her she was like all women—an ashtray. "And when you're all filled up, I'll get another." Beverly felt devastated as scenes of her objectification surfaced. She realized that their marriage might not survive.

Beverly became depressed. She cried uncontrollably. "In a way I feel like I'm going to die. I feel so defective. I have never been loved for who I am." She felt her losses. Beverly began to see that she didn't create this alone. She also realized that when she saw Ted, she was seeing both her mother and her father and went through several months of shutting herself off from Ted. When she brought her mother into therapy (her father refused to come), she told her mother she was no longer going to take care of her feelings. She now felt alone and isolated. She wasn't sure she wanted to stay married, yet felt financially dependent on Ted. She said, "I think I'm going crazy." I reminded her that this was part of the way through the shame; she was letting herself see and feel her story. As she came to see that her self-hate was her shame, she began to vent her anger and set limits. She began to shut down and make her own decisions. In parenting, she started to become firm and yet remained a good listener. She began to become playful.

Beverly found it easy to recognize her physical boundary violations; she had more difficulty recognizing her intellectual and emotional boundary invasions. We can recognize bruises or incest or rape. The insidious incestuous emotional invasions like the kind experienced by Beverly are more difficult to discern. Often the invasions occur early in life, leaving its victims robbed of their own growth. Whether known and visible or invisible, these invasions are tears in the screen of the self. The budding self then can't grow naturally.

Boundary Neglect

While boundary invasions are common in dysfunctional families, we see neglected boundaries as well—often in the same family.

Monica was a mother of three adolescents. She was an active parent and substitute teacher. A compulsive helper, she gave herself to anyone, often before being asked. Having drawn no defined line between herself and her children, she lived her life through her children's grades and achievements, beaming with their successes, becoming depressed with their disappointments. She had no awareness of any line between her and the rest of her world and either invaded the space of others or was invaded herself, with little knowledge of what happened.

Monica's history revealed she had been neglected as a child. She had no bed of her own when she was small (she slept in a drawer) and no room of her own until she was twelve. Her educated middle-class parents ran their downtown antique business together and had turned her over to the streets at age seven. She took the bus alone to her doctor's and dentist's appointments and bought her own meals in restaurants. Monica grew up with almost no feedback about what she thought, felt, or did. She said she could not remember ever being touched or held. Her parents had set no limits around bedtime hours, activities, friends, or money. Repeatedly her parents abandoned her. She had no modeling of what was appropriate behavior and no guidance. She felt helpless about taking charge of her life; she had turned her life over to fate. She relied on television, films, and media to learn how to be a woman. She often agreed with what others thought at any given moment; she did not know or trust her own thoughts. She also thought she was not intelligent.

Monica was distraught and exhausted over the constant emotional tirades between her husband, daughter, and two sons. She felt tugged in many directions, even doing school work for her children, yet feeling disrespected with the lack of cooperation or appreciation. She also handled all the family "business" and picked up her husband's and children's clothes. She could hardly talk for more than one minute about herself; all her energy seemed to focus on her children or husband. Out of touch, she wanted to solve all their problems. Her feelings were not available to her and yet she felt bad about some of her caustic remarks when her children and husband often responded with tears. Monica faced a powerful challenge to find her true self and grow up emotionally. This challenge involved her learning about her personal boundary.

The personal boundary, which is like a cocoon made of fine, strong mesh screen, encompasses and protects our whole self. Our boundary has a "zipper" so we can regulate what enters our personal space. Monica's boundary seemed more like a chain link fence than a good mesh screen. Moving from depressed to anxious, Monica made decisions that reinforced her shame and sense of rejection. Monica learned how likable she was after she joined the same women's group that Beverly was in. With feedback from the women's group and with the help of an ACA group, she began a recovery program. Monica changed her behaviors, allowing her children to reap the natural consequences for *their* behavior. She recognized she could not protect them from their pain, any more than she could have saved herself from her own.

Monica and Beverly both focused on their boundaries, setting limits with time, space, money, and helpfulness. They focused on listening to their own thoughts and feelings and changing their own

behaviors. They now understood that the combination of their socialization and their family abuse accounted for their undeveloped boundaries. They found respect for their own and others' boundaries—they
were moving their zippers from the outside to the inside.

Finding Our Zippers

I sketched a drawing of the self with the boundary screen around
it. Drawing a zipper pull on the outside, I then drew another one on
the inside. The goal is to get the zipper on the inside so we can protect
the growing self within us and gain control of our own lives with our
internal "zipper" (Fig. 8).[16]

External Zippers. How often have you felt that your sense of control
was totally outside of you? And how often have you felt vulnerable
when someone comes close to you and gets inside the invisible yet felt
space, but you aren't sure how? Frequent invasions indicate undeveloped, or blurred, boundaries. When control is totally outside of us,
we seem to have a zipper sewn on the outside of our screen, our personal boundary that encloses our intellectual, emotional, and physical
selves.

Intellectual boundary blurring results from mind reading, prying,
or mind raping. It occurs when someone is trying to get into our
heads. We experience it as blaming and criticism. It comes wrapped
in sweetness, in rudeness and sarcasm, or in "specialness." Have you
ever felt "special" when someone gossips with you about someone
else's secret? We hear blurring in unrequested advice fraught with
"you should" and "you ought to" messages. We see women who have
not learned to say no. Raped after accepting a ride from a truckdriver,
Holly said that she couldn't say no because he had been nice enough
to stop. And typically in rape, the woman is charged with "asking for
it." When cultural messages hold women responsible for men's behavior, it makes working through the shame even harder. Intellectual
boundary blurring also occurs when our thoughts are ignored or dis-
qualified. The child with little positive feedback about her thoughts
grows up with uncertainty and mistrust about her ability to think.

Emotional boundary blurring occurs when our emotional space has been invaded or neglected. A needy, lonely parent who wants love desperately often turns to a child. What is easier to love than a child? Beverly's mother had tried to fulfill her need through her daughter; Beverly's father sulked, yet denied all emotions. Some children feel

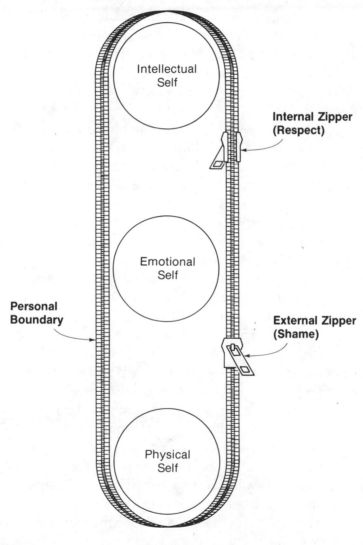

Figure 8
Boundaries and the Zipper to the Self

special because parents discuss their intimate secrets and thoughts with them. On one end of the continuum, blurring creates emotional sponging, in which women become receptacles for the family's feelings. They feel for anyone and everyone. On the other end of the continuum is emotional anemia, in which feelings, if they have any color at all, are painted in pale watercolors. The emotionally anemic have difficulty accepting any closeness and maintaining eye contact. They fear connection. Many of us have been negatively reinforced for honesty or openness of expression. How many of us were told to go to our rooms if we cried or were angry? We may be very reactive and seek emotional highs, or we may shut down. We learn that emotions are not trustworthy.

Physical boundary blurring stems from physical abuse, battering, incest, and rape. We are invaded when others satisfy their own needs for affection through excessive hugging and holding. Boundaries are also blurred when children are deprived of affection and touch, leaving them yearning and constantly looking outward for their physical needs to be met. These violations, whether from intrusion or neglect, result in young women who become passive, open receptacles to be used by others. Many adult women look back on childhood hospitalizations as a time when they were "objectified" with various probes, instruments, enemas, bandages, and all those varied ways in which children are "done to" by professionals.

Other, more subtle physical invasions come from sexualized affection in families, in which children feel the sexual energy from adults' affection but don't know what to call it. Typically, the adult is some "apparently" affectionate relative, "nice Uncle George" or "sweet Aunt Abby." How often have we as parents gently nudged our children toward their violators? Children do not understand this confused affection; they often protest with such words as "weird" and "icky." This can be the foundation for confusion later when, as adults, they experience violations with affection as well as sexual abuse.

Such family intrusiveness is accompanied by cultural messages for women to be objects or things, and we see the results in high rates of sexual abuse in girls and women. Eighty percent of sexual abuse victims are women, eighty percent of whom were abused before twelve.[17] Violence is so pervasive that high percentages of young women victims misinterpret violent acts as love.[18] Between 20 and 50 percent of premarital couples experience violence in their relationships.[19] Some violated children grow up to be violating adults, intruders, "aggressive victims" who use "I'll get you before you get me" as a defense.

Socialized to give ourselves away, our "stuff" can be taken in a variety of ways. In the very moving play *For Colored Girls Who Have Considered Suicide When the Rainbow Is Enuf,* the "Lady in Green" clearly reacts to her "stuff" being taken:

i want my own things/how i lived them/& give me
my memories/how i waz when i waz there/you cant have them
or do nothin wit them/stealin my shit from me/don't make
it yrs/makes it stolen/somebody almost run off wit alla my
stuff/& i waz standin there/lookin at myself/the whole time
& it waznt a spirit took my stuff/waz a man whose ego walked
round like Rodan's shadow/waz a man faster n my innocence/
waz a lover/i made too much room for/almost run off wit alla
my stuff/& i didnt know i'd give it up so quik/& the one
running wit it/dont know he got it/& i'm shoutin this is mine/
& he dont know he got it/my stuff is the anonymous ripped off
treasure of the year/did you know somebody almost got away
with me/

i gotta have me in my pocket/to get round like a good woman
shd/& make the poem in the pot or the chicken in the dance/what
i got to do/i gotta have my stuff to do it to/why dont ya find
yr own things/& leave this package of me for my destiny/what ya
got to get from me/i'll give it to ya/yeh/i'll give it to ya/round
5:00 in the winter/when the sky is blue-red/& Dew City is getting
pressed/if it's really my stuff/ya gotta give it to me/if ya
really want it/i'm the only one/can handle it.[20]

This experience is universal for women, crossing all age and ethnic groups. Whether stolen or given away, we need our own "stuff."

We need to find that place between becoming an angry aggressor and a helpless victim. When our zipper is on the outside, we pay a high price of boundary violations and boundary neglect. We enter relationships with an invisible lasso tightly binding us. Intimacy is a distant, untenable experience we're not entitled to know. We accept being left. Our broken connection results in broken dialogue; we feel isolated but often don't admit it. We feel empty. This empty space fills with anxiety and becomes the reservoir for addictive behaviors and relationships. We desperately try to fill the void of anxious detachment with food, chemicals, exercise, work, or other compulsions. We turn to others in our codependent search for our missing self. We experience emotional cutoffs as normal. If others try to praise or compliment us, we tell ourselves they must be crazy because if they had any intelligence at all, they could see that we really aren't very much. We then diminish those who see the good in us. It becomes a lose-lose situation.

Beverly said, "I think I need to add more to my life besides recovery." Beverly knew that she was in another phase of finding her self, working on her internal zipper.

Internal Zipper. When we are in charge of ourselves and can regulate ourselves intellectually, emotionally, and physically, we have an internal zipper. We then can experience the "five freedoms" family therapist Virginia Satir writes about—the freedom to hear, smell, see, touch, and taste—*and* the freedom to comment on all five.[21] When we identify the historical self, the child in us, we can develop boundaries and allow the self to grow. In knowing our self, we must recover the child-self who shut down to survive in her family. In workshops I lead women through guided fantasy experiences to meet their child-self and their childhood perceptions. They identify perceptions born out of fear of closeness, inability to speak out or ask questions— perceptions born out of the dysfunctional family rules and power imbalance. The child-self needs validation for the shutting down and needs to know that she did the best she could at the time. She was the child; it happened *to* her. As women recognize the child and the belief and meaning systems that were formed early in life, they can then move on to adult meaning systems. I suggest that they not go alone, but that they take their adult competent self with them. I ask them to hold their left hand, representing the child within them, with their right hand, representing the adult self. The woman who downclimbs into her history with her child-self can gain compassion for this part of her who shut down to survive pain.

In the fantasy, as they walk through rooms and note people, pets, smells, and favorite childhood things, women typically find buried feelings and have new understanding of what life was like for their child-self. Women also can see how the base of their perceptions was distorted by living in a dysfunctional family. Often I ask if there is anything they would like to say that they were unable to voice at that time. This they later put into letters or graveyard or in-person visits. As women take responsibility for protecting the growing part of the child-self within them, they are able to recognize that it is the voice of the child in them who has been dictating much of their intellectual, emotional, and physical life.

We find our own voices as we work through our childhood beliefs. Breaking rules, we begin to find our own voices.

Beverly said formerly her voice of shame had constantly been monitoring her interactions. She described its incessant whispering self-doubt: "I wonder if I'm doing okay; I wonder if they'll like me. I hope I don't get found out." Beverly said she knew at some deep level that something was missing. This something was her own true voice. Finding her true voice required cutting through the layers of denial and delusions that made up her provisional self.

Beverly took a course in assertiveness training and a course in women's self-defense. By facing her shame, she was no longer held prisoner by it. As my friend and colleague Marilyn Peterson says, "This freedom to expose who we are is hand in glove with knowing what our rights are, saying yes and saying no." Beverly's fears of being punished and of failing dropped away. She began to trust herself. Recognizing the long periods of childhood memory that were still blocked out, she continued to grieve.

She hung up the telephone when her father talked disrespectfully, teaching him how to treat her. She set limits with Ted on their physical and sexual relationship; this naturally raised his anxiety. They struggled while he entered therapy as well as a Twelve-Step group for his sexual addiction. From her women's group, Beverly was able to get honest feedback and support to take her stands. Beverly also said she was ready to work on her connections with her two stepdaughters. Letting go of her guilt, she found the ability to connect with them. Her relationship with her daughters also stabilized. She also did informational interviews for work possibilities. Beverly said she now experienced some extraordinary moments; she said she thought she was glimpsing what serenity was.

Beverly was learning the positive function of shame—that it is an interior warning system that can tell us that we revealed too much or we trusted the wrong person. As Beverly was identifying her own value system, she was able to see the positive ideals she held and how essential self-respect was to protect those values.

Beverly had reached a new place in her long-term marriage; it was the crisis of loving. Beverly could not yet admit this to herself. Aware that she didn't like or respect the bit of the self she did know, she had to downclimb through five "self messages" to find her core voice. She spoke to Ted.

VOICE ONE: "I am really angry with you; you never support me."

VOICE TWO: "I focused on you because I'm afraid of loving me."

VOICE THREE: "I am unlovable."

VOICE FOUR: "I don't trust. The marriage is not going to work anyway."

VOICE FIVE "I can always get a divorce if this doesn't work out."

CORE VOICE: "If I'm to love him, I have to love me."

Here was the crux of the matter, "If I love me . . ." Beverly had decided during her growing years that she was incapable of loving. She brought this meaning system into her adult relationships; the denial in her "voices" protected her from the risk of commitment to her husband. Long focused on her husband's failings, she discovered her own fear of loving. (Of course he had his own fears as well.) Overpowered by the cultural messages that hold women responsible for relationships, Beverly felt like a failure. In time, she came to know that there is no genuine equal relationship without a self. She realized she couldn't have a self until she had well-defined boundaries. Central to her lack of boundaries was shame, imprisoning her in the trap of self-hatred. Now she knew that shame is an emotion with a signal—a signal to repair her broken relationship with her self.

Claiming Our Selves

Now we're at the heart of the matter, the heart of *our* matter—our selves. Many, if not most, of us have spent years devoting our energy to how to love thee, how to know thee, how to please thee, how to accommodate thee. Dancing chameleons, we asked, "Who do you want me to be?" The I-Thou relationship was often a little "i" with a big "THOU."[22] So we live with the dilemma: "I am responsible for this relationship; yet I should be who *you* want me to be." We carry impaired perceptions from our childhood in addition to the cultural void concerning women's experience. Our "knowing" is "received knowing" that comes from parents and authorities outside ourselves, usually men.[23] Beverly grew up with an unknown self; after down-climbing to find that budding self, she now had compassion for it. Until Beverly could see how her "subjective knowing" voice had been muffled not only by damaging cultural messages but also by the many defenses she had created to survive in her family, she could not find her true voice. Beverly realized that she found what had been missing in her relationships, her self. She turned to Ted and asked, "How could you love *me* if I do not know me, my self?" Now, after several years in therapy with and without Ted, she knew her zipper was on the inside. She trusted her own perceptions and her own feelings.

Replacing our external zippers with internal zippers involves facing our feelings. The feelings come in spurts, in bursts, in indirect "gotchas" at first. We are surprised and feel out of control. And we are! We begin to express our feelings and set limits with people. And it is natural for women moving through this to be angry with men, sometimes all men. We can generalize our anger toward the patriarchy. Some women find their dormant lesbian feelings and act on them. We face rage at the oppression and the family myths and cultural lies. Our boundaries firm. We learn our limits, sometimes by exceeding them.

We make mistakes and we don't always "do it right," but we learn what is right is within us; we increase our self-trust. We question the spiritual. We gain optimism and have a sense of control in our lives. We move to "subjective knowing," the knowing based on our intuition. We find our personal authority and our own truth. We learn that we are entitled to express ourselves, to know ourselves, to act on the messages from our own inner voices.

Beverly was feeling positive about herself after moving through her downclimb into her self. She now knew about her shadow side; she also filled up with new images of respectful "others" in her life and let herself take in new messages. As she did so, her self-respect grew gradually. She now had a distinction between her self and others and knew what she thought and felt. She could discuss openly her relationship with me. In therapy she had experienced a "safe place" to proceed with her growing. She used this relational context and support from her women's group to focus on other relationships—with her children, her parents, her brothers. She talked empathetically about her mother after her mother revealed more of her own story, shedding light on the missing empathy in Beverly's life.[24] Her relationship with Ted brought waves of intense fear. She had numerous opportunities to assert her own relational needs in her marriage. Her husband returned to therapy to do some individual work; we followed up with couples work. They had truly begun changing their process in relationship to one of greater mutuality. In her growing empathy, she could finally forgive herself for her mistakes and even began to laugh at herself. At this writing she is the loving grandmother of four, has a comfortable relationship with her husband, and has a new career working with grief and loss. She has truly deepened her "self-in-relation."[25]

Beverly found in her growth that there was indeed another way to view "self"—a relational self, not a "separated-individuated," lonely, cutoff self. The "self-in-relation" has always been women's way.[26] We have cared deeply about our relationships. Finding the self does not mean staying obsessed with the self and individualism. The benefit in facing shame and finding the self leads us to yet another shame, a genuine, moral shame coming from integrity, self-respect, and respect for others. This is the deepening of our ethical self, the natural outgrowth of natural caring.[27] With this growth of our selfhood, we find our "ideal self." This "ideal self," which grows out of our relatedness, has moral standards of goodness and ethics; to sustain our ideal self we develop an "I must" stance.[28] As women awakening to our true selves, we naturally become more expansive and fully connected to the rest of life and all of nature.[29]

It is no surprise to see most of us encountering the dawn of a self between our twenties and our fifties. To recover our selves, we must also recognize our need for rebirth into a world including the "self-in-relation" experiences of women.[30] This rebirth process is the challenge of forming a mature identity.

CHAPTER 4

FROM ANONYMOUS SELF TO TRUE SELF:
The Challenge of Forging an Identity

I believe that true identity is found ...
in creative activity springing from within.
ANNE MORROW LINDBERGH

The clear blue sky and crisp fall Wisconsin breezes made it a perfect day to climb. Joe and I had had a lovely hike up the trail to our new climbing site; our spirits were high. Joe had done the "lead climb" and, anchored securely at the top of the quartzite rock spire, he was ready to belay me. My last knot tied at my waist, my helmet adjusted, I was ready to climb. I trusted Joe's belaying; we frequently climbed together. "On belay," called Joe. "Climbing," I responded. "Climb!" was Joe's final command, signaling he was set to belay me. The climbing contract was set. I was ready to climb.

Then it happened. Glancing down to my left, I saw about 5 feet away from me a clearly defined edge with a dropoff of about 150 feet to the valley below. We were higher than I had realized. The "edge" was certainly not dangerous; after all I was climbing up the rock facing me, and I was standing on a solid rock-earth base. I had no reason to fear this edge; it had nothing to do with my climb. Still, I felt queasy as I glanced over and down; I remembered my downclimb. Fear rose within me; I became irritated that I was allowing something so external to my climb to affect me. I was ready to climb! I glanced over at the edge again. The damn fear again! I felt angry. "Facing Our Edges!" was the title on my climbing brochure; "Facing Our Terror" would be more accurate. "Who needs this?" I asked myself. "Why am

I compelled to look when I know it only frightens me?" Then Joe's voice trailed down, "Is something wrong?" "No," I lied, "I'm ready to climb." Facing the rockface, I began breathing deeply to relax. It didn't work; I was stuck. I couldn't raise my foot to the little rock nubbin immediately before me. "Damn, I've been here before; why did I look down and get frightened?"

Joe, realizing I must be stuck, called down, "Marilyn, go inside." I got it! "Go inside! That's it!" It was just what I needed to hear. Joe and I had talked often about the "inner climb." Closing my eyes and breathing deeply, I shut out the fear-awakening "edge." Suddenly I felt calm; a stillness rose within me—I felt almost serene. I had my self. Opening my eyes, I placed my foot on the narrow rock ledge before me, put my hands on the rock, and began to climb. Steadily I moved up the rock, focusing only on what was immediately before me, moving deliberately. I was hardly aware of Joe's gathering in my belay rope as I climbed. The "umbilical," as we teasingly called the powerful rope life line, was an ever-present reminder that I wasn't climbing alone. When I reached the top of the climb and said "Off belay," Joe beamed saying, "Congratulations! I've never seen you climb so well! What happened?" I smiled. This was so different from the downclimb at Devil's Tower! This time I had turned within and I found someone there. I now knew more of me.

FROM ANONYMITY TO FORGING A TRUER IDENTITY

Reflecting on the downclimb at Devil's Tower, I realized I did not know then what was "within" to call forth. Now I could trust my inner self, my true self, and count on what I had within me to climb. The phrase "Go inside" was no longer a foreign language. I knew what it meant. The external world induced fears of falling and fears of failing. I was just as powerless over the "edge" as I was powerless over the position of the rock footholds before me. These externals fed my insecurity, my self-doubt. But when I went inside and relied on my self and what I knew, I could let go and allow my trust—in me, my belayer, and the climbing process—to get me up the rock. What had been anonymous to me when covered with shame was now becoming more known to me. I had begun to trust the process, knowing there would be times I would be stuck and fearful. The climbing metaphor transferred over to my daily life. When I got off route, I could count on good friends, some family members, my belayers, to tug those invisible belay ropes of our relationship and keep me on course. I knew I didn't climb alone.

My friend Norma says we don't *form* an identity; we *forge* one out of some real tough stuff, that is, our families, the thicket of cultural myths, and gender-prescribed roles. "Beyond my roles I am a person," said the French philosopher Gabriel Marcel. I think he had that wrong; I believe that "*behind* my roles I am a person." Roles are what we *do*; our true self is our *being*. Since our sense of true self is the core of our identity, we need to unwrap the layers of roles to discover our budding self within.

FROM OBJECT TO SUBJECT

Jessica had not realized how deeply she had fused her self with her roles. Civic-minded, she played a vital role in Santa Monica community organizations. While attending a leadership training seminar, she had a jarring awareness. The leader asked participants to identify themselves by writing three self-descriptions on adhesive tags and sticking them on their shoulders. Jessica wrote quickly. On reading Jessica's tags, the leader assumed that Jessica was teasing about her identity and exclaimed, "What a great sense of humor! You are really creative!" Laughing at Jessica's clever "joke," she turned to the group and called out, "Come, see what Jessica did!" Shocked, Jessica sunk into shame as she stared at her tags: "Daniel Goodson's wife," "Dean Anderson's sister," and "Kathy's mother." Suddenly realizing that there was nothing of herself on the tags, Jessica quickly masked her feelings and laughed along with everyone else. She knew how to pretend. Whenever she told the story to others, she always ended by laughing at herself. Some years later, haunted by the feelings she had walked away from that day, she connected with the pain behind the laughter.

95

Jessica realized that she had learned that her sense of self was to come solely through her relationships with others. Jessica had added her roles so naturally over the years that she was unaware, as many of us have been, of how enveloped and sealed shut she had become in all her roles. In each of her sticker descriptions, she was the object; each phrase contained an apostrophe and implied possession. She belonged to many others. While she highly valued these relationships, she had totally ignored her true self; she remained anonymous.

Jessica later commented, "I know who I am as a daughter; I know who I am as a sister. I know who I am as a mother; I know who I am as a wife. But what I don't know is, 'Who am I?'"

Jessica's question is the question of many women who grew up in dysfunctional families. Many "adult children" with highly developed false selves play their public roles with great success but in their inner psychic world they continue to play out their childhood family roles.[1] While all women struggle with identity, women who have grown up in dysfunctional families have an additional strain when unraveling childhood and adult roles simultaneously. The process is complicated because the rules of shame have kept the budding self anonymous. If our socialization were viewed as a sentence to be diagrammed, we would see that women are the "objects." If you recall, the objects are done *to*. It takes most of us *years* to reconstruct this cultural "sentence structure" and become "subjects."

Two young girls were on our family climbing trip. I was leaning over the rock to encourage them as they climbed. Not long after their initial spurt of energy they got stuck. I watched, waiting to see what they would do. Then one turned to the other and said, "This isn't working; let's try something different." They did, and they were free to continue.

I was amazed to see this! What a valuable lesson! They obviously didn't have their egos invested in the climb; they were free to make mistakes and try new approaches. I wondered at what age that left me. Most of us adult climbers would stay jammed in one spot for too long and keep beating our bodies against the rock until exhausted. What wasted energy! As we climb, we *do* get stuck. In fact, most climbs have at least one "crux," that is, a most difficult "pitch," or section, of a climb. Moving from our anonymity to our true identity means facing more than one crux.

CRUXES IN OUR CLIMB

There are three identifiable but not obvious cruxes where women can get stuck as they move toward true identity. These cruxes are not obvious cruxes to us because they stem from our sociocultural myths and seem natural; they are in the very air we breathe. We may be at a crux in our climb and not know it. The three cruxes are unconscious role playing, role loss, and role deviance and deconstruction.

Unconscious Role Playing

Jean's children were shocked as they talked to her. "You've got to be kidding, Mom. Do you mean that you didn't really *choose* to have kids?" Jean said, "No, I didn't, at least not *fully consciously*. Wanting children was automatic; you came after college and marriage—next on life's list. And it was easy to be asleep; there were no decisions to make. That is where a lot of us were then . . . on automatic pilot." Jean went on, "I became the image of a woman other people wanted me to be instead of the woman I want me to be. I'm not afraid anymore."

Jean had fused her growing self with her roles because she did not realize how deeply they blanketed her. She revealed that she thought only men did that. Not knowing her self, she turned outside herself for her identity, using media images and other women as models.

Young girls from dysfunctional families are especially vulnerable. With poor role models and parts of the true self sealed off, they turn to media images and develop a pseudoself. Carol Gilligan was surprised to find assertive and active girls shutting down emotionally as early as age eleven or twelve.[2] When girls join the adolescent subculture, they take in the cultural myth of what a young woman should be—an object to be desired, to be pleasing, and to be used. Our culture continuously reminds us that women's family roles of wife and mother are crucial to women's psychological well-being; therefore the natural response to children in trouble is mother's role failure. Women need to be aware of how culturally inoculated we are as we interpret our lives. When I saw the book title *No More Lies* I said to myself, "That's it!" No more cultural inoculation![3] Because our feelings about ourselves are shaped by the ever-present prescribed behavioral roles, we are often unconscious about how tightly fused we are to our role selves. And we can carry the best part of those roles with us. This part of the climb is difficult; we cannot know where we are going and can only dimly see the next ledge. We must risk to continue our climb.

Role Loss

When I presented my first workshop on "making our lives our own," I had a jolting surprise about the fusion of self with roles. I asked women to draw their role life line across a large sheet of paper from birth to the present time. Along the line they were to list all their roles from childhood to the present. Then they were to draw lines down from the roles they had acquired after age eighteen and mark with a C only those roles that they felt they had truly chosen. I asked them to mark with an "O" those roles that they felt were prescribed by others. I also asked them to bracket the periods when they experienced "role pileup" and "role loss" (Fig. 9).

On entering each of several small-group meeting rooms, I was surprised to find many women quietly crying as each viewed her life laid out on a sheet of newsprint. They told me they had been unaware of all the multiple roles they had juggled and were grieving over the loss of their complex roles. "At least the role self was *some* self," they said. "We didn't realize how dependent we were on our roles to provide our good feelings about ourselves."

As we move through life, our children grow, our spouses and partners die, our lovers leave, we divorce, we retire. Such "necessary losses" can be easier to accept when women have a strong sense of self, other valued roles, and the support of other women. We need to grieve — but not alone.

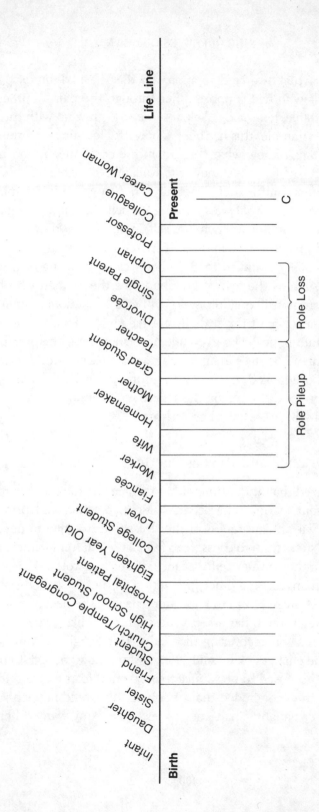

Figure 9   *Role Life Line*

C = Chosen

O = Others Prescribed

As Jean's actual divorce date approached, she had a dinner party for her friends who had supported her through the painful process. Seated at the table, Jean said, "Well, for one who grew up with the 'I'll do it myself' syndrome, this has been a powerful learning experience. A year ago I didn't know what the 'gift in the crisis' meant and now I have the gift—of the constancy and availability of each of you."

We resist our painful grief, especially when our true self is anonymous, because we feel that we are losing the self. Actually, facing this crux means making our anonymous self more vividly known to us. The fear and anxiety of facing grief can keep women unknowingly stuck. This anxiety is linked to the unconscious knowing of a very painful loss, such as the loss of childhood for the woman who had been the overresponsible "adult child" in her dysfunctional family or the loss of innocence of the sexually abused child. Since women are expected to automatically be in charge of relationships, the overfunctioning daughter who lives in anxiety and fear that her world will fall apart is often overlooked. Again, moving through this crux is difficult because it requires us to trust in the self, to not abandon our grieving, growing child-self but to take her with us.

Role Deviance and Deconstruction

Jean realized that at the time of her divorce she took on the roles of single parent, dating adolescent, student, teacher, and primary breadwinner with no awareness of the stress that it added to her life on top of the stress from role loss. Jean felt a little different, almost like a deviant from her former self, because of her new roles.

As Jean changed, so did her interaction with others; she became more honest. As Jean began to know her true self, she began to speak assertively, even though her assertiveness often felt like aggression to her. She was now a "recovering nice lady." Her daughter, Amy, also recognized the changes. Amy said, "I can't stand how you talk to people anymore! You used to be so *nice* to everyone." Jean flinched for a moment but then concluded that of course this would happen. She wasn't who her daughter had known her to be; Amy wanted her to "change back."

Two years later Jean and Amy sat together laughing about this time when a mother and a daughter were both learning to be assertive. Jean was finding more of her true self under her roles. Jean naturally felt "different" when she chose choice; she became a role deviant.

Just as we resist becoming conscious of our roles and facing our loneliness and losses, so too do we resist being cultural deviants. Given our socialization, it is natural for us to fear our changes and we may feel we are wrong and think the problem is us. Facing this crux means facing role conflict—conflict created when our new behaviors do not match others' expectations. In violating the stereotypic expectations for the feminine, we feel the upset and the control of others. Many younger women today realize their sense of self does not reside in the role of mother. Often criticized, they stand tall in defining themselves as "child free" rather than "childless." Women struggling with infertility see themselves as child*less*. Childfree couples can be looked at with disdain or sympathy, depending on whether their situation is voluntary or involuntary. Unmarried women past their thirties, women in lesbian relationships, childfree career women, and working mothers with young children all risk social disapproval. Single women (not men) at couples' parties and lesbian couples in public social settings are subject to criticism. Women need many belayers to continue to climb and get beyond this difficult crux.

IDENTITY—CHOOSING CHOICE

Many women have not felt they have had choice; millions of women do not have choice economically, politically, religiously, or often socially. At first glance it would appear that economic freedom and choice go hand in hand. Yet we find that most women have been unaware of the very idea of choice. There are many ways in which women *can* make choices in their own behalf. Choice means making *conscious* decisions about how we live our relational lives on a daily basis.

Women who choose choice can forge an identity. Although choice can be frightening if we have not learned how to be intentional about our choices, it can also be exciting. We have to give ourselves permission to see when we are off our direct route, to find a new route and be true to it, to keep going, to make mistakes, to rest, and to continue to climb. Because the process is erratic, we do not always see the growth gained from risking. We won't always be congruent when we move off our former route and spiral down into our true selves.

Kay had decided to become involved in a nonviolent civil disobedience action at a local defense manufacturing plant. She planned to risk arrest by climbing over a chainlink fence with a "No Trespassing" sign. As the rest of the crowd moved strongly across the street to begin the action, Kay hung back. She waited for the stoplight to turn green before crossing the street to risk violating the law against trespassing!

The process of forging a new identity requires new ways to think about ourselves; it will take years to assimilate our now acknowledged truth into our psyches. Indeed women have needed to turn outside the family to find new models and perspectives for maturity. Yet many of us have not been aware of the models available to us *within* our families. One model lies in the mother-daughter relationship; another powerful model is the black woman model.

Mothers and Daughters: Redefining the Relationship

Since our identification with our mothers is primary in our development, it is a natural place to turn for a model for identity. Our receiving of caring and our reciprocal caring form a relationship in which both mother and daughter experience emotional sensitivity. This is where empathy is learned as well.[4] While it has been important for women to look back to deprived childhoods and mothers who were in denial, it is equally important to identify what *was* there in our learning. Our mothers are in us, and it is essential to understand the context of our mothers' mothering and have compassion for their oppression.

In working with women and encouraging competencies, Marianne Walters guides women to focus on what women *know* and do well and to trust what they know. In their mother-daughter workshops, Marianne and her daughter Suzanna emphasize that we have not had good models for the mother-daughter relationship; the negative stereotypes so prominent in our society result in mothers and daughters being disconnected or bound together with blame and resentment. Fortunately, we are learning to move beyond responding to the word "daughter" as young, small, or lesser. Maturing daughters need to form an adult relationship with their mothers to learn more about "daughtering." Marianne and Suzanna report being approached by people who applaud them for being such good *friends*. Their clear response is that their relationship is not about friendship at all; rather, it is a new model for the mother-daughter relationship: adult daughter with adult mother.[5]

For years we heard that successful women in the workplace had good relationships with their fathers; this supports the "daughter against mother" theme. Today we know that the work status of *mothers* is a very high predictor of success for *both* daughters and sons. Recent research shows that successful women executives had good relationships with their mothers, whose educations equaled those of their fathers.[6] Gradually we're finding truth in our own models.

The Black Woman Model: Seeing the Obvious

Although we often talk about the lack of competent models for women, we have overlooked for generations the model of black women. Historically black women in this country have known that paid work is necessary; indeed, they have worked outside the home for centuries, usually in subservient and often degrading jobs. They also have developed remarkably effective coping patterns, providing continuity and stability in the family.[7] Although today many black women have jobs, not careers, their work outside the home reinforces their sense of being equal to men. These strong and independent women know well how to live without a man.

Recently, in fact while writing this chapter, I attended a fashion show. My friend Iris was modeling in this fund-raiser for young black women's education. Seated with us at the table was a distinguished, friendly seventy-eight-year-old woman who began chatting with us about her family. I was reminded of my mother as I listened to her proudly tell us about her life's work—her children, grandchildren, and great-grandchildren. Later in our conversation, I asked her who belonged to this organization. "Why, this is a national organization for black women," she proudly stated. Then, beaming with pride, she went on, "It is an organization of highly motivated professional women and, of course, those of us homemakers who *motivated* these professional women." I gasped in astonishment. Ida Mae Young clearly *knew* what her life had been about! For the first time in my life I heard a woman proudly claim it! It was not that she had defined herself in terms of relationships; I often hear this. Rather, what stood out was that she *knew* she had an equal place; her identity was strong.

I turned to others to ask if they had ever heard a woman "claim it." No one had, but the black women at the table said it was much more likely to be heard in the black community. I often hear women young and old take credit for their work, but this was the first time I had heard a woman take credit for her caring. She knew her relationship "work" was equal, if not more than equal, in importance to other women's professional work. Ida Mae clearly knew and took credit for the relationships she had been nurturing through the years.

But black women also know they live with white values—individualism, autonomy, accumulation of goods, achievement, efficiency, competition, and privacy. Black, other racial minority, or white, women share an overwhelmingly difficult challenge in facing patriarchy, the absence of fathers, and a deeply entrenched socioeconomic caste system. The challenge requires an entire rethinking of self and identity.

In contrast to many young black women who have romanticized the roles of homemaker and mother (a dangerous turn say some), most black women know it is "idle dreaming" to think that black women can stay at home, caring for their children and homes. Also, they expect their children to do household chores, and there is less stereotyping of sex roles among black children. Black women know about support and don't limit their friendships to the workplace; they model interdependence.

FROM PSEUDOAUTONOMY
TO THE RELATIONAL SELF

Earlier I discussed the male theories that present adulthood through separation and individuation, the pathway to autonomy.[8] But children *don't* really distance from their mothers as they grow in skill and competence. Rather, they continue to redefine and reconstruct their relationships, which increase in complexity as they understand more and become more aware of differences.[9] That self that is growing through relatedness is the *interdependent* self, the relational self. She maintains a balance in her attachments to others. She has a strong sense of self and simultaneously she can both give and receive to others — in interdependence. It is probably going to take many more years to unravel the myth of autonomy (pseudoautonomy) that has pervaded the adult development literature for years.

Pseudoautonomy

Indoctrinated with male theories, women have learned, falsely so, that autonomy is the outcome symbolizing mature adulthood. Unfortunately, our environment is saturated with cultural messages whereby men shape women's identity and women's roles are devalued. Traditional thought in women's psychology contended that women should become more like men. As a result, many women who had found their voices moved into male-dominated professions and then took on the voice of the "male baritone."[10] Women must be careful not to get caught in a trap of a "female tradition of autonomy." In my women's group for women in management, I saw women dressing in neckties and striped suits, drinking alone, and feeling outside.[11] A great many women have left the workplace because of value conflicts. More and more women and men know that reinforcing autonomy, individualism, and separateness results in isolation, disconnectedness, and emotional cutoffs, all of which wholeheartedly support our "addictive society" and the lives of those raised in dysfunctional families. Indeed, in our culture, shame and pseudoautonomy have equaled corporate success. With shame as the powerful motivator, no wonder we find that 35 percent of male corporate executives in this country come from alcoholic families![12] They know well how to live with emotional cutoffs and isolation. However, what brought these men success has also made them candidates for psychotherapy. On numerous occasions I have teased emotionally shutdown corporate and professional men by saying that if their emotional functioning were manifested physically, they would be parking in the disabled slots in the office parking lot. Many of these men now nod their heads in agreement. Rather than use the terms "disengagement," "separation," and "individuation," feminist psychologists now refer to the "relational differentiation process."[13]

In truth, men have not achieved autonomy. Rather, they have only achieved *pseudoautonomy* and have done so only because they have always been supported by women—sisters, wives, daughters, secretaries, lovers, and mothers! We know that emotional dependence persists even in the face of geographical distancing. The remarriage rate among divorced and widowed men is clear proof of men's dependency on women. Many men know this at some very deep level and get angry because they neither feel powerful nor own their power, often strangers to interdependence.

Interdependence

Historically we had learned that women (socialized to be near mother and home) need to be more separate and men (socialized to distance from mother) need to connect. Carol Gilligan's work has shown that this is not the case and insists that we must revise our whole way of thinking about the self.[14] Gilligan asserts that women have an ethical base grounded in our knowing of human relationships—self and others are interdependent. Women's experiences have taught us that care and responsibility for the well-being of others—not separateness and distance—are the qualities to strive for. Although as women we have always known this, we have struggled with identity because we did not consciously realize that our identity includes morality. Gilligan finds that moral people treat others as their equals.[15]

So the identity issue becomes more complex as we add the word *moral* to *relationships* and *mutual* to *interdependence.*

In writing this chapter, I became frustrated while searching for a single word to describe women's sense of self. I talked with women; I read other women's work. I felt stuck; how could I write about women's identity and not have a term for the mature adult self who is both separate (relationally differentiated) and connected? While some writers have suggested the word "mutual self," others, including Jean Baker Miller, say they can find no single word to describe women's sense of self.[16] So what word can depict an adult identity that encompasses competency and caring? At this time many use the term self-in-relation, judging that term to be the most honest reflection of what is being described.

What we are living with today is the result of our climbing out of a dependent, oppressed subculture.[17] As we stand on our ledge and look back, we can see quite clearly where we have been but we can't see a pinnacle yet; we can only see what is right before us. In time, more language will change as meanings change to reflect the lives of women.

Yet we live in a public world in which the ethic of care is not valued in the marketplace and has kept women imprisoned. Not long ago a woman in a workshop audience, upon hearing me talk about Carol Gilligan and an ethic of care, challenged the emphasis on caring—that it might be used to the detriment of poor women who already are doing all the caring for parents and children. We discussed the fact that we must take our caring into the public world where social changes can be made. Another woman in the workshop audience responded, "But what we are talking about here is inherent in life. It isn't just about what we *do*, . . . it's about who we *are*. This is in our unconscious, our historical self that is connected to all of life." Her words strongly remind us of all life moving naturally toward continuity and care, developing relationships, while understanding that without social change, women will continue to be oppressed.

As Martin Buber implied, the "individual" is a fact of existence insofar as it is a unit built of relationships.[18] Carol Gilligan says we gain our strength by weaving ourselves into the world of relationships, not by accumulating power.[19] Women's identity develops through our interactions with the environment. We risk traditional "safety" for a life with no warranty; we continuously modify and demythify our relationships—with self and with others. Since we are the integration of *all* our life relationships, women's identity must encompass the context of relationship, the "between."

Jacqueline, my dear seventy-four-year-old friend from France, was preparing to say goodbye after her visit here. Looking at her dark brown eyes set into her richly lined skin, I had tears in my eyes. Jacqueline asked what they were about. I said, "It's because you are leaving, and I will miss you." Jacqueline, placing one hand on my shoulder and her other hand over her heart, looked lovingly at me as she said in her thick French accent, "But oh, my dahling, you know, don't you, zat I take you weeth me; I carry you een my hot (heart)." So it is; we carry our relationships within us. They are part of our true self. As we claim our true self and say "I am . . . ," we move from being the object to being the subject in our relationships, relationships in which there are two subjects mutually meeting. We see relationships balance.

All climbers eventually learn that climbing is about balance, not physical strength. Women must balance their sense of care and responsibility for others with their need for public competence. Public competence involves obtaining financial equity, political parity, and marketable skills—while not overvaluing male patterns. Women's identity, or true self, includes a developed boundary encompassing both a self of relatedness and a competent role self. Relatedness and roles are not separate domains; through integrating these we move toward interdependence.

Because we still struggle to integrate interdependence, or mutuality, into our psyches, this chapter on the challenge of women's identity at this time in history has been the most difficult to write. What I have written here can be shot at and criticized; however, with our collective stories about our own identity, we are redefining and modifying our relationships with our selves and with our culture.

Knowing our true self involves self-awareness, awareness of how others see us, of our feelings about their perceptions, and of our capacity to respond to them. This is simple; it just isn't easy.

Knowing our true self intimately requires a safe growing place for our anonymous self. We create this safe place by simultaneously delineating our true self from our role self while replacing the rules of shame with rules for being real. As our true self grows, we gradually internalize the rules for being real. Over time, we present our waffling identity to the world and reach the "I am." This is not a narcissistic "I am" identity but an "I am" that includes *self and other* empathy. This identity will constantly be polished, allowing a fine patina of character to develop. Whether we lose or gain roles, this identity can remain intact.

A MUTUAL EMPATHETIC PROCESS: RULES FOR BEING REAL

Some time ago some clients came to me saying, "We know what we're doing wrong now and we're catching ourselves at it, but we don't know how to do it differently!" All too familiar with the rules of shame, they knew little about the rules for healthy mutual relationships and reminded me that neither their family nor their culture had been a dependable teacher.

No one can have a true identity unless she has guiding rules. Rock climbing has rules; the ethics in climbing parallel the ethics in daily living: stay on course, resist cheating, trust your belayers, rest, and ask for help. Just as it can be hazardous to climb without any instruction, so is it dangerous for our anonymous self to climb toward an identity without rules. We already know what the rules of shame can do; we need rules for being real.

While our former relationships were founded on need, our healthy mutual relationships can be built on our affluence. We are entitled to be real; we are entitled to respect. We are entitled to nurture our anonymous self into our known, true self. Since we define ourselves in relationship, we need to govern our relationships with growth-enhancing, affirming rules, a process for empathy. With these rules we teach others how to treat us. As we internalize this new set of rules, we convey to others that they matter to us and we matter to them. Socialized to nurture others, as women we need to learn to matter to ourselves.

Rule 1: I'll Face My Emptiness; You Need Not Fill Me Up

It is natural to feel emptiness sometimes; now I know this is normal. Before I can find solitude in my life, I must face my emptiness by sitting face-to-face with my basic human aloneness, my craving to be whole. I don't need you to take away my loneliness or to fill me up, and I don't need to fill up with work or cookies or chemicals or exercise or chatter. I can simply know that this is part of being human, the other side of solitude. Often we don't recognize our emptiness.

Rose felt despondent; she had gained 20 pounds and didn't know how to make changes. With both daughters away at college and her husband happily settled in his work, she found herself longing more for her native Puerto Rico. "Yet, I'm not sure I could ever live there again; I do like living as an American woman. And, after all, both our families have come here with us; that would hardly be fair. And yet I don't want to end up like the 'folks'—with their dependency on us to fill their lives. I don't miss *that* part of Puerto Rico."

Rose's friend, Lucia, commented, "You sound like you're feeling empty." Rose looked directly into Lucia's eyes; she asked, "How do you know what that is? No one has ever said that out loud to me, but that *is* it." Rose wept. Lucia understood. As they talked, Rose realized how she had been so actively parenting, wifing, and daughtering that she had not considered her own needs and what she might want to do for the next thirty years of her life. Rose went to the women's center for life/career assessment and took a part-time job in real estate, working with low-income families. By facing her emptiness, she was also able to face years of bottled-up feelings and move from depression to anticipation. She no longer was a passive, reactive object; she was now a self-motivated subject, writing her own story. She used her first paycheck to visit family and friends in Puerto Rico.

Most of us seldom acknowledge emptiness, and that's easy to understand. When we experience the "nothingness" along with the absence of any connectedness to anyone or anything, we feel frightened. Yet facing our emptiness is part of the process of being human.

Many women in transition get depressed or, fearing emptiness, turn to alcohol or addictions to medicate their feelings. More than

60 percent of women over age sixty are on psychoactive prescription drugs![20] The woman dependent on her children for her sense of self will feel a wrenching tear when they leave home or when they surprise her by violating her role expectations. But her "tornness" may well be the recognition of how alone she is, how lonely her marriage is, how depressed and anxious she is about an uncertain future. When we no longer deny our emptiness, we no longer have to incessantly fill up with busying activities and substances that block our spiritual core.

Rule 2: I'll Trust and Tell You When I Don't

Trust is the reliance upon the nonverbal communication of another in a high-risk situation. Our nonverbal communication is five times more believable than our verbal; we need to trust our own intuition and our "infallible gut knowing." We have to let go of "shoulds." And we need to trust our distrust. It can be difficult to know our own mistrust; words lie.

Paula and Cynthia were struggling with their upcoming visit to the West Coast to visit Cynthia's parents for a family reunion. Cynthia was visibly upset, saying she didn't know what to do with Paula's anger toward her dad. True, he had been rude to Paula when they told Cynthia's parents about their commitment to be in relationship together, but that had been over a year ago. Now Cynthia's mother had extended invitations to Paula and Cynthia to visit them. Paula admitted she was and had been angry with Cynthia's father for his rudeness and "cold shoulder" when they disclosed their relationship. Paula also told Cynthia that she felt betrayed when Cynthia did not stand up to him. "You seemed more concerned about his feelings than about our relationship," Paula said. Paula continued that she was fearful of going to Cynthia's parents' home and being emotionally abandoned.

Cynthia reassured Paula that she had concentrated on her "protectiveness" in therapy. "I want you to trust me," she declared. "Give me another chance. I have decided that if you and my dad do have a fight, I will not interfere. I know it's not right."

When Paula and Cynthia arrived at Cynthia's parents' home, Paula did comment to Cynthia's dad about how she had felt the last visit. Cynthia's dad glowered at Paula, as if to push her away. But Paula continued and they proceeded to heatedly talk together—at first defensively and then more openly. Cynthia did keep her word; she left the room and went outside for a walk; she knew Paula could hold her own.

When Cynthia returned home, she found her father and Paula drinking coffee together. They both reassured Cynthia that they had just had a good fight and both felt comfortable with one another now. Cynthia sat next to Paula at the table and took her hand in hers. Paula's trust in Cynthia took hold.

Trust is primary to a relationship. Our mistrust of whether we can truly count on someone or on ourselves can surface in any stressful situation. Paula and Cynthia's experience only made apparent what was interfering in their relationship. Both Paula and Cynthia said that this was a major turning point in their relationship; within two months after this visit, they had a wedding ceremony.

Rule 3: I'll Be There; You Can Count on Me

All I can give you is my word; my behaviors must follow through. My "being there" will be based on my responsibility and availability but with limits rather than blind devotion. I am committed to me as well as to you. I am grown up enough to know that there will be times when I won't want to be there and I will not always be as available as I might like to be. But you can count on me.

Deborah and Natalie had broadened and deepened their friendship when they joined their local affinity group that did civil disobedience in protest of nuclear weapons manufacturing. Natalie was going to risk arrest by trespassing on the grounds of a weapons manufacturing plant in remembrance of Hiroshima Day. This was a first for Natalie; she had always been a part of the action from the periphery. Weighing her decision and intention for almost a year, Natalie had asked Deborah to be her support person, the one designated to be with her throughout the process. Natalie and Deborah both noticed the strong spiritual connection in the group's circle that evening after planning their action. They talked on the way home about the unity and purpose they both experienced. Natalie commented, "I'm so grateful we can act on these values together. I feel so rich." At 12:30 that night Natalie's telephone rang. Groggy, she bolted up in bed when she heard Deborah's pain-filled voice. "Terry's on a rampage; he said he doesn't want me to have any part of any actions tomorrow. He told me I'm not to go, and if I do, he's through. And I don't even know what that means, but now he won't talk about it. I'm sleeping down in the den and calling you from there. I am just furious and also scared. He sounded serious."

Natalie felt an inner sinking; feelings of compassion for her friend, irritation with Terry, Deborah's husband, and anxiety for herself were all boiling together. After talking for about a half hour Natalie said, "Well, Deborah, I'm sorry about your struggle. I'll still get arrested. I have counted on your being there; naturally the decision is yours." The "former Natalie" would have put her friend first and said, "That's okay, I don't need support." Natalie no longer put her own needs last. But she did sleep fitfully that night. In the morning she felt vulnerable and shaky as she drove over to the plant. It was too late to call someone else. She knew the group would give plenty of support. As she walked up to the site, she thought she saw, yes, it *was*— Deborah! Natalie and Deborah embraced and then, with a somber facial expression, Deborah said, "I guess we're both taking risks today. It's time to grow up and live my own values and that includes being here today." "I'm glad you're here," Natalie responded. "I'm glad I can count on you."

Deborah had realized that she had to make her own responsible choices. She had felt torn but she had said, "I'll be there." She also realized that her "no" to Terry was a "yes" to her self.

Rule 4: I'll Tell You If I'm Leaving; I'll Be Honest About Where I Am

Rule 4 includes psychological leaving as well as physical leaving. If I can't be psychologically present with you, I'll tell you rather than pretend. No one can be 100 percent present all the time.

Sharon felt exhausted; she had worked a long day and had gone to a committee meeting that evening. When she arrived home, her doorbell rang. Over the speaker she heard, "Please, Sharon, let me come in. I need to talk to you—*badly*." "Of course," Sharon replied, recognizing the voice of her old friend Millie.

As Sharon waited for Millie to arrive at her door, she told herself that she would have to muster up a little more energy; her friend was in need. Millie entered the condo and sat down like a slumped rag doll. She began to cry, saying that her ex-husband, Dan, called to tell her he was remarrying in a month. In a sobbing voice, she said it brought back all her pain, even though she would not want to be married to him any longer.

Sharon listened empathetically; she knew that her friend's divorce, although behind her, had been very painful since her ex-husband had become involved with an old friend of theirs when leaving their marriage. Sharon felt sad and angry for her friend, and then something washed over Sharon. She felt herself drifting off; suddenly she knew she was too exhausted to listen anymore. "But this is my dear friend!" she said to herself. "Shape up!" Now she saw Millie stare at her, as though she was checking to see if she was still listening.

Sharon knew she was discovered. "Look, Millie. I know this isn't going to feel good to hear, but I must be honest with you. I just can't be here any longer with you. I am so exhausted that I am tuning you out, and it's nothing to do with you. I feel just wretched, but I can't pretend to listen any more. I am truly sorry. I can plan on having dinner with you tomorrow night if you're free, and I do want to hear your feelings." She paused. "God, this is hard to do," she commented.

Sharon knew anyone can sense when someone leaves psychologically. Since we have been socialized to be focused on others, we look to others for cues about ourselves. Often when someone leaves us, we think it is because of us, not that person. We tell ourselves we are boring or dull rather than challenge the rudeness. I remember my young children tugging at me when I tuned out psychologically. They charged, "Hey, Mom, you're not listening." As adults we have become dishonest with ourselves in being overresponsible to others. When our friends and family members have grown up with fears of abandonment, whether physical or psychological, we can reassure them by telling them when we're leaving.

Rule 5: I'll Let You Know My Thoughts and Feelings to the Fullest Extent Possible

Since I am human and not 100 percent aware, I'll not always know just what my thoughts and feelings are. So I may need to take care of "unfinished business" later. And I'll consider the context when I let you know me. I'll let you know my thoughts and feelings to the extent they are appropriate; honesty without sensitivity is brutality. Some people assault others by saying "I was only being honest," thereby justifying their disrespect. I will consider the context when I share my honesty.

Liz saw her eleven-year-old daughter Maggie sitting, sadly staring out the window, waiting for her dad to pick her up. He was four hours late; Liz could not reach him by telephone and her anger at him was at the boiling point. He had seen Maggie only once that month and Liz realized how powerless she was over his meager visitation. Liz was all too ready to "do" her daughter's anger for her; she had tried many times to "help" her daughter see that she did nothing to deserve this and had a right to be angry. Maggie had retreated. Liz did not want Maggie to accept her dad's behavior but knew that if she spoke to Rick, he would only "punish" Maggie more. Liz felt caught in a bind. She wanted to blow up and let Maggie know what a jerk her father was being; yet he was her father and Liz knew she did not want to polarize her daughter. She had heard bitter stories of divorced parents who drew their kids into their divorce battles.

Liz went to her bedroom, picked up a tennis racket, and started whacking it on her bed, releasing her boiling anger toward Rick. Then the tears came, and she fully realized she could not prevent Maggie's hurt; she knew from experience that if she came on too strongly, Maggie would defend her father. Liz knew all too well about father forgiveness and father protection; she had taught Maggie well. She saw herself in Maggie and was angry with herself and felt guilty. Liz telephoned a friend from her ACA (Adult Children's Anonymous) group and got support for her anger. Liz knew this was between her and Rick; it would not be appropriate to release her intense anger in front of her daughter. Liz returned to Maggie and lovingly and firmly said, "We're going to eat lunch now; afterward you can return to the window if you choose, but now it's time to eat." She knew Maggie would have to work out her own relationship with her father.

Liz had worked hard to know and express her thoughts and feelings, but she knew it would be inappropriate to share them with Maggie in the same way she could with a peer. Liz was grateful that she had found her anger; it helped her see clearly. Psychologist Harriet Goldhor Lerner says, "The taboos against our feeling and expressing anger are so powerful that even knowing when we are angry is not a simple matter."[21] As conditioned as we are to being pleasers, we all struggle both with being in touch with our negative feelings and with expressing them. We can model this for others and yet we must be sensitive to the power imbalances in our relationships, as with children, when we choose to express ourselves.

Rule 6: I'll Be Vulnerable as Often as I Can

It is said that to be authentically naked in the twentieth century is as difficult as being born again. I need the ability to be vulnerable; I will find my own truths in order to be vulnerable. When I remove my mask spontaneously, I am letting you see me and know me.

Louise had been upset about her marriage of ten years. In therapy she was discovering how untrue to herself she had been while being so protective of her husband and his career. Louise and John were each in their second marriage and were parenting four children together. Louise said she was afraid to find her feelings, yet she knew this wasn't who she wanted to be. She was well aware that she was totally financially dependent on John and was comfortable with their child-centered life-style. She said, "Look, I divorced once; I can't go through that again." Admitting to herself how lonely and isolated she felt, she realized she needed to be honest with herself and with John. "He's never vulnerable with me!" "And," she added quickly, "I am never vulnerable with him."

Louise began her journey through her family of origin while also receiving career counseling. In the process she learned she had shut down in her covertly abusing family and had buried her anger from her childhood and from her first marriage. As she recovered her feelings, she dropped her masked expression. She had learned to be vulnerable and was ready to face John. "But I'm afraid this could be the end of our marriage. He is perfectly satisfied with this pseudomarriage. And surely it's not fair to him since I'm the one who changed!" The next week John called for a joint appointment. I knew he was unconsciously sensing the change in Louise, but he said he just realized he had not been in for a while. Louise immediately began, with an honest expression of pain on her face. "John, I have been lonely in this marriage for too many years. I want you to know that I no longer intend to protect you from my pain. I have had a lot to do with this brother-sister marriage, and I own that. I don't know what this means, but I am no longer accepting this pattern. And I'm terrified that we won't make it." Her eyes filled with tears, her face red, Louise sat tall and was congruent. Louise realized she could not change John; she could only be vulnerable about herself. She realized she could not know what the outcome would be; being vulnerable was a great risk for Louise.

A woman with an anonymous self cannot be vulnerable. As Louise found her true self, she found her honest voice, a voice filled with all her feelings. Like other women who can touch the core of their true self, Louise had become motivated from within. She could not turn back.

Rule 7: I'll Disagree and Say When I Do

"And *stay* when I do . . ." could be the rule for many of us who learned to leave psychologically or walk away when in conflict. We don't have to think alike. Remember, if the two of you think alike, one of you isn't needed! Our fused and dependent relationships demanded agreement; healthy relationships foster accuracy.

Jean and her sister and brother-in-law were sitting at the dining room table with Jean's aunt and uncle. Their discussion was typical, focused on broad social problems and young people. Years earlier one of Jean's children had been involved in drug abuse and Jean, guilty about upsetting her children's lives with divorce, had blamed herself for years. Like other overresponsible mothers, Jean had difficulty in her early postdivorce years accepting that her family's disruption wasn't all her responsibility.

Then, like a comet hurtling down from nowhere, Jean's aunt said, "Jean, you're probably not going to like this." Without pausing, she continued, "Do you want to know what *I* think caused the problems in your family? I think it all began when you got so absorbed in your own life that you just weren't there for those kids." Jean was stunned! "How could this be?" Jean asked herself. Her mind flashed to memories of staying up until two in the morning doing schoolwork after evening courses so she would not interrupt her roles of wife and mother. She felt defensive at this attack; anger surfaced. The others froze while Jean gasped and responded, "You're right; I don't like hearing that. It's just one more 'blame the mother' story, blame the woman. I am very deeply hurt by your blaming. Did you ever consider for one moment that the kids might have needed their father? Did you ever consider that someone other than me, the mother, could have contributed to any problems?" Sarcastically Jean's aunt said, "Well, I suppose you'll never forgive me for saying this." Jean firmly replied, "I might not." Then silence. A wall rose between them. Jean felt tears coming and struggled to hold onto herself. She did not feel safe enough to be vulnerable. Jean's sister supportively joined in, reminding her aunt about her own children's adolescent struggles with drugs; it fell flat. Her aunt, uncle, and husband didn't respond. All three shared an age-old assumption: women are responsible for all family problems.

Jean's self waffled. She suddenly felt alone; her self-doubt surfaced once again. The old messages about being a good mother returned. Yet Jean felt different; this time the feeling of "inappropriateness" was only a momentary flashback; she realized she had been honest with her aunt in speaking her own truth. She had certainly heard murmurs of this from her aunt before, but never out loud. At least this time she had stood up; her anger had helped her to speak clearly. She had not been inappropriate; she was no longer the dutifully respectful niece child. She now felt like the adult niece, a peer.

Jean realized that this was not about her at all; it was about her aunt being culturally brainwashed and, like many women her age, she had had no deprogramming possibilities. Jean knew it would be nearly impossible to get her aunt's support for any identity that did not encompass the traditional roles of wife and mother. Jean valued her long history with her aunt and uncle. Jean knew their disagreement did not mean leaving or ending the relationship with her aging aunt.

Rule 8: I'll Comment on My Reality

I shall speak of what I know. In my commitment to growth, I shall speak aloud of what I see and what I hear. It will be my perception, my reality, and I shall affirm it, even if I am alone in it. I am committed to being true to my experience. I shall no longer lie to protect others.

In Henrik Ibsen's play *A Doll's House,* Nora has decided she must leave her husband, Torvald, to understand and know herself. Nora states:

> But our home has been nothing but a playroom. I have been your doll-wife, just as at home I was papa's doll-child; and here the children have been my dolls. I thought it great fun when I played with them. That is what our marriage has been, Torvald.

Torvald, upset, reminds Nora about her roles:

TORVALD: It's shocking. This is how you would neglect your most sacred duties.

NORA: What do you consider my most sacred duties?

TORVALD: Do I need to tell you that? Are they not your duties to your husband and your children?

NORA: I have other duties just as sacred.

TORVALD: That you have not. What duties could those be?

NORA: Duties to myself.

TORVALD: Before all else, you are a wife and a mother.

NORA: I don't believe that any longer. I believe that before all else I am a reasonable human being, just as you are—or, at all events, that I must try and become one.[22]

Nora had awakened to find herself buried under her roles. Our culture continues to reinforce our playing out our self-sacrificing roles of wife and mother. Eventually, however, many women awaken to seek maturity on their own terms. Some stay married during this process; others separate or divorce. An implicit, culturebound marital contract would not survive Nora's newfound integrity; a new contract would be essential. My friend Pat says she has been married seven times, each time to the same man.

Rule 9: I'll Take the Consequences for What I Say and Do

When I choose choice, I know there will be consequences for myself and for others. There will be hurt. All genuine relationships include hurt at times. In my willingness to wrestle with choice I do not take the easy way out, but I practice the courage and strength to live according to my convictions.

Elsie was breathless as she entered group. Intensely focused on the faces of the women there, she disclosed, "I love a woman." Elsie was overwhelmed; she had met Elaine at their local school board meetings. Elsie was anguished as she continued, "I tried to tell myself I could make this go away. It is awful; it is wonderful. I am married; she is single. I have been living with this secret for far too long; I must now do something about it. I cannot live with my dishonesty."

This was the beginning of Elsie's coming-out process. Initially, in individual therapy, she was so fearful and anxious that she could not even sit back on the chair. As she continued to get support from a few close friends and her women's group, she became more settled with the idea. She entered a group for married women exploring sexual preference and let herself know that she had been lesbian since adolescence. Her sexual shutdown at adolescence continued in her sexually unfulfilling marriage. Elsie struggled with keeping the secret, yet she knew she was not yet ready to tell her husband and her family. She then faced the weighty decision-making process of who to tell and in what order. Afraid of losing her children to a punishing husband, she got legal consultation.

Elsie's consequences were high priced; she was deeply concerned about her two adolescent sons and her ten-year-old daughter. Her commitment to live an honest life and her commitment to her marriage and family were in direct conflict. Elsie and Elaine proceeded slowly, carefully reflecting on all their decisions until eventually, two years later, they were established in a relationship that was solid and accepted by most of their family members. They parented together with Elsie's ex-husband, Michael, and the children entered an educational support group for children of gays and lesbians.

Elsie's choosing choice entailed facing strong cultural prohibitions. To be a lesbian, or to be a feminist, is considered unnatural by many men and women and male-dominated institutions. In response to the strident voices from outside, many lesbian women have gone underground. Feminists face penalties for defying traditional sex roles; lesbian women experience even greater penalties for preferring same-sex relationships. When lesbian women discard accepted sex roles, their emotional development is commonly referred to as psychopathology or mental illness. This flies in the face of what many of us know to be true: homophobia is a pervasive illness in our society. Elsie had the courage and maturity to take the consequences for claiming her sexual preference and her identity.

Rule 10: I'll Be Receptive to Giving and Taking

"Love is an investment," says Carl Whitaker.[23] We need to collect our dividends. We surely wouldn't put our money in a bank that didn't pay interest! Relationships require reciprocity—giving to one another, as well as feeling good about receiving from one another. The giving and taking exist in behaviors as well as emotions.

Since her hospitalization for depression and subsequent therapy, Ginger was no longer the overresponsible wife who took care of everything at home plus five children plus a part-time job. Formerly a domineering, paternalistic husband who was deeply engulfed in his career, Jim was now overly solicitous. He had taken over all the meals and household chores without Ginger ever having to ask.

Furious, Ginger wanted to scream. She asked, "Am I crazy? I should love this, right? Well, I don't. He always looks like he is suffering and seems to sulk once guests leave." She continued, "And he won't ever say no, so I don't trust him. His 'all taking' is now 'all giving.'" They had just exchanged roles. Ginger realized that Jim was manipulating her; he controlled her through his pleasing. Moreover, the fact that many of their friends commented on how wonderful he was also infuriated Ginger. "Why is it a man becomes a hero when he does what I've been doing all our married life?" asked Ginger.

Jim's role behavior, however, did not stem from his intent to share responsibilities. Rather, it served only to help him feel better about himself. Jim, an accountant, revealed in therapy that he was fearful of Ginger's anger and felt guilty about how much he had taken and was attempting to balance the ledger. Ginger sensed his insincerity and Jim felt trapped. He truthfully told Ginger that his helpfulness was to help *him*. He was afraid she might leave him. Ginger and Jim decided to work on an honest giving-and-taking relationship.

Working on their love investment in therapy, they came in with lists of their unstated expectations of each other. Their lists began "If you love me, you will . . ." and "If I love you, I will. . ." Making the implicit explicit, they changed the "I give, you take" to "I give and take and you give and take." Their power struggle diminished as they became vulnerable and shared their fears with one another. Both Ginger and Jim were eventually able to both give and take.

Rule 11: I Promise to Respect and Have Compassion—for Your Struggle as Well as Mine

It is important to value and befriend the healing self within us. I will not judge you. I will make a safe place for you as well as for me.

Margie, a highly successful career woman, struggled with anxiety. She never knew when it was coming, so she had developed her breathing, relaxation, and speaking skills in an attempt to overcome it. While these had given her some symptomatic relief, she lived in total dread of her anxiety attacks. When the anxiety surfaced, she felt little and needy and ashamed. On the day she entered therapy, she was in the midst of an anxiety attack. Asked to close her eyes and picture herself at this moment, she saw herself sitting on the stairs in her childhood home; she was seven. Her five-year-old sister was sitting next to her. On questioning, she revealed that her mother and father were out drinking again and she was worried that they might not come home. Both her parents had left the two of them every night, saying they were going out to "party." Now Margie had a clear context for her anxiety; she learned that she had focused all her childhood anxiety into her professional role as the head of her human development corporation. Her "adult" voice had always told her to be brave and strong and all would be okay. Now she could speak aloud of how frightened she was; she cried hard with the sobs of a child. Margie had denied herself her fears—fear that her parents might not come home and the even greater fear that they might fight when they came home. Margie had not realized how much she had lost in childhood. Childhood was serious; she had never felt secure; she had never learned how to play.

Margie began to grieve the loss of her childhood—the loss of being an innocent child. Margie learned that her anxiety was the anxiety of the child in her who had shut down and was now awakening. As Margie developed compassion for the hurting child within her, she respected her fears and anxiety and asked friends to support her in her newfound struggle. On befriending the child within her, Margie's anxiety vanished within four months.

Rule 12: I Understand That My Needs for Intimacy May Be Different from Yours

Each of us has a very personal experience of intimacy. Two persons can long for or demand intimacy and have two very different experiences in mind; there is no right way or one way.

My friends Ethelyn and Howard fought long and hard over intimacy. "I want intimacy," Ethelyn demanded. "Well, I want intimacy, too," snapped Howard. The word was the same, but their messages were bypassing each other because the word meant something different to each of them. Ethelyn said, "I don't think I should have to depend totally on my women friends for my emotional intimacy!"

Howard responded, "Well, I know that's where it's at for you, but that's not as high on my list. You just never like to be outdoors with me, and it's an almost sacred place to me." Clearly, both had defined intimacy according to their own known experiences. Ethelyn wanted more emotional closeness through shared feelings. Howard wanted the closeness he enjoyed so fully when they sailed or biked together. Yet, they had never talked about what intimacy *meant*. As they focused on respecting each other's intimacy needs, Howard became more vulnerable with his feelings and Ethelyn bought a new bicycle and became more competent at sailing. Ethelyn and Howard had stopped trying to change each other and could accept and respect each other's choices. Ethelyn's and Howard's changes reflected their mutual respect for each other; Ethelyn and Howard had each held fast for what they wanted. Loyal to herself and trusting herself, Ethelyn could stand up for what she wanted. I smiled when I received her postcard from a Lake Chatauqua seminar last summer. It read, "Having a great time; I just returned from a bicycle ride and Howard is off in a dream seminar. Love, Ethelyn."

With these twelve rules for being real, we can continue to discover our true, core self and develop an identity that is known to us and others. Living these rules provides us with a boundary to protect the relational self within while screening what we take in from the outside world. As we move up in our climb, we become more of who we are, from our own experiences. The climb will not be a direct route; we must often stand still and prepare for the next pitch of the climb in moving from an object identity to a subject identity.

In order to move toward modifying our relationship identity with our culture, we must first face the challenge of coming to terms with our sexuality.

CHAPTER 5

EMBODYING OUR BEING:
The Challenge of
Sexual-Spiritual Integration

The first problem for all of us, men and
women, is not to learn, but to unlearn.

GLORIA STEINEM

My friend Jacqueline revealed her annual spring ritual in the country-side in southern France. After she planted her potatoes and her roses, she climbed to the top of the hill adjacent to her property where she took off all her clothing. She stretched her arms openly to the sun-filled sky, took in several deep breaths, and gave thanks. She then lay quietly in the grass, feeling her connection to the earth while absorbing the warmth of the noontime sun on her naked body. Saturated and nourished with earth and sun, she then turned over onto her side, and rolled, tumbling like a child, down the hillside.

Jacqueline's story describes her acceptance of *all* of herself. She had integrated her sexuality with her spirituality, feeling her sense of connection with all of life's creative energy. The catalyst for this integration was her sensuality. By "sensuality" I do not mean the old dictionary meaning of "carnality" and "lust"; rather, sensuality is openness to our senses. Jacqueline's senses were fully alive; thus, she could take in all that she saw, heard, smelled, tasted, and touched. Jacqueline's integration is a constant reminder to me of sexual-spiritual embodiment.

Embodiment is a challenge because most of us have had to—or need to—reconstruct our sexuality to some extent. We must unlearn our sexual fallacies, for example, the confounding message, "Sex is bad, wrong, and dirty; save it for the one you love." Only then can we claim our sexual rights and values and awaken our flattened senses and spirits. Through a process of recovery from fear, ignorance, abuse, cultural myth, and objectification, we can heal our sexual dis-ease. Our challenge begins by redefining sexuality. Perhaps the following definition we used at the medical school at the University of Minnesota can serve as our base: "Sexuality is, in the broadest sense, the human/psychic energy that finds physical and emotional expression in the desire for contact, warmth, tenderness, and love."[1]

Yes, this *is* a broad definition. We are sexual beings from the top of our heads to the tips of our toes; we cannot *not* be sexual. Unfortunately, many people define sexuality as genitality, which is merely *one* of its aspects. To broaden the meaning of our sexuality, we must examine the context in which we learned to understand and express our sexuality—the *sociocultural* context. Our culture has defined sexuality according to deeply imbedded cultural myths that we all have absorbed as "truth." Although we now recognize this "truth" isn't working for us, we still are vulnerable to these ever-present, often subtle myths.

Recently, while preparing a lecture on women's socialization and addictive relationships, I was surprised to find how much of my past was still in me. I had decided to use popular songs to illustrate women's socialization, and as I listened to some old records, to my amazement, I could recall the exact lyrics to songs I had learned forty years ago. I found I was still susceptible to the music; I was flooded with memories and feelings. Why was I having such a powerful emotional response when surely my head knew better now? Hadn't I unraveled the confusion around sex and gender? Hadn't I been lecturing on "*sex* as *biological,* referring to our femaleness" and "*gender* as *social,* referring to our social tasks both learned and assigned"?[2] Yet my emotional warehouse of nostalgia seemed to dismiss what my head knew. My emotional memory had its own feeling-filled responses. As I listened to "You're Nobody Till Somebody Loves You," I realized how unconsciously I had swallowed this myth in my prefeminist years. I accepted that the sexual revolution, feminism, and social sciences would never eradicate past memories and feelings. My past is within me, to be revisited and remembered.

Realizing how very different society was for those who grew up in the late 1960s, I asked a younger friend, a corporate executive, what the hit tune of her day was. She said, "That's easy—Tammy Wynnette's 'Stand by Your Man.'" I bought the tape and heard:

> But if you love him, you'll forgive him,
> Even though he's hard to understand ...
> And if you love him, always be proud of him,
> 'Cause after all he's just a man ...
> Stand by your man, give him someone to cling to,
> And something warm to come to when nights are
> Cold and lonely ..."

I was surprised; the explicitly stated "taking care of" message to women hadn't changed. Despite our age difference, my friend and I had both internalized the same message, just as today's young girls do. A contemporary film is entitled "Sex, Lies, and Videotape." Perhaps it should read "Sex, Lies, and Media."

DEMYTHOLOGIZING OUR ROMANTIC MYTHS

Unaware of the powerful grip of our cultural messages, we live in sexual confusion, often with arrested sexual growth. Indeed, we have paid a high price for accepting these myths as "truths." Before we can integrate our sexuality and spirituality, we must first understand this culture's romantic myths—and their outcomes. Only when we can demythologize the romantic myths can we see the reality. It is then that we can move toward sexual-spiritual integration.

A word about romance. I am not making an argument to eradicate romance. Who of us doesn't like a romantic environment? Surely none of us wants to live in a nonaesthetic world without music, the beauty of the human body, and the expression of our passions. To walk onto the deck of a restaurant hidden in treetops where we fully open our senses and drink from the sky, to carry romantic melodies of old favorite songs, to sit before a quiet glowing fire alone or with another, to know those special moments where we truly meet and touch each other—all these we need. All these are possible.

Romantic Myth One:
A Woman Is Not Complete Without a Man

"You're Nobody Till Somebody Loves You" illustrates how women are socialized to be sexually fused with men. In subordination we learned to have identity through relationships, by being someone's "other." That a woman is "nobody" until "somebody" (male) loves her suggests a woman's sense of self comes through her needing, and being needed by, a man.

Outcome. Although we know it to be cultural propaganda, the myth of unhealthy fusion hangs heavy over all women. Young girls longing for genuine affection turn to fused relationships and, losing themselves in another, call this sexual fusion love. Young women from dysfunctional families, who have permeable boundaries and impaired perceptions of relationships, are even more vulnerable to becoming sexually fused.

As Betty reviewed her written sexual history, she read, "My first sexual encounter was in eighth grade—as I began to 'have' boyfriends and kiss. There was no petting until ninth grade. From the day I learned about 'how to get' boyfriends I always had one. By tenth grade I didn't care; I had intercourse on a regular basis. When I look back on junior-high days I now recall utter fear—to the point of *shaking*—when standing with a group of kids—feeling like I'm giving something up to be accepted."

We can hear the pain; the young girl is shameful because she *knows* she is giving something away in the hope of being accepted. Early on Betty defined her pleasure solely as sexual pleasure and took this belief into her adult life. Betty is not alone. As a sex therapist I have found that many women are totally dependent on their partners for their sexual pleasure. They never learned to pleasure themselves, never having considered that self-pleasuring is natural. Disrupting this pattern goes against our strong cultural injunctions that women are to be sexually needy for men. Women learn that self-pleasuring is "selfish"; you exist to pleasure others. Women who enjoy and want sex are called nymphomaniacs.

Reality.   Each of us is both male and female; the "other" is within us. Women's loss of self in fused relationships became clear to me during sexuality seminars for the general public that I conducted during the 1970s. Using a guided imagery exercise focused on androgyny to deepen the awareness of the "other" in the self, I asked females to picture themselves as males and males to picture themselves as females. As I guided them with questions, men experienced their tenderness and ability to nurture, whereas women discovered their strength, competence, and aggressiveness. Not uncommonly, the men broke into tears as they found the "other" within themselves. Some saw themselves holding and nurturing babies. The women sat up straight and smiled as they "saw" parts of themselves that had been denied. Both groups learned that such characteristics are not biologically based but instead are *socially* learned. Clearly, all of us have internalized *to some degree at least* the sex-role stereotypes promulgated by our culture through the media.

When I conducted this same exercise for professionals in alcoholism and chemical dependency at the Johnson Institute in Minnesota, I was astounded. Women did not find the "other" within themselves; rather, they *became* their husbands or sex partners! Clearly, their identities were fused with their male partners; they were dependent on them for parts of themselves that were actually available to them from within. Many in the audience were adult children from alcoholic families. With underdeveloped boundaries plus strong cultural messages, they had little choice but to internalize another as their "other."

Romantic Myth Two:
Romantic Love Is "Real" Love

The lyrics "I Think I Am Falling in Love . . . Falling, Falling, in Love" come from the romantic assumption that we *fall* into love. Only a few relationships that begin romantically mature into deep, rich, mutually affectionate relationships. I don't want to imply here that all romantic love is *always* fraudulent. It *is* true that a few relationships *do* maintain romantic love and mature into deep, rich, mutually affectionate relationships, but romance alone does not guarantee a strong, enduring relationship.

Outcome. "But I thought it was love," Jean said. "I thought it would last forever. How could I experience something so wonderful and not have it mean something special, something forever? I had never felt anything that powerful before. No one had ever told me that you *grow*, not *fall*, into love. No one told me what love would feel like; my experience surely fit with what I had seen in films and read in books."

Jean had experienced romantic love. With Jean's strong sexual awakening, amid her cultural messages about love and marriage, she had not known the difference between loving, being in love, and falling in love. Jean had *fallen* in love. Romantic love was a catalyst; her heart fully opened. The entire foundation for her relationship was *feeling*. "Feelings, nothing more than feelings . . . ," as the song says, strongly overrode any common sense or reasoning. Just like the characters in books and films, she and Bob had been ecstatic; Jean was in love with "being in love."

Sociologist Dorothy Tennov describes the commonplace adolescent state of "being in love" as "limerence."[3] In limerence, our relationship with our love object eclipses all other relationships, probably because of the intense sexual attraction involved. Limerence has the following characteristics:

- acute longing for reciprocation
- dependency of mood on love object's behavior
- fear of rejection
- shyness in love object's presence
- aching of "heart" with uncertainty
- buoyancy when reciprocation occurs
- ability to emphasize what is admirable in love object and avoid the negative
- cognitive obsession[4]

Tennov says that by late adolescence 97 percent of American men and women have fallen in love, often more than once.[5]

Limerence is overwhelming because of the heightened feelings of euphoria and energy. With powerful feelings of passion, desire, and lightheartedness, we soar. We are also victims to it, lost in another and feeling totally helpless. Many women who grew up in dysfunctional families are romantics, that is, they "fall" in love and, idealizing relationships, deny the negative aspects. Women denied a solid attachment in earlier life take their longing and unfinished grieving into adult relationships and interpret their *romantic* attachment as love. Girls are prone to romantic love—love that is almost always fleeting and fraudulent. Too often daughters in dysfunctional families look to their mothers as models and see fraudulent love, the love of trapped women, many of whom are economic captives. Many of our mothers and fathers' relationships probably started as romantic, but by the time we were old enough to become aware, we were looking at romantic love that had died. Seeking genuine love, the girls turn to the romantic myths that pervade books, films, and television programs where women are depicted as desired objects. Unfortunately, women as objects of desire also become objects of attack and violence. Romantic love, often a hiding place for abuse, can be the "holding" environment for the girl who believes that "somebody is better than nobody." Some women, addicted to the initial highs of relationships, become "relationship junkies" dependent on the adrenaline (epinephrine) rush and increased concentrations of phenylethylamine (PEA) in the brain.[6] These women mistake the biochemical and neurochemical aspects of romantic love for genuine love. Fearing withdrawal and resulting depression, many women seek an amphetamine-like exhilaration. Dorothy Parker writes about this in "Symptom Recital."

> I do not like my state of mind:
> I'm bitter, querulous, unkind.
> I hate my legs, I hate my hands.
> I do not yearn for lovelier lands.
> I dread the dawn's recurrent light:
> I hate to go to bed at night.
> I shoot at simple, earnest folk.

I cannot take the gentlest joke.
I find no peace in paint or type
My world is but a lot of tripe.
I'm disillusioned, empty-breasted.
For what I think, I'd be arrested.
I am not sick, I am not well.
My quondam dreams are shot to hell.
My soul is crushed, my spirit sore:
I do not like me any more.
I cavil, quarrel, grumble, grouse.
I ponder on the narrow house.
I shudder at the thought of men . . .
I'm due to fall in love again.[7]

As true today as when Dorothy Parker wrote in the 1920s, we now recognize that many of us normalized *falling* in love. Highly charged romantic love *cannot* last forever; believing this myth is a setup to fail. And women typically blame themselves for the failure.

Reality. The reality is that we *grow* into love. "It is only with the heart that one can see rightly . . . ," says Antoine Saint Exupery.[8] Many women don't realize that love doesn't feel the same for both sexes. Many men experience *carnal love,* love based on physical attraction. Women admit to having more symptoms of romantic love than men and report greater degrees of euphoria during love relationships.[9] And although women are likely to fall *out* of love earlier than men, we are slower to *be* in love relationships.[10]

With all our focus on love, have you ever asked what the function of love is for women? How does it work for us? Romantic love has often been pragmatic for women; that is, it has had a positive function. Since women once contributed less economically to marriage, they brought their love contributions to marriage, along with their emotional and social strengths.[11] When we look at the economics of marriage, we can readily see how women would value romantic love in practical terms.[12] Romantic love was not just love for love's sake; romantic love was a basis for marriage. We had a real payoff for falling

132

in love. "First comes love, then comes marriage, then comes (girl's name) with a baby carriage." What we did not consciously know was that this sequence we chanted also meant we were walking into economic dependence. We all learned that "husband and wife are one, and that one is the husband."

So if love was not available, we took a facsimile, limerence, as the foundation for decisions affecting our whole lives. Perhaps romantic love is why women are happiest during their first two years of marriage. By the time they reach long-term marriage (Jean was married twenty years), women are very dissatisfied—*no matter whose studies you read.*[13] As Thelma Goodrich states, "Women are in subordinate positions and love was called upon as a way to galvanize women's attitudes and behaviors in the service of their exclusive role as housewife and mother."[14]

Although we live with myths of an addictive society, we do see changes. Learning about limerence and awakening to the biochemistry of love helps our unlearning.

Romantic Myth Three: Seductive and Highly Feminine Behavior Will Bring You Love

"Hold Me, Thrill Me, Kiss Me" says the seductive song title from the 1960s. Today's titles are even more suggestive, such as "Let's Get It On." Our social mandate is to seduce males by becoming objects. Sanctioned to be sexy, not sexual, young girls buy into the cultural messages *and* the fake promises attached to being "highly feminine." Advertising persuades; men's appearances communicate *power* and women's appearances communicate *presence.*[15] Women are to be noticed so they can "catch" a man.

Outcome. Sexiness is a means to an end. Outcome-oriented sex is goal-oriented sex, and the goal for women is love. Sexuality is equated with *genitality* and is viewed not only as an outcome but also a product, a commodity. Often genital sexuality involves "scoring" or measuring and comparing frequency of behaviors. In our capitalistic, shame-based, product-oriented culture, we often quantify sexual behaviors and equate quantity with quality. During the sexual revolution we focused on performance, on *doing*. Individuals learned how to *come* together, not to come *together*. Women searching for love barter their sexuality. For women longing for an identity and longing to be loved, media advertisers offer hope: if you buy our product, you will get what you want. Given our culture, as long as dollars can be made on limerence, limerence will be touted. Addictive love, limerence, and sex are big business; women spend billions of dollars on aids to enhance romance, sexuality, and beauty. Women are used to promote products of sexual stimulation; and women are themselves marketed, objectified, and often victimized.

Children with violated sexual boundaries become adults who feel like passive, open receptacles. Indeed, incest victims account for 70 percent of the prostitutes in this country.[16] Seeing themselves as sexual commodities, they learn early to barter their sexuality. A woman who feels angry and powerless learns to gain power through sexual manipulation. This evolves into a pattern of sex as revenge. Diane wrote in her journal: "My feeling about sex in general is that men use you and you let them. Sometimes I like to take a man in bed and make love to him so good that it nearly makes him weep. I sometimes feel very powerful and angry and like I want them to never forget me. Other times I'm like someone who 'puts up' with the whole thing and sometimes hates it. I always think the next man is going to satisfy me and we'll have good sex—but I've had so many men and it hasn't been good yet. It makes me sad to think of how ugly I get when I try to destroy them—I feel sad and abused and angry and stupid for how I've handled things."

At first Diane blamed herself for what she had not learned. She long ago had foreclosed on sex in love when her father betrayed her with his frequent alcoholic sexual abuse.

Reality. We need to love and accept ourselves. In process-oriented sex, the focus is on the relationship, and for many this causes a greater fear than the more lustful, nonperson, genital approach that we call "sex with nobody home."

Carol Gilligan reminds us that preadolescent girls know what they think and feel; they have their true voices and are resisters.[17] We see it in the "tomboys" who have enough "boy" in themselves. But by age fifteen they go underground with what they truly know as they are socially pressured to become women. We all certainly know that physically attractive women do draw attention, attention to their outer selves; they date more and get better grades in school. We also know the other side. These same women, knowing that they "show well," often feel inadequate because they do not feel accepted for who they truly are. Eventually we must realize that it is our true self that will attract people to us. Acting seductive results in women getting hooked into genitally charged, deluded relationships that end when the stars fade. Physical attractiveness and sexual openness are certainly enhancing, yet neither will make an empty relationship full. Women who enter relationships as *friends* will be respected and can *grow* into love. In the grand scheme of things, we are loved for who we are.

Romantic Myth Four: Love Relationships Stay the Same

The song "When I Fall in Love, It Will Be Forever" is but one anthem for this cultural myth. Our relationships often begin with romance. We surround ourselves with romantic stimuli—candlelight, soft music, the warmth of a fireplace, a beautiful setting indoors or out. All these social stimuli enter our brains as we associate our feelings about our relationships in these romantic settings.

Outcome.   The outcome is delusion and illusion. When we experience the powerful feelings of romantic love in a romantic environment, we naturally want to hold captive our feelings of intimacy. As our relationships change, we tell ourselves lies, we deny. We tell ourselves to be patient, we rationalize. We often return to familiar songs, places, and letters to recapture the romantic state. The romantic experience becomes "learned"; it has entered the unconscious.

Reality.   The reality is that relationships are *always* in the process of change. We cannot *not* change. And we recognize that not all change is growth.

Jean felt frightened when she realized she did not deeply know either herself *or* Bob. She realized not only that she was far different from the person Bob married, but that her original marital contract with him had dramatically changed. She was no longer living her life to please him, yet their relationship did not have any rules for discussing the changes. Neither had ever acknowledged that they were growing, changing, dynamic organisms and that their relationship, like their sexuality, was on a spiraling circle of change. While each of them could admire the other for growing, they both clung tenaciously to their myths of who they *had* been to each other. Age, relationships, life-cycle issues, sexual experiences, family events, and roles had all affected their relationship, yet they were frozen in time.

Sexuality, like loving, ranges widely as we grow through periods of learning bursts, periods of flatness or disinterest, periods of abstinence, and periods of full bloom. Sometimes it is difficult to accept our changes. As we grow older in an ageist culture, we must make decisions about how we choose to enhance our aging through diets and cosmetics. There is often a fine line between what we do to feel good about ourselves and what we buy into from cultural myth. At this point having a self is essential. In a youth-valuing culture, many aging women strive to look "youthful." When I look in the mirror it takes me a few days to adjust to my new lines, wrinkles, and increasingly supple skin. And it takes even a few days longer for me to become friendly with those changes. "We don't age, we ripen," says poet Meridel LeSeuer.[18] This process of change does not wind around in smooth circles; it is an uneven spiral. We continue to dip down into our past sexual history and integrate that meaning into our adult self, each movement making us a little bit more of who we are.

Romantic Myth Five: Combining Sex with Chemicals Guarantees Intimacy

As the movie *The Days of Wine and Roses* attests, women without permission to be sexual can count on alcohol and drugs as powerful permission-giving catalysts. With them we can quickly become aroused, and we all know that becoming aroused can be an impelling force in relationship attraction. Indeed, the release of control, the surrender, and the rush can be highly romantic. So *initially* the use of chemicals is almost a guarantee for lowered inhibitions, sexual arousal, and sexual experimentation.

Outcome. Many women who awaken their dormant sexuality through using chemicals have had positive experiences. However, sex and chemicals can be harmful for women raised in alcoholic or dysfunctional families. Do you remember a few pages ago when I talked about the guided imagery where women from alcoholic families internalized their partners as the "other" in themselves? One longitudinal study of adolescent girls showed that 72 percent of the those who were identified as being "highly feminine" with the stereotypic sex-role characteristics (sweet, demure, passive) became addicted to alcohol.[19] The same study also showed that in families in which both parents are alcoholic, a child's risk of becoming alcoholic is *four* times greater than average. Dependence on chemicals for release of control quite obviously leads these women away from a healthy sexual start and toward sexually addictive relationships with emotional shutdowns.[20] Trapped in their shamebound process, they often use alcohol or drugs not only to be sexual but also to ease their self-contempt and pain.

Nina said once she was on the track, she couldn't stop. In tenth grade the excitement turned to lack of control and generally a fear of sex. She wrote, "As I got more heavily involved with drugs, I also got more involved sexually—to the point of sex for sex's sake and many one-night stands. I always felt terribly opened up and used the next day. I often felt I couldn't say no and I just didn't care. I look back and I see many more times of losing self-control and self-esteem than I thought. It was pretty yucky. I felt like a tramp."

Nina, with an intense desire to be recognized and accepted, was drawn like a magnet to "users." She did not realize addictive drugs were structurally quite similar to naturally occurring brain chemicals. Nina had inherited a biochemical predisposition to addictions. Do you remember the brain chemical PEA that I talked about in regard to limerence? This, along with the fact that Nina was the victim of childhood sexual abuse, gave her very few choices. Like 74 percent of alcoholic women in recovery, she drank to numb painful memories of abuse.[21]

Because drug treatment centers were originally set up for men, women in treatment have faced many "blame the victim" problems. Socialized to be desirable sexual objects, women were seen as manipulators and seducers, impeding men's recovery. Drug treatment centers today have made great gains in this area. In addition, many women in Twelve-Step programs have been troubled by the male language used to define the concept of a "Higher Power." Jo-Ann Krestan says, "It doesn't matter what your Higher Power is—as long as *you* ain't it!"[22] Some women, uncomfortable with the concept of powerlessness, have joined a Women for Sobriety group.[23]

Reality. Both sex and chemicals can be barriers to intimacy. Some women who describe themselves as "open" later realize that their underdeveloped boundaries made them vulnerable. Terror of intimacy is not always terror of sexuality. Some women drank over their fear of being close; being close could result in being sexual. Other women covered their terror of emotional commitment with sexual competency and "apparent" comfort. Also, women who numb themselves with chemicals often experience blackouts and do not even remember sexual encounters. Some chemically dependent women face terror when they become chemically free; we can live without chemicals but we are always sexual. Women in recovery may experience an adolescence that was denied. Actually, many of women's sexual problems are biochemical problems and social problems.[24] Many women accused of "loving too much" have *inherited maladaptive biochemical responses to certain chemicals.*[25] Now we know that an enzyme deficiency is at the genetic basis of alcoholism.[26]

Sexual health professionals today report that more than *half* of their clients are in chemically dependent relationships.[27] And at least half of those who seek chemical dependency treatment have sexual concerns.[28] Many professionals believe that sexaholism and alcoholism are essentially the same disease or dis-ease, depending on how you define them. In my practice I see women from alcoholic families who resolved not to marry an alcoholic but ended up marrying a sex addict. The romanticized relationship of sex and chemicals is a major barrier to women's sexual and spiritual growth. Being honest with ourselves and with others is the key to genuine intimacy.

Romantic Myth Six:
True Love Is Heterosexual Love

"You Make Me Feel Like a Natural Woman" the song says. This song presumes the cultural myth that "natural" is always heterosexual. The song further implies that women are dependent on males for their sense of feeling loved. According to this romantic myth, not only are women's friendships secondary to their relationships with men, but lesbian relationships could not be "natural." These would certainly be at the bottom of the relationship hierarchy. Some women have normalized other associations — such as girlfriends being referred to as "lezzies" in some families — with the result that women feared women.

Outcome. Despite the strong support women receive from women friends, many women have learned to expect that women friends will be there for them only until a man comes along. Many women have accepted such rejection as natural. As a result, their friendships have become holding places for them "until . . ."

Another outcome of this myth is that women fear loving women. Although there is more sexual openness than ever before, we still live in a culture that overvalues heterosexuality. Any behavior outside heterosexual loving frightens women. Lesbian women willing to pay the price of being denied the benefits of the sexist system, including financial security and recognition of domestic roles, can live and love exactly as they please. In doing so, lesbian women are threatening to both men and women.

Jacqueline, my French friend, had come to visit me. Curious about the university's Sexual Attitude Reassessment seminars (SARs) in which I lectured, she decided to participate. The seminar approached sexuality from the perspectives of anthropology, biology, theology, and sociology. We explored sexuality over the life cycle; we looked at alternative relationships, including gay and lesbian relationships, using lectures and films. Jacqueline found her small-group experience stimulating. On the last night of the program Jacqueline said in her deep, husky voice, "My dahling, zare is something I must say to you. Do you know, my dear, that I was a leetle bit frightened by my experience in zare? Zare was something I did not know about. . . . I did not know about zis thing, zis affection I hold for you. I did not know if perhaps I might be lesbian . . . my love for you is so strong." With tears rolling down her deeply lined cheeks, she continued, "And what I discovered is zat I just love you so very much. Zare, now you know."

Touched deeply by Jacqueline's honesty and courage, we hugged and we talked about our deep and loving friendship. Like other women, she was afraid of allowing herself to love a woman, just as was I. Because we had learned that love is heterosexual, there was no way to explain our loving friendship without it being lesbian. Jacqueline was delighted with her discovery; we both gained from her disclosure.

Some women struggle with homophobia. Women who have loving sexual feelings for a woman often shut down, fearing the friendship may become a lesbian relationship. Often, when women awaken sexually, they learn they can be sexually attracted to women. Some women recovering from alcoholism do become sexually involved with women. At one time treatment centers referred alcoholic patients to me for sex therapy, asking me (indirectly, of course) to tell them this same-sex attraction is just a "stage" they must move through to regain their "natural" heterosexual self. Because of my lack of cooperation, those referrals stopped.

Reality.   Because their emotional connections are often much closer with women friends than with spouses, many women depend on their friendships to survive lonely marriages. In feminist friendships, as in deeply expressive loving Victorian friendships, women have greater freedom to let themselves love.[29] In *The Second Sex* Simone de Beauvoir expresses her idea of the natural response of women:

> If nature is to be invoked, one can say that all women are naturally homosexual. The lesbian, in fact, is distinguished by her

refusal of the male and her liking for feminine flesh; but every adolescent female fears penetration and masculine domination, and she feels a certain repulsion for the male body; on the other hand, the female body is for her, as for the male, an object of desire.[30]

Many women at various times in their lives are bisexual, capable of having relationships with both men and women. A majority of lesbian women believe this is not a true preference, countering that bisexual women are fearful or tentative about their lesbianism.

BLOCKS TO SEXUAL HEALING

While these six myths have hindered us, they also illustrate that gender learning, not biology, is the culprit here. We have come a long way from seeking romantic salvation; women are now taking charge of their own healing and experience sexuality within a broader, deeper context—the context of relationship. Two major forces—the rhetoric of avoidance and sexual shame—can block our growth.

The Rhetoric of Avoidance

Our avoidance of sexuality through the conspiracy of silence reinforces irresponsibility. We are without a natural sexual language; thus, we discuss sexuality using medical terms, euphemisms, or street talk. Given the limited attempts at sex education by families, schools, and churches, we enter adulthood in sexual ignorance. Not permitted to learn through experience, we struggle to escape sexual imprisonment. Sara's journal reflected her meager sex education. "My husband was the first one who told me about my clitoris—I never masturbated until I was engaged to my husband, and with much shame. Sex after marriage wasn't fun—I didn't like it. I had *never* since eighth grade had a boy or a man try to please me. I was always a hole in the bed."

Sara said aloud what many women dare not say. Deprived of an adequate sex education, Sara, like so many women, thought the vagina to be the counterpart to the penis and, in ignorance, loved the first man who touched her clitoris. While most parents do not name the clitoris as a sex organ, virtually all name the penis as a sex organ.[31] Sara was angry and blamed her mother, with no mention of any expectation of her father.

As we hear the varied stories about our mothers' awkward attempts to be our sex educators, we laugh, but only until it becomes our turn to be educators. Then we find compassion for our even more poorly educated mothers.

Jean and Jan were pleased that in their long years of friendship, their daughters, Amy and Susan, had also become friends. Jean and Jan decided that their daughters might feel more comfortable if the four of them discussed sexuality together. The girls reluctantly agreed. Jean began, "We don't know how to do this well, and we're not going to do it perfectly, but let's start talking about sexuality. We don't even know what you know!" Together they talked—awkwardly at first, with the girls teasing about their "weird mothers" who wanted to talk about sexuality.

They also agreed that if one of the girls felt uncomfortable talking with her own parent, she could talk in assured confidentiality with another parent in their friendship circle who shared their values.

Some years later Jean and Jan, on asking their daughters what this attempted sex education had been like for them, commented on how comfortable it must have been for both daughters to be together. Amy and Susan burst out laughing, exclaiming, "Why don't you both admit it? You probably did it that way because it was more comfortable for *you two!*" Jean and Jan, startled, glanced at each other and laughed in agreement.

When our mothers and fathers and churches haven't given us permission to be sexual, we must give it to ourselves. Jean discovered after her divorce to what extent her role as wife governed her sexual behavior. Her role clearly defined the parameters of her sexual expression. After her divorce, she discovered her sensuality was flowering. Now a forty-two-year-old woman excited with feelings and unlimited choices, she felt overwhelmed. Because she had shut down her sensuality at about age fifteen as a way to ensure being a "good girl," she was now flooded and frightened by her feelings. Describing herself as "middlescent," she fully realized that she was unclear about her sexual values. Neither age nor role was a reliable guide. Desperate, she wrote, "As a Sexual Person I Have the Right to . . ." and then listed her rights and her responsibilities. Unaware that she was defining her sexual values and ethics, she now had self-chosen rather than role-prescribed guiding rules for her sexual life.

Comfortable with her internal permission, Jean found external permission when she went to her gynecologist for her regular checkup. Her doctor began, "Now that you are single, what do you want to choose as your birth control?" Jean blushed. He had acknowledged her as a single person; but more importantly he acknowledged her as a sexual person.

Women are giving themselves permission to be sexual, permission to talk, to learn, to ask questions about socially transmitted diseases; many women not only talk about birth control but carry it with them. We cannot afford loyalty to no-talk rules; the consequences are too high. Our silence and avoidance have resulted in generations of buried pain and shame.

Sexual Shame

Our shame is often the reservoir for our sexual pain. Women who have been abused feel shame; so too do women who have cancer, physical disabilities, and infertility. Secrets give shame power and can keep women stuck for years. Attractive forty-two-year-old Meg entered therapy because she couldn't stand the lack of intimacy in her marriage. Sex, she revealed, was perfunctory and without passion. "You see, I don't think I *do* want Jack closer," she revealed. She felt trapped and discouraged.

Meg's sexual history revealed that at age fourteen her first sexual encounters with her sixteen-year-old boyfriend had resulted in her being used sexually and then degraded and rejected. Her second partner, age twenty, also used her and forced himself on her. She felt her whole inner self had been torn open by those experiences. Burying her shame, she had decided she was a sexual failure. In therapy Meg saw she had internalized the shame and had punished herself for the acts that were committed against her. After blaming herself for years, Meg now could see that her early sexual experiences had set the foundation for her carefully choosing a "safe" mate, a professor, whose greatest turn-on was his long list of published academic articles. She was surprised when she found the rage about her first sexual experiences. As she expressed her rage, she also found her voice. "I do want to be a sexual woman," she exclaimed. "Do you think it's too late?"

By facing her shame, her truth, and Jack, Meg redefined herself. This created a relationship crisis in Meg and Jack's implicit contract to be sexually inhibited. This changed dramatically, however, after Jack reluctantly entered a men's group and worked through his own sexual inadequacy and they worked together to restructure their marriage and their sexual relationship.

As women struggle with sexual secrets, they often become stuck. Our sexual secrets are often our sexual concerns, concerns for which there is help available. Secreted, the concerns keep us circling around in the shame reservoir. The shame in turn feeds the secrets. Trapped in the downward spiral of shame, we become blocked not only to ourselves but to those in our closest relationships. If we are to integrate our sexuality and spirituality, we need to face our sexual secrets and sexual concerns.

SEXUAL SECRETS, SEXUAL CONCERNS

Sexual concerns most frequently revealed by women often lie in secreted shame: sexual abuse, including incest, rape, and sexual assault; abortion; extramarital sex; anorgasmia; sexual addiction or sexual compulsivity, and sexual preference issues.

Sexual Abuse

Often women struggling with intimacy are *unknowingly* struggling with the trauma and stress caused by early childhood sexual abuse. One of five women has been sexually assaulted; 38 percent of all female children are assaulted by age eighteen.[32] In alcoholic or drug-dependent women, we see *differences in the quantity, quality, and extent of the abuse.* For example, they are twice as likely to be incest and rape survivors than are nonalcoholic women.[33] In addition to sexual abuse, we see an intolerable percentage of women reporting emotional and physical abuse. Many women describe the sexual near-orgasm experience that accompanies physical beating; they normalize this early association. The abuse occurred in closeness and in closeness it typically continues. Women recovering from early sexual abuse often blame themselves, not realizing they have internalized someone else's self-hatred. Unaware that their victimization was not a sexual act but rather an act of aggression, they are caught in the downward spiral of shame, pursuing a course of mutilating and/or starving themselves. "In their own flesh, they bear repeated punishment for the crimes committed against them in their childhood," says researcher Judith Herman.[34]

Incest

Incest is probably one of the most obvious results of objectification of females in our culture. This year 400,000 new cases of incest will be reported.[35] There are other alarming figures: in a recent survey, 29 percent of women who were abused sexually before age eighteen identified their father as their first abuser.[36] Fifty percent of incest victims are from alcoholic homes.[37] Chemical dependency treatment statistics show that 47 to 75 percent of women are incest survivors.[38] In my work as a clinical consultant to drug and alcoholism halfway houses in the Midwest I found that 75 percent of women were incest victims.

Stolen innocence and boundary violations leave women vulnerable to being assaulted and used by other males. Women incest survivors need time to heal, to build support, to work through the shame and rage, and to learn to trust.

Acquaintance Rape, Marital Rape, and Sexual Assault

Rape is about violence, not sex, but since it affects our sexual functioning so greatly, I include it here. The highest percentage of rape is *acquaintance rape*: 60 percent of rape cases involve a known perpetrator.[39] Also, staggering numbers of women experience marital rape or forced intercourse. In alcoholic families more than 60 percent of women have been victims of rape.[40] Women with unresolved childhood sexual trauma or marital rape are often misdiagnosed as having inhibited sexual desire, painful intercourse, or anorgasmia.

Sexualized Affection

Women are often victims of sexualized affection; as girls they received touch and affection that not only met someone else's needs but contained sexual energy. Young girls directed to sit in someone's lap or give someone a kiss knew something wasn't right; they often referred to relatives as "weird" or "icky" and we did not listen to them. Today we would name it—sexualized affection. These young girls have taken their violators' shame as their own.

Abortion

Abortion is a heated, controversial, and often shame-filled issue for women today because it involves choice. For many women, abortion is a moral dilemma born out of the loss of a possible relationship; for many others abortion is not.[41] Although we view abortion from religious, moral, biological, and legal perspectives, we must also view it from political and ethical perspectives. Many women are surprised when they learn about women's history regarding abortion. For centuries, women attended to the medical needs of one another. Then, women were coerced to trade their healer role for a patient role—with men being in charge of women's lives. Although abortion had been legal in the United States for a hundred years, abortion was criminalized during the nineteenth century, not because it was immoral, but because physicians wanted to do away with midwifery.[42] Obviously, women who were denied the right to vote had little influence on the legislative system. In 1973 with *Roe v. Wade*, the U.S. Supreme Court stated that the Constitution protected women's as well as men's rights to privacy with regard to their reproductive lives. Because of recent changes in the makeup of the court, we again face a charged issue. Therapist and author Deborah Luepnitz states, "A woman can accept or reject even the possibility of contraception as well as abortion, but she can no longer accept a condition in which she makes no decision about these matters."[43]

Extramarital Sex

Extramarital sex is often a guilt and shame issue for women. The number of women in extramarital affairs has increased greatly during the past decades (statistics ranging from 26 to 70 percent).[44] Some women's magazines have even suggested that women should enter affairs with young men to take care of their loneliness, but this is just another way for women to be used.[45]

The causes of affairs include women's entry into the behavioral world of men, an attempt to disprove dependency, an intention to end or "open up" a relationship. It is not the affair itself, but rather the betrayal of a covenant between spouses, the breaking of trust, that harms a relationship. We tend to think all extramarital affairs are sexual-genital, yet many lonely women have emotional affairs that may or may not be charged with sexual energy. The guilt here usually lies in the fact that the primary investment is being made *outside* the partnership. A small number of couples do live with "open and consenting" extramarital sexual relationships, but for most couples, infidelity arises when affairs are lied about or kept secret, betraying the marital contract.

Anorgasmia

Once called frigidity, anorgasmia is common among women. Anger and fear of lack of control are both contributors to anorgasmia. Women have faked orgasms to please partners. Often they fear orgasm because they have experienced sexual trauma or painful intercourse.

Repressed anger over forced intercourse can also result in anorgasmia. Many women fear sex, thinking that if they like intercourse, they may become "street women."

A woman needs to know she has some control before she can let go. When women are ready to face their barriers and find their feelings, they are highly successful in becoming orgasmic. Learning how to pleasure themselves and masturbate seems to be the most useful means of helping women to know their body-selves and become orgasmic.

Sexual Addiction

Sexual addiction, hypersexuality, and sexual compulsivity are as prevalent as alcoholism. With the 1970s sexual revolution sanctioning any behaviors between "two or more mutually consenting adults," we gave license to sexual compulsives to remain addicts. By the end of the 1970s, sexual openness was called boundary ambiguity.[46] Women who had totally "unzipped" now zipped up their boundary screens. Most people changed with the culture and its shifting norms of constraint; now only the sexually compulsive stood out.

Women in transition after relationship breakups or divorce often go through an experimental dating phase. Women working through a denied adolescence are not sexual addicts; we must be careful not to label them as such. However, many women who come into treatment settings and therapy have covered their sexual addiction with drugs or alcohol. Women have been socialized to be partners to sex addicts — by being passive objects. Woman can ask three questions to see if their sexual behavior is addictive: Can I control when I start it? Can I control when I stop it? Does it interfere with my relationships?[47]

Sexually Transmitted Diseases

The sexual revolution of the late 1960s and early 1970s brought sexual openness — and an increased risk of sexually transmitted diseases. Chlamydial infection (affecting 50 percent of partners of males who are carriers of the pathogen), genital herpes (500,000 new cases will be reported this year), and gonorrhea have been the most common.[48] Because of advances in medical treatment, sexually transmitted diseases are not as alarming as they once were.

The same cannot be said of AIDS, the fatal sexual disease of the 1980s. Women now are taking "safe sex" openly and seriously. Out of necessity we have drawn back tightly on the continuum of sexual openness. Women are taking responsibility for safe sex practices: (1) Be informed. (2) Be observant. (3) Be selective. (4) Be honest. (5) Be cautious. (6) Be promptly tested and treated.[49]

In reviewing the sexual concerns and sexual secrets, we cannot be surprised to see that abuse of women can be a real source of sexual concern. The violence and trauma are intertwined with women's concerns, secrets, and shame. I always recommend that women share their secrets with a trusted friend or two to relieve the painful isolation.

Sexual Preference Issues

How is sexual preference a sexual concern? It is a concern in that many women keep their lesbianism a secret. Many professional women choose a secret life-style because they know the high cost of coming out in professional circles. Raised to believe that their lesbian relationships are inferior and invalid, many women often feel ashamed of their same-sex feelings. Moreover, women who are awakening sexually and examining their sexual identity often feel confused about their sexual preference. Given the high social costs to lesbian women who come out, these women clearly need a solid support system. While writing this chapter, I questioned whether to include the material on sexual concerns. After all, don't they really belong in a book on women's sexuality? To date, I have not seen a book that discussed the relationships of women from dysfunctional families and their sexual concerns. We are looking more fully at gender and the context of relationship; by talking more and sharing stories, women are becoming part of a worldwide spiritual movement. As we hear the stories of women from other cultures, our awareness that we are part of a spiritual shift, a shift in consciousness, deepens.

RE-VISIONING OUR SEXUALITY

A woman's sexual recovery is only as full as her spiritual recovery. By spiritual I mean our connectedness with all of life. I do not mean religion, although for some there may be a religious connection as well. We learn that all we know is in us; we listen to our inner knowing as we deepen our compassion for our growing self. We learn to accept ourselves, our own values, our body-selves, our sensuality, and our feelings. During this process we may find that, just as the song says, "Love Will Get You Through Times of No Sex Better Than Sex Will Get You Through Times of No Love."

This rebirth involves an embodiment of our beliefs and attitudes, our feelings and our body-selves. With a plethora of materials from the social sciences, we find it takes time to change our deeply held beliefs and feelings. As we begin a sexual reconstruction, we enter the three stages of our sexual-spiritual integration.

Stage One: Our Relationship with Our Self

To develop our relationship with our true self, we must focus on three areas: education, age, and body image.

Education. We need information about our bodies and our attitudes. We can learn from such books as *Our Bodies, Our Selves,* films, lectures, group discussions, and experience. But we also need our own internal history, our stories. Writing our personal sexual history can be invaluable, and placing a sexual lens on our family story can be illuminating. Knowing how we learned our sexuality is a part of the cognitive reconstruction essential to our sexual-spiritual integration.

Developmental Versus Chronological Age. Many women sexually shut down during adolescence or earlier because of sexual abuse and/or fear of pregnancy. When we return to our early years to work through our thoughts and feelings, we honor the child within us who was frozen in time and guide her into growing up. However, as my friend Marianne recently said, "My God, my child within has finally grown up and now she has gray hair!"

For some women, facing chronological aging is more painful than growing up. Women show no decline in sexual satisfaction with age; in fact, many women report increasing growth in sexual interests and responsiveness. Yet, older women encounter very real restrictions in expressing sexuality. For heterosexual women the most outstanding is the lack of a partner.[50] As my friend Kate says, "It's the possibility that's missing." Widowed or divorced older men remarry quickly— usually to younger women. Despite the beauty of older women, our society values youth. As a result, three-fourths of all men over age sixty-five are married as compared with one-third of all women that age. Mid-life women need support so they don't become lonely and invisible. They need to learn that late-life singlehood can open doors to a freedom never known.

Body Image.   Most women spend years disliking their body-selves. A poor body image is the result of the media-supported, thinness messages in our culture. Young women in search of love are particularly vulnerable to the cultural myth that "thin will win." Whether thin or overweight, their body is a stranger to them. I have heard many women refer to their body as "it." Such distancing language is a sign of women's sexual cutoffs. As a result, they externalize their body— "dressing it," "exercising it," "feeding it." Poet Carol Connolly states the view clearly in her poem "Last Resort":

> I am trapped here in a second rate body.
> I. Me with the proper address,
> and acceptable blood lines
> and the appearance of a decent bank balance.
> Trapped here at the pool
> during the thigh show.
> Sins of the flesh
> are punished here. Exposed.
> Sagging tits and a stretched belly
> negate a person at this spa.
> Here the only interest is in bones
> and sinew and teeth and tan.
> No flesh need apply.

Attention. Over here. I would
like to say that I am terribly sorry
if I have visually assaulted you.
I want to explain. I followed the rules.
It was seven pregnancies for me
and twins and nine pound babies.

Do you know that
if you want to have your cake,
you must eat it.[51]

As women take responsibility for knowing their body-selves and learn about self-pleasuring, they increasingly integrate "I" into their language.

Jean, just coming out of the shower, was surprised when her daughter, Amy, entered the bathroom. As she toweled her stretch-marked, full-bodied self down, Jean said to Amy, "You know, I feel so good now that I have finally accepted my body." Amy, age thirteen, stared wide-eyed at her and exclaimed in near disbelief, "You *have?*" Jean smiled in recognition of the difference in their age and values. This scenario might have been very different had Jean not joined a women's sexuality group and had learned to accept and respect her body. In doing so, she had moved through the first stage of her sexual-spiritual growth; she was now in touch with her body. Women in this culture have not been socialized to live in their bodies. The expectation is to be "built well and don't do anything with it." Unlike men, who are socialized in their bodies, women learn to trust their bodies more with more physical action. This trust in our physical self strengthens our self-trust, self-image, and self-worth. This became clear to me from my research on rock-climbing trips with couples. Unlike their partners, most of the women had never tested themselves physically. Pre- and posttrip assessments and tests revealed that the women's self-trust scores were *triple* the men's scores after the climbing experiences, and their self-esteem scores *doubled.* In women-only climbing trips, women who initially described themselves as "mermaids" found their dormant physical self-support awakened through climbing. They then were able to translate this self-support into their daily lives. The invisible became visible. "The body is the word in the language of God," says theologian Karl Barth.[52]

Stage Two: Our Relationships with Others

In this second stage we learn about respecting and being respected. And respect, after all, *is* the greatest aphrodisiac.

Defining Sexual Boundaries. All too often women have learned their sexual boundary through violation. As we acknowledge what we feel and believe, give voice to our true self, and set limits, we strengthen our sexual boundary. We draw a clear line between self and other by standing up and speaking out. Our sexual assertiveness allows us to nurture our self-respect.

Clarifying Sexual Values. By learning about our own attitudes and feelings, we clarify our sexual values. The exercise I described earlier, a "Sexual Bill of Rights," is really a values-clarifying exercise. Doing it often entails facing our overabundant sexual guilt. Our "guiltometer," our sex-guilt barometer, is a positive index for knowing our values. Since our values are linked to our conscience through feelings, we feel guilt when we want to or do violate our values. By guilt I refer to mature guilt that comes when we are dishonest to our *own* values. When our guilt rises, we must first tune into ourselves and ask whose guilt it is. Does it come from our own values, is it mature guilt? Or does it come from neurotic guilt, guilt stemming from family and church values?

Risking Intimacy. To risk being intimate is both exciting and frightening. Intimacy does not begin in bed. Women who have foreclosed on hopes for respectful intimacy are terrified in intimate connections. Feelings from both the past and the present surface and we need to befriend ourselves as we separate them.

Intimacy is a process; this process is the same whether we are talking about a paired permanent relationship or a garden of intimate friendships. It has to do with where we are in life.

Jean told the story about her children teasing her. "We think you're married to being single," they commented. Jean said she retorted, "Look, I've been married, and I've been single, and . . ." At this point her daughter interrupted her, saying, "But you've never been separate *and* paired!" "Touché," Jean said and smiled. She said at least she knew her adolescent children understood what had taken her many years to learn.

While teaching an all-women's singles course at the University of Minnesota, I discovered that many highly successful women felt "lesser than" because they weren't paired. It took some weeks before they could debunk the cultural messages that intimacy with a "significant other" is the *only* intimacy.

At times it is important to value our "insignificant others" and recognize that we do have intimacy even if it is not sexual-genital intimacy. When intimacy was initially categorized by men writers, there was no separation of affectional and sexual-genital intimacy, only "affectional-sexual intimacy." This indeed fit with what men had learned—that the two are one. Being single doesn't mean we cannot have intimacy. Being in a paired relationship is no guarantee that we have intimacy. There is no greater loneliness than loneliness in relationship.

So we need to expand our meaning of intimacy. Intimacy is the co-creation of an experience with shared closeness and connection in a variety of activities that are deep and personal. To know connection, oneness, and intimacy as a process requires new ways of being.

Intimate connections occur in a variety of contexts: social, emotional, intellectual, physical, recreational, affectional, sexual, aesthetic, and spiritual. We each can order these contexts according to our preferences and experiences. When we do have intimate moments or intimate experiences, we long to re-create them. But even though we experience an intimate moment, that does not mean we will have an intimate relationship. An intimate relationship exists only when we have shared intimate experiences with someone in at least four or five of the above areas *with the expectation that the experiences and the relationship will continue over time.*[53]

154

Sexual Celibacy. To build trust and work through sexual fears, women often limit sexual-genital expression. We need to listen to our inner knowing, to our own timetables. I often quote Jim Nelson's belief: "The physical expression of one's sexuality with another ought to be appropriate to the level of shared commitment."[54] A redefinition of celibacy can be the reward.

I like Joanie Gustafson's statement that celibacy is "that dimension of me which can never be given away, exhausted or comprehended. It is the embodiment of my fullest potential, my entire personality, the solitary I in any relationship. It is my integrated character, my interior freedom to love and to receive love."[55]

This quotation comes from a book whose title I shall long remember. Newly single and intent on rediscovering my sexuality and sensuality, I attended a seminar in a retreat center. After hearing rave reviews of the book *Celibate Passion*, I went directly to the center's bookstore and, approaching the clerk, eagerly asked, "Do you have a book entitled *The Passionate Celibate*? I froze in blush as I saw the clerk stare at me in response to my question. Politely composed, she said, "I believe you mean *Celibate Passion*." I smiled inwardly as I realized my "revised" title told her just where I was in my life.

Stage Three:
Our Relationship with Higher Powers

This stage involves surrendering ourselves to the creative spirit, the sacredness in life, our respect for our earth. (I cover this in greater detail in Chapter 7.) This connection to the spiritual may or may not encompass religion. Some women may be feminist in their approach; others may be nonfeminist. Our connection may be pagan, Native American, Buddhist, Catholic, Christian, Muslim, New Age, or Goddess. Or our connection may be to the universe itself or to whatever universal mysteries we feel drawn to.

As we examine this band of the spiral of life, we know that this stage is not a one-time, steady state. We will dip down into our past and emerge with more spiritual connectedness. As we move closer to sexual-spiritual integration, we come to know "I am my body." To know the Goddess within, we must come to our senses and allow ourselves to be fully open—to hear and be heard, to see and be seen, to touch and be touched, to smell and be smelled, to speak and be spoken to. Opening our senses allows us to be fully connected to life's energy. We know that our being is within, relentlessly nudging us to be fully human.

As we connect more deeply with our spirituality we recognize this rising consciousness is universal. From the far corners of the world we are hearing stories of hope from our global sisters. Perhaps you have heard of the women in Iceland who held a sexual strike in an attempt to get their right to vote. They got it! This is a clear reminder of couples researcher Pepper Schwartz's message: by women's assuming a position of sexual openness and gaining sexual equality, women gave away the only power we had in relationships.[56]

Another recent story comes from a small village outside Arusha, Tanzania, in East Africa, where clitoridectomy, a ritual rite of puberty, has been performed for centuries. Clitoridectomy is the surgical removal of the clitoris but is referred to as female circumcision.[57] If males were to have the parallel surgical procedure, they would have the tip of their penis removed! When the mothers in the village, all of whom had had a clitoridectomy, learned that the term "female circumcision" is a misnomer for genital mutilation, they gathered together and decided to take a stand for their daughters. They went en masse to the village chief and his council saying, "There will be no more clitoridectomies for our daughters." To date, no young woman in the village has had one.

As we unlearn our myths and broaden our meaning of sexuality, we can truly embody our spiritual in our beings and in our separate and collective union of souls make some necessary changes. To write honestly about women's sexuality means having to write about abuse. Although some women do enjoy and celebrate their sexuality, I always assume that much of this is luck; we do not choose the families into which we are born. Far too many of our sisters are victims of abuse. The goal for all women is to live with respect so we can express and celebrate our sexuality and enjoy being women. Our entitlement is to allow our passions to run fully, to know relationships based on mutuality and warmth, to experience deep romantic attachments with affection, bonding, and intimacy. This challenge of sexual-spiritual integration takes many years. Our intimacy needs change throughout our life cycle, but we will always be sexual. Our sense of feeling like a full woman is empowering.

We feel empowered as we express ourselves. The next challenge, expressing our personal power, is tightly woven with our fullest sexual-spiritual expression.

CHAPTER 6

STANDING UP AND SPEAKING OUT:
The Challenge of Expressing
Personal Power

Somewhere along the line of development we discover
what we really are and then we make our real decision for
which we are responsible. Make that decision primarily for
yourself, because you can never really have anyone else's
life, not even your child's. The influence you have is
through your own life and what you become yourself.

ELEANOR ROOSEVELT

Marcia showed up for church at her regular time, as she had for twenty years. Seating herself on her familiar, worn organ bench, she began to play the Prelude. Then suddenly, something took over— Marcia began to pommel the keyboard, her fingers expressing the most intense feeling she had ever felt. Congregants stared as they entered the church; those seated in their pews turned their heads and looked up at her in contained disbelief. The sounds thundered louder and stronger. Marcia, very present, was also very present with her self. What her congregation did not know was that Marcia was playing the Prelude backward!

All her life Marcia had been obedient to her family, her religion, and her community. Recently, however, she had been reflecting on how trapped she felt and had been reading women's books in her Women's Identity course. Her agitation grew about as rapidly as her awareness. She described her act as something that just happened; she had not planned it. She realized she had made a statement. When

159

she told me about it later, I commented, "Well, you surely were expressing your personal power!"

Personal power? Just what *is* personal power? How does personal power, our real power, differ from role power and power by association? Where does personal power come from? What do we do with it once we feel it? Before we exercise our power, we have to search for meanings that fit our life experiences.

JUST WHAT IS PERSONAL POWER?

I thought of Rosa Parks, the courageous black woman who became the "mother" of the civil rights movement by sitting in the whites-only section of a bus in Selma, Alabama. I thought of Bella Abzug, a powerful role model for women in politics, and activist Dorothy Day, whose inspiring words "speak truth to power" are reflected in Betty Friedan's *The Feminine Mystique* and Jean Baker Miller's *Toward a New Psychology of Women*.[1] I thought of Gloria Steinem who founded *Ms.* magazine, and Carol Gilligan, who in her book *In a Different Voice*, refuted the traditional (male) thinking on women's moral development.[2] All these women acted on personal power in the public domain.

Whether expressed through action or nonaction, in public or private, power simply *is*. The word power comes from the Latin word *potere*, which means "to be able."[3] The essence of personal power is reflected in the way we live our daily lives through our everyday acts. Lecturer-author Janet Hagberg describes personal power as, "the extent to which one is able to link the outer capacity for action (external power) with the inner capacity for reflection (internal power)."[4]

We exercise personal power when we tell a doctor that we no longer will be his or her patient because we refuse to be kept waiting for more than one hour each visit. We exercise it when we say no to our children and refuse to deny them their own life struggles, even though a part of us wants to protect them from life's pain. We exercise personal power when we confront a friend who has hurt us. We act on personal power when we write a letter on the abortion controversy to the editor of the local newspaper. Jean felt personal power when, several years after her divorce, she moved from the "passenger" side to the "driver's" side of her bed. My friend Ann has exercised her personal power by influencing a great many women to enter doctoral programs. Clearly, personal power means acting on what deeply matters to us. When we express and act on our personal power, we honor our inner knowing, our "infallible gut."[5] Each act of "personal authority" shapes and enriches our life story, of which we alone are the "author." Acting on our inner power to give and to nurture is also called actualization power.[6]

My friend Moira is a glowing example of actualization power. She and Dan, her husband, share an equal commitment to work in the social justice movement. A psychologist, Dan's primary role is to earn the family income; Moira's primary role is to engage in acts of civil disobedience, which has led to her spending several months at a time in jail. With each passing year, Moira's voice has grown stronger and more passionate. As a result, she has empowered many others to act with purpose and face life's challenges.

HOW DOES PERSONAL POWER DIFFER FROM ROLE POWER?

Power has been and, for the most part, still is bound to status and success in our patriarchy, where domination, whatever the cost, is the name of the game. No one in this society has escaped the domination, authority, and control inherent in the role power wielded by parents, bosses, clergy, teachers, and political leaders. (And a good share of us exercise role power ourselves to negative or positive effect.) Moreover, women and men alike know only too well about power imbalances imposed by language, appearance, class, age, ethnicity, and race. For women, gender heads this list.

Lacking real power in the male-dominated public domain, women tend to adopt power by association, that is, power bestowed through relationship with someone else's name or role.[7] Socialized to accept and value this "unreal" power, many women either are unaware of the flimsy security it affords or fear the consequences of asserting their "real" power. One such consequence is poverty; another is the stigma attached to powerful women, who traditionally have been viewed as dangerous, devouring, and castrating.[8]

The meaning of power is gradually changing. Today we are rediscovering the old ways of ancients like the Cretans to whom power meant responsibility, care, and nurturing.[9] We dip back to the past to move forward. The movement is universal, not limited to American women. Remember the women in the African village who en masse demanded that their daughters not be subjected to clitoridectomy? Connected by their values of responsibility and care, they exerted their nurturing power to face and overcome a challenge to their daughters' physical and sexual well-being. These women made a moral decision. They took responsibility for their relationships.

WHERE DOES PERSONAL POWER COME FROM?

Personal power doesn't just show up one day in our psyches. Personal power grows out of our integration; it is our expressed integrity. Personal power begins with our relationship with the self and then extends to our relationships with others (i.e., interpersonal power).

In moving along the bands of the spiral, that is, in meeting the challenges after the awakening crisis—leaving home, facing shame, forging identity, and integrating sexuality—we continuously reinforce our commitment to growth and healing, making new growth possible. As we take risk after risk, we add to the uppermost band of the spiral: it is here that we act on our own values by giving voice to our personal power. Again, this growth process is gradual and never-ending, for we revisit our challenges, but we meet them on a new (higher) plane because we are more than what we were. Indeed, we share much with a natural, living spiral, the ancient chambered nautilus. Throughout its lifetime, the nautilus adds to its shell (life), whether in deep or shallow waters. Each is unique; no two are alike (Fig. 10). Crystos says, "In this circle I pass each of you a shell from our mother sea. Hold it in your spirit and hear the stories she will tell you."[10]

WHAT DO WE DO WITH IT ONCE WE FEEL IT?

It is not enough to know; we must give voice to our knowledge and we must act. Kathleen Michels, freelance editor, says, "Only if you can disclose what's real do you have personal power." Those around us sense it when we have personal power; we don't have to advertise it or lean on a role or someone else to express it.

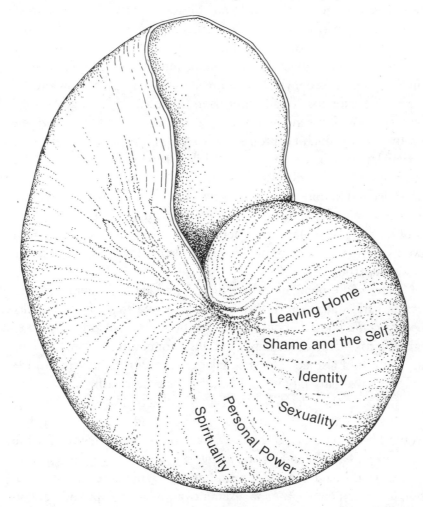

Figure 10
Integrating Personal Power: The Nautilus

Finding Our Voices, Speaking Our Truth

In live burial for many years, my personal power did not have a clear, direct route of expression. Calling myself a "recovering nice lady," I felt overwhelmed and frightened when I began to move from my anonymous, unknown self and recognize my personal power. I can recall words getting stuck or coming out in "fast forward" or sometimes even in "reverse." And I can still recall with some embarrassment those times when I was discovering my anger, seeing it flash out inappropriately, not only toward those around me but myself as well. My unconscious seemed to speak loudly and clearly, almost without my filtering. I asked myself, "Did I really say that?" I saw how hurtful I could be. Not that I had never been hurtful to others; of course I had. But now I was *aware* of my personal power and felt responsible for the way in which I expressed my voice. Others probably called me a troublemaker or deviant. For a while I thought, "Maybe I'll have growth with no friends." But of course that was not the case; I was a beginner and in transition. Disclosing what is real is a risk. Sometimes we can disclose and don't, sometimes we can disclose and won't. I could list pages of incidents when I didn't speak up because I didn't even see the injustices or hear insults. I hadn't known what personal power was then.

Later came incidents when, after I *had* learned about personal power, I still walked away. I walked away feeling shameful and guilty because I *did* know and did not act. At those moments I was afraid to take the risk—fearful of disapproval, anger, or confrontation. As I look back, I would also add that risk taking was often politically unwise. Often I have felt guilty when I heard myself recounting my stand in a risking scene in much fuller strength than I actually took at the time. Other women tell me that they too have reported scenes the way they would *like* to have heard them. Perhaps these are rehearsals for the next scene; each "stand" is still a victory.

As we develop our voice, we often experience a real transformation in our self-concept. As we examine our relationships and develop new ones, we often feel a waffling of the self as our integrated voice strengthens. Moving through our adult challenges we listen and develop empathy, including others with differences. But we must also listen to our own self.

The integration of the layers of our voice takes a long time. First, we find our voice within us by hearing our own voice. You might remember the earlier chapter's examples of the inner voices that told us to follow the family's unspoken rules—that voice that meant survival in a pain-filled family. That voice tenaciously held the delusional beliefs. Learning more about the language, voices, and meaning systems of women, we find our true voice is often muffled by delusional messages we tell ourselves to survive and to protect others.

Polly found her voice to be delusional. When she heard herself tell the police, "Everything is okay," after Tom had tried to throw her out of the car, Polly realized she was in trouble. She had just lied about a life-threatening event; this time she heard herself.

Polly had to hear herself before she could claim her core voice and talk back. In "talking back," we express our movement "from object to subject—the liberated voice."[11] Polly began acting like a subject when she let herself hear her words of denial. Polly knew she had to act after hearing her delusional voice. She told herself she was going to live, and that meant taking responsibility for her life. Polly told her husband she was through being self-deceptive and would no longer be party to his self-destruction. She affirmed that she truly cared about him. Then she said she was going for help on her own, since he refused to seek outside help. She made it clear that she would no longer live in terror.

This was her "different voice," coming from her caring and her responsibility to herself.[12] No longer would she focus on understanding Tom and neglect to care about herself. She had "had it" with the selfless, overresponsible caretaking into which women are socialized. Polly had begun meeting the challenge of expressing her personal power.

MEETING THE CHALLENGE

Polly's statement to her husband was a dramatic turning point in her life. Polly's story is her story; yours will be yours. Each of us will find our own way as we recognize and master the five underpinnings of personal power: valuing, finding our feelings, setting limits, taking risks, and giving up control.

Valuing: Acting on What We Know

Polly's decision was based on her values. She valued her marriage and her commitment to it. She cared deeply about their child, families, and friends—all of whom were tightly intertwined in her life. Reflecting on the scene after the car episode, she realized her values of self-respect and honesty meant little unless she acted on them. Our moral decisions require acting on our values, which means we unravel our own concealed values from those we internalized from others. Our "truth" is trusting our intuition, our "gut." This is our "homebrewed epistemology," the part of us that simply knows and knows that we know. When we *know* that we know, we must act.

Finding and Facing Our Feelings

Polly had been unaware of how resentful she had been. In her denial, she had lied to herself, telling herself to be patient. In therapy, she took a good look at the smoldering chamber in her gut that burned each time she faced another drinking scene. She said it almost felt like an internal organ.

Have you ever noticed how clearly you see situations when you are angry? We often have a near shift in consciousness when this clarity illuminates our inner knowing. When we feel the injustices, our center is touched, and we know. We cannot have grown up in an oppressed group without being totally unaware of the injustices and discrimination of race, class, and gender. Many women go through several years of anger, working through the buried wounds of the past. Socialized to please others, we have often directed our anger against ourselves or our children. When we speak directly, we will often be labeled a "hostile bitch." This, of course, is often a way for others to control our voices.

We know when our anger is true; we also eventually learn to discern when our anger is expressed through manipulation, defensive rage, or survival tactics. It becomes easy to blame the victim when we encounter this anger and rage. This defensive power is, for some women, a necessary pendulum swing in their process of developing real power out of victimization experiences. Therefore, for many women the feelings aspect of personal power involves facing hurt, sadness, and unresolved grief. Any of these feelings can be motivating.

Setting Limits

When Polly took a stand that day, she knew she was doing it for herself. Her feelings reflected her values; and her values tugged at her emotional cords. As we learn and live our values, we become more definite in saying no and yes. Often we have been saying no inwardly before we express it outwardly. Polly had been taking stands in other places in her life; now it was time to make a statement to her husband. Drawing our lines, setting limits, our boundaries become firmly defined. No longer walking away from our values, we no longer walk away from our core self, going deeper in nourishing our self-worth.

Taking Risks

Polly had to consider the outcome. She knew about Tom's temper and his control over the money. She also knew her work as a nurse could never bring in enough to keep her in their present life-style. She also knew that she would be working full-time if she left her marriage and would probably end up with responsibility for child care. She also knew as a woman in her late thirties that she would most likely be single for the rest of her life. We consider the relationship consequences as we take risks. Polly wondered about being made to feel guilty by Al-Anon friends, rejected by some neighborhood friends, and called an "uppity feminist" when she wanted something for herself.

When we face our challenges and set limits, we risk. We often go through an internal dialogue, reviewing all aspects of the situation. We may call a friend and ask him or her to listen while we think out loud. When we are motivated by our morality, our ethic of care, we consider others as well as ourselves.

Giving Up Control

Polly knew there was little she could accurately predict. When we express our personal power, we have to recognize that we are unable to control outcomes. She realized she could not control what others would think of her; she knew some would disagree and caution her to change her mind. Some would say, "You're really risking!" But others would say, "Of course you must; I respect you."

On the one hand, we have control; on the other hand, we don't have control. We can do what we can; that is all. We can be responsible to ourselves and considerate of others, yet not be responsible for the feelings and actions of others. Some situations will be satisfyingly smooth; others will test our voice. The Serenity Prayer of AA helps us in our choices about where and when we express our voice: "God grant me the serenity to accept the things I cannot change, the courage to change the things I can, and the wisdom to know the difference."[13] But we always voice personal power in relationship.

EXPRESSING PERSONAL POWER
WHERE IT MATTERS

Several areas call us forth to claim our personal power in relationships. These are not mutually exclusive relationships; they affect one another. With our spiritual self at our center, we have relationships with physical things that matter; with people who matter greatly— friends, family, and heartmates; and with issues that matter—work, money, and community, and environment. We rely on our spirituality to feed our core self so we can express our voice with people and issues that matter.

Physical Activities That Matter:
From Mystery to Mastery

Early in our growth, succeeding at some physical act we were socialized to believe women cannot do may put us in touch with our personal power for the first time. We may push our body to the utmost while rock climbing, skiing, white-water canoeing, or backpacking. Whether mundane or risky, physical acts nurture the self-trust and self-confidence so essential to the growth of our personal power. Simone de Beauvoir expresses the need to risk: "Let her swim, climb mountain peaks, pilot airplanes, battle against the elements, take risks, go out for adventure, and she will not feel before the world . . . timidity."[14]

Many of us were socialized to believe that fixing things was a mystery whose secrets were to be only understood by men. Interestingly, many women reported finding personal power through the challenges of changing a flat tire, buying a car, putting on storm windows, or fixing a broken household appliance.

Two years ago I took a bicycle repair course. From the outset, the instructor, Mary, never asked us how we felt or reassured us that we would be successful. Empathy didn't seem to be a part of her teaching. She simply said, "Put your bikes up on the rack. Anchor them tightly. Pick up your wrenches." Her play-by-play directions were oddly refreshing! (On reading this story, Kathleen Michels remarked, "And I'll bet you never asked the infamous question, 'Why?' during the course, did you?") On reassembling my bike and adjusting the tires, I felt a real sense of accomplishment. Since taking this course, I not only "know" my bike in a different way but I "like" it. I have a genuine relationship with it. Consequently, I now pay greater attention to it; I listen to its workings.

This experience reminded me of how both men and women are stereotypically socialized into mastery. Males are socialized to "fix things" and gain the concrete sense of mastery that can result. In this society, women aren't expected to be mechanically adept; in fact, all too often we ourselves subscribe to the stereotype that we are too weak or too dumb to master the mechanical. Socialized to think only of our relationships with people, we forget that we too have relationships with inanimates. So we learn that personal power comes from our relationships with *its* as well as with people. And while the *"it"* (tire, window, bicycle) doesn't have a relationship with us, *we* have a relationship with *it*. Women can gain mastery through traditional women's activities, such as cooking, sewing, painting, canning, redecorating, and needlework, but also through those typically reserved for males, such as car maintenance, rock climbing, playing in jazz groups, stock investment clubs, driving taxis, and being corporate executives. In her journal, author Marguerite Ickes quotes her great-grandmother about a quilt it took many years to make:

> It took me more than twenty years, nearly twenty-five, I reckon,
> in the evenings after supper when the children were all put to
> bed. My whole life is in that quilt . . . my hopes and fears, my joys
> and sorrows, my loves and hates. I tremble sometimes when I
> remember what that quilt knows about me.[15]

Today both men and women are crossing over into one another's stereotypic mastery areas, expanding their mastery. Adding to our sense of mastery can indeed enhance our personal power and give support to us as we face other challenges.

People Who Matter:
Friends, Family, and Heartmates

Our relationships with our relationships! How are we doing with those who matter most to us—friends, family, and heartmates?[16]

Friends. I remember so clearly the day one of my therapy clients committed suicide. After I got the call, I sat frozen and stared—until the tears poured forth. Then the tormenting questions began: what took her over the edge? She was so young. Why did this have to happen? And, of course, the typical: what had I not done? How did I fail her? The pain tore at my insides. The phone rang again. It was my friend, Ethelyn, and through my sobs I told her what had happened. She softly suggested a plan. I agreed. She and another friend, Jeannine, met me at my apartment where they took over, listening as I thought out loud, vented my anger, and wondered. They then put cushions on the floor, had me lie down, and began to massage me, gently, deeply. I hadn't had to ask; they were just there for me. Their loving, nurturing care deeply touched and comforted me.

In friendship, we do touch each other with our thoughtfulness. And we stay in touch — by clipping articles, noting ideas, giving small gifts, making telephone calls. (My closest women friends and I "check in" with each other almost daily by telephone.) We honor birthdays, celebrate accomplishments, and gather for farewell and welcome-home parties. Through such rituals we keep our connections viable and make change more palatable. Surely we have all learned the traditional life-cycle rituals, but in friendship we often create rituals that acknowledge identity redefinition (such as the story I told earlier of tearing the tags off the pillows), ethnic traditions, and healing. I know many women who have ritualized significant life shifts by buying or finding themselves a small gift.

When I think of my friends I picture flowers blooming in a Minnesota summer garden — some in clusters, some in pairs, others alone. I treasure tending this garden, even weeding it. As friends, we are vulnerable with each other, we support each other, and we know and accept each other's flat sides. Each knows how to be a friend. Out of our constancy and openness has come intimacy, so essential to a rich life. Before I became a single mid-life adult, I think I took some friendships for granted. I have since learned to value friendships and to invest in maintaining them. Often in the world of singles, the "bouquet" of friends constitutes a primary relationship.

Tending this garden sometimes involves weeding. And weeding often calls for personal power when we know we have to say something. Jean told me such a story. She said that through the years she and Bob had become good friends with another couple, Nancy and Gary. It was not until Jean and Bob had children that they became deeply concerned about Gary's racist comments. One Sunday while their children were watching television together, Jean heard Gary making derogatory remarks in response to a newscast about a series of crimes that, in this particular instance, had been committed by people of color. Jean said she asked him to stop, explaining that she was dead set against teaching children to hate. When he continued

171

to make nasty remarks, she walked over to him and said, "I know we have had long years of friendship, and I have valued our friendship, but I no longer will tolerate such talk in my home. I am asking you to leave." She said she did not ask Bob about it or talk with Nancy; she just did it.

Family. My friend Anita, a California therapist who often works with blended families, said that when she suggests clients bring in their family, they ask, "Which one?" I think most of us could ask the same question. In the not-too-distant past, we spoke about families of *procreation.* Now, given adoption, foster parenting, and artificial insemination, we talk about families of *creation.*

Moreover, the United States has not only the highest divorce rate but the highest remarriage rate in the world.[17] Since 1970, the number of remarriages among divorced Americans has increased by 80 percent.[18] The result is an ever-increasing number of yet another family of creation — the *binuclear,* or postdivorce family.[19] In 1987, of 14 million divorced people in the United States, 8.5 million were women and 4 million were men.[20] By 1997, of *total* marriages, more will be remarriages than marriages.[21]

My family of origin is one family; my family of friendship, my family of affiliation, is another.[22] I created the latter. Many of us feel more strongly attached to our family of affiliation than we do to our family of origin. My son reminded me of the emotional entitlement in my family of affiliation when he exclaimed one day, "Gosh, one mom flips out and another flips in!"

Our personal power grows with the challenges we face by creating these new family forms. What matters is how we give voice in all our family relationships — past and present.

Beverly, whom you met earlier, had many issues with her verbally and sexually abusive father. She had worked hard and long struggling through the messages of her shaming self to find her core voice. In a different place with a "different voice," Beverly had been grieving her "old" dad. In doing so, she had made several trips back home to visit her father, who was dying of cancer. This time she had returned home at her mother's request to help discuss finances. Her father, retreating in his suffering, would not let anyone get near.

En route to the hospital for more tests, Beverly's father threw one of his ugly, contemptuous remarks at her. Instead of shutting down and backing off as she once had done, she turned to him and said, "I don't like it when you talk like that! You sound like a cantankerous old man." Her father gruffly snapped, "Well, that's who I am." Beverly's voice grew stronger as she retorted angrily, "No, that's *not* who you are; that's your cover, and you know that I know that!" Her final statement did it; her father sat silent and, within a short time, started talking about finances. As she reflected on the story later, Beverly smiled and said, "And he never spoke that way to me again." Empowered, Beverly was reaping the rewards of her hard work; she had befriended herself and had broken ground for an honest relationship with her father.

Heartmates.   "I wonder why love is so often equated with joy when it is everything else as well," writes Florida Scott-Maxwell.[23] Love carries almost intolerable burdens; it can push us hard. The ancients have told us that perhaps the heart breaks in order to open. We mature in our love when we realize the "everything else" of it and learn to become more emotionally and/or physically naked with our lovers, husbands, or life partners, our heartmates — the relationships we carry within us.

Jean spent time in therapy discussing her divorce. She reported having difficult times through her divorce, with power struggles over the children and household goods. In fact, in the early stages, anything was fair game for conflict. Attached to Bob in anger, she gradually worked her pain over time. As she continued to heal, she could see him and their marriage more clearly. Jean knew she had some things to say to Bob. She had moved to this town years ago with Bob and now, since she was divorced and since their last child had left her home, Jean felt free to move away. She wanted some closure, yet feared that he would laugh at or be sarcastic with her.

Jean said she had felt awkward when she called him. "Bob, I have something I've been wanting to say to you for a long time. I wanted to thank you for introducing me to the outside world, to your world of nature." Bob paused for a moment and then guardedly and softly responded, "Well, thanks; I like hearing that." Jean then said, "You know, Bob, I am leaving town and I wonder if you would like to come over for dinner with the kids and me." Bob replied with some tentativeness in his voice, "Well, I guess that might be okay."

Jean said she had felt tense; she had prepared everyone's favorite dishes. The start of the dinner was awkward, but the children immediately loosened up the conversation. They began asking questions about Jean and Bob's relationship and soon Jean and Bob were reviewing their history together, telling about the day they met, their courtship, and their early married life. They assured the children that each of them was wanted; they then continued telling family stories that included the children. Amy asked, "Do you mean you would have married even if it wasn't just to sleep together?" "Of course," they replied in unison. The children asked more questions of both of them. Jean said that what began as a goodbye dinner ritual became an act of healing. "Now," Jean said, "both Bob and I can honor our long history together."

"There's no such thing as divorce," says my mentor Carl Whitaker.[24] When there are children, the relationship goes on forever. Jean's story reminded me that our personal power is not always risking to say the hard and critical; sometimes it is more difficult to express the caring.

Julia was concerned. She had met the man with whom she could have a good life; he enjoyed the arts as much as she did. Divorced two years ago, Bart had been busy parenting his three children, ages seventeen, fourteen, and twelve. Julia had been involved in several primary relationships but had never married. She knew she wanted to marry and have children. She also knew that at age forty-one, pregnancy posed some risk to her. Bart made it clear that he loved Julia and that for financial reasons, he did not want more children. Julia knew she had to decide whether to break off the relationship or allow her love for Bart to deepen. Together they sought help from some friends who helped them talk it through. Julia came to the realization that it was

Bart she wanted to spend her life with. She did make the commitment to marry Bart and continued to grieve about not having children with him.

Issues That Matter:
Work, Money, Community, and Environment

Because women are socialized to focus on caring for people, we often minimize the importance of our relationships with work, money, community, and environment. Moreover, these are the arenas in which we traditionally have had severely limited power.

Work: An Unwelcoming World for a 70-Cent Woman.   Barbara, age sixty-two, felt desperate when she came into our women's group for support. Her husband was involved with his thirty-year-old office manager and refused to stop seeing her. Angry, Barbara wanted to leave the marriage, but she was totally financially dependent on her husband. In exploring her options, we found ourselves in a dilemma: we wanted to support her decision to leave, but we didn't want to support her out of marriage into poverty. We suggested she examine the economics of divorce and work.

Like most women of her generation, Barbara had worked in the home—raising four children, managing the household, and entertaining her husband's associates. In addition, she had done volunteer work for several community organizations. Now, at age sixty-two, she was not marketable. She felt trapped and furious at her mistaken belief that it was "until death do us part" and that the "us" meant joint ownership of all assets. Now she learned that her husband was making large withdrawals from their savings and stock funds, all of which were in his name. When Barbara saw an attorney, she learned she did not have to prove her worth regarding her share of the marital assets. A recent change in the law deemed that marital assets are assumed to be equally obtained and that unpaid work—not just income-earning work—is a contribution to the joint assets. Yet, like other women, she didn't trust the new law. Hadn't she just learned that the higher a man's income, the less he paid proportionately in maintenance? Hadn't she learned that one year after divorce, the standard of living for mothers and children falls 73 percent, whereas fathers' standard of living rises 42 percent.[25] Also, many states report that only a little more than one-third of child support orders are being paid.[26] Barbara came face to face with the fact that author Riane Eisler states: "globally women are half the population, perform two-thirds of the world's work in terms of hours, earn one-tenth as much as men earn, and own one-hundreth the property that men own."[27]

Barbara started reading about women and work and heatedly reported her findings to the group:

- Today, more women than ever are working outside the home *by necessity*. Between 1947 and 1980, the number of women in the paid labor force increased by 173 percent.[28] Today's young women can expect to spend about 30 years in the work force.[29] Many experts predict that we will look back on the 1980s as a decade in which women constituted two-thirds of the labor force.[30]
- Regardless of their income, hours, or status outside the home, women do more housework than men.[31] Women with paid jobs do roughly 35 hours of housework per week in addition to their 40-hour week.[32]
- Women earn only 70 cents (actually 70.2) for each dollar earned by men.[33]

We agreed with Barbara that the picture was rather bleak. I decided to call economist Geraldine Gage, a professor at the University of Minnesota who testifies on women's worth. I began by asking about women's work at home. She replied that, "For most women their *nonpay* contribution exceeds their paid income over their lifetime. Women start younger and work longer; we never get out of working at home while we *do* get out of our paid jobs."

She continued, "Currently, the conditions in the labor market are such that domestic work has a higher wage rate than other types of work. Domestic houseworkers earn $8 to $10 per hour—in sharp contrast to women who make the minimum wage doing low-status officc work. Yet, women working for $5 to $7 per hour consider their job to be more valuable than domestic work. Clearly, women outside the home work for less wages because work in the marketplace is more valued than housework. In fact, their work at home is more valued *on an hourly wage basis.* Women who work outside the home need to delegate work, so there is a demand for domestic help. Since not everyone will do such work, the requests for domestic help outnumber the offers by two to one." I said, "You mean that women will work for status for less money!"

Geraldine went on to say, "The trend today is to not give benefits anyway, so many women working outside the home do not get better benefits than domestic workers. It won't be long before those willing to do housework can earn $10 per hour with no benefits rather than work for $5 per hour in an office with no benefits." I asked, "So can you sum it up?" Geraldine replied, "Over a lifetime for the average woman without a degree, the most significant part of her contribution will be in what she does as a homemaker."

This conversation jarred me. Add to this another disturbing fact: wages become depressed when large numbers of women enter a field (e.g., law, medicine) once dominated by men. Obviously, we have a long way to go.

Today, many women are choosing to work with a career focus; many others have a career-family focus. No matter what our focus, women must realize that we need to be marketable in the public world; we cannot know what life will bring. The work need not be a career-slot position; it could be tutoring, accounting, teaching, bus driving, clerking, or secretarial work. Women gain a sense of mastery from work inside and outside the home, and mastery feeds our personal power. Many women whose primary work was raising a family are surprised to discover the remarkable management skills and flexibility they have developed—as well as a sense of competency. For many divorced women, the postdivorce period is a time for developing mastery, often out of necessity. Many single women in middle adulthood became competent in at least one area early in life (teaching, office management, investment business, engineering, medicine) and are extremely invested in and satisfied with their work and enjoy their economic independence.

Money: Virgin Territory?   Many women are like Barbara, who called herself a "financial virgin." Most of us have not been socialized to think about money. Indeed, until recent years, a woman could not get a charge account in her own name.

Yet money, like sex, is a power base. An examination of couples' relationships has revealed that lesbians are the *only* group for whom money does not determine the power balance.[34] Given this deplorable situation, it is difficult for women to become responsible about money.

Laura, separated from David, took her two boys, ages twelve and ten, to the store to buy their dad's birthday present. Her friend, Mary, questioned her about using *her* money to pay for the gifts. Laura responded, "I always have!" Mary argued, "Isn't it time to allow them the satisfaction of paying for the gifts themselves?" "But you just don't understand," Laura protested, "that would be fake; I never *have* done that." Mary asked, "Do you mean you do not know how, or did you never get it?" "I never got it," replied Laura. As they continued their discussion, Laura stated that her parents always gave her money to save; it wasn't to spend. "I just saved and saved—in fact, it's all still there."

Laura, like Barbara and many of us, had an unsophisticated attitude about money. A smart and well-educated woman, Laura had no idea of how money really works or what money means to her. While she valued her interpersonal relationships, she denied her relationship with money. Indeed, until Mary confronted her, Laura was unaware that she was handling money in her adult world just as she had learned to do as a child—and was teaching her sons the same lesson.

Women need teachers. Fortunately, we can learn from women who are financially empowered. Some women in the workplace are using personal power to awaken both men and women.

Joy joined the estate planning department in a large metropolitan bank, where the estate planning model called for meeting with the husband and having his wife come in to sign the final papers. Despite the protest of her older male colleagues, Joy insisted on working with both spouses from beginning to end. Joy is now the manager of the trust department, making certain that women's financial equity is reflected in estate planning.

It may take a long time for many of us to awaken to *all* aspects of money management. Long after her divorce Jean and her financial consultant, Vivian, were planning Jean's money management strategy. "And what disability insurance do you have?" Vivian asked. Jean stared at her long and hard. "Disability? I don't understand." Vivian said, "You're self-employed. Who will take care of you financially if you cannot work?" Again, Jean stared. "You mentioned your sisters," Vivian continued. "Oh, no, I couldn't expect that of them," commented Jean. "Well," Vivian replied, "there's always your mother." "Oh, no, that isn't possible; she's living on a tight fixed income," Jean retorted.

As they continued to discuss possibilities, Jean realized that she had never faced the fact that she was now totally responsible for her well-being for the rest of her life. Jean said, "I feel embarrassed about this. God, I'm an educated woman and have never even considered this." Going from her parents' home to marriage, Jean had always been financially dependent on men. She was not alone; Jean later learned that several of her women friends were in the same virgin territory. Jean learned that knowledge is power and that financial knowledge adds to her personal power.

We often hear that women control the money in America, but in fact, women have the money *in name only.* As women gain *real* financial power, they gain personal power through equity in their marriages.[35] Some family therapists now ask financial questions as naturally as they ask questions about education, health care, and religious affiliation.[36] They are assisting women to get their share of the family finances in their own names. Women's economic independence appears to be critical in coping with divorce and old age, in protecting against abuse, and in building self-esteem. Until women have financial equality, we cannot move toward transformation.

Community: Taking Our Place. Expressing our personal power in public, in our community, is a risk of a special nature because we are vulnerable to ridicule and shaming. Patty Ann, a school principal and a lesbian, had agreed to address the Gay Pride Rally. Highly respected in the community for her outstanding leadership of many years, Patty Ann was at the point in her life where she knew that she could no longer be silent at the cost of the next generation. Patty Ann had neither hidden nor flaunted her lesbianism in school, a private academy for high achievers. She said she thought most people in the school community knew but that no one said anything.

As the large crowd gathered, a group of "closeted" teachers mounted the outdoor stage and stood behind Patty Ann. Each wore a brown paper bag over her or his head as a symbol that it is not okay for teachers to be identified as gay or lesbian. Patty Ann reminded the audience that about 4,300 of the 43,000 elementary and secondary teachers and principals in Minnesota are gay and or lesbian if the "one-in-ten" rule applies. Patty Ann began by talking openly about the vicious cycle of prejudice and bigotry to be broken—to let young people know that there are adult gays and lesbians who are happy, whole, courageous, and respected by their communities. She then ended her speech by saying: "My name is Patty Ann Markham; I am a high-school principal—and I'm proud to be a lesbian!"

The crowd gave her a standing ovation. In the midst of the overwhelming outpouring of emotions, those standing behind her took off their bags and a few other teachers from the audience came to the stage.

When I later asked Patty Ann about her fears, she said, "I always get up before school functions and say the first two lines, 'My name is Patty Ann Markham; I am the high-school principal.' But to say the third line aloud to people who are not close to me, but are part of my public life, *that* was what shook me." As far as retribution, she said the only telephone calls she had received so far were calls of support.

Patty Ann expressed her integrity with clarity; she gave voice to her personal power to empower others. She belongs to that community of often invisible American women who have formed supportive systems—systems that have become our training schools for effecting social and political changes.

The Environment: Our Natural Bond. Susan Griffin, poet-author, clearly describes our alienation from the land:

He breaks the wilderness. He clears the land of trees, brush, weed. The land is brought under his control; he has turned waste into a garden. Into her soil he places his plow. He labors. He plants. He sows. By the sweat of his brow, he makes her yield. She opens her broad lap to him. She smiles on him. She prepares him a feast. She gives up her treasures to him. She makes him grow rich. She yields. She conceives. Her lap is fertile. Out of her dark interior, life arises. What she does to his seed is a mystery to him. He counts her yielding as a miracle. He sees her workings as effortless. Whatever she brings forth he calls his own. He has made her conceive. His land is a mother. She smiles on the joys of her children. She feeds him generously. Again and again, in his hunger, he returns to her. Again and again she gives to him. She is his mother. Her powers are a mystery to him. Silently she works miracles for him. Yet, just as silently, she withholds from him. Without reason, she refuses to yield. She is fickle. She dries up. She is bitter. She scorns him. He is determined he will master her. He will make her produce at will. He will devise ways to plant what he wants in her, to make her yield more to him.... He names all that is necessary, nitrogen, phosphorous, potassium, and these he says he can make.... What device she can use to continue she does. She says that the pain is unbearable. *Give me something*, she says. What he gives her she takes into herself without asking why.... He says she cannot continue without him. He says she must have what he gives her. And he has devised ways to separate himself from her. He sends machines to do his labor; no longer praying, no longer imploring, he pronounces words from a distance and even with his back turned to her as she yields to him. What he possesses, he says, is his to use and to abandon. And with his machines and his chemicals, he has created the distance and depersonalization we live with today.[37]

It is no surprise to see so many women returning to Native American and Goddess spirituality at a time when we are so painfully aware of our estrangement from our Earth, Gaia. From the power of domination, the power of the blade, we are returning to the actualization power, the ancient power of the chalice, to give and to nurture in an egalitarian world.[38] Riane Eisler states, "They [the children] will be taught new myths, epics, and stories in which human beings are good; men are peaceful; and the power of creativity and love— symbolized by the sacred Chalice, the holy vessel of life—is the governing principle."[39]

In ancient Crete, "the whole of life was pervaded by an ardent faith in the goddess Nature, the source of all creation and harmony."[40] The myth of Demeter, the goddess of the earth, and her daughter, Persephone, reflects the feminine perspective on power honored by the Greeks.

"Persephone was playing in a meadow with her friends. When she picked a lovely narcissus blossom, the earth opened and Hades, god of the underworld, kidnapped her. Tormented by grief, Demeter refused to let anything grow! When the life-giving crops and animals began to die, Zeus, the king of the gods, convinced his brother Hades to return Persephone to her mother. As she was leaving the underworld, Persephone ate some pomegranate seeds, an act that ensured her spending part of every year with Hades."[41]

This myth clearly reflects the need for strong interdependence, the building of resources, and giving. It reminds us not only that "narcissism leads to death but that *the fertility of the earth is tied to the continuation of relationships*—here the mother-daughter relationship."[42] The earth is basic to our existence. Once we understand our relationship with our environment, we realize we must play an active role in preserving it.

As my friend and I walked up to our favorite climbing site in the Black Hills, the holy ground of the Sioux, we spoke in low whispers. We had come to say farewell because we knew that our continued presence in this fragile meadow would eventually ruin it. As we took one last, long look at the rose quartz waterfall spilling over the granite rocks like a strawberry milkshake, I flashed on what could happen in a nuclear holocaust. Out of both fear and awe, I wept. The earth had spoken to me. Its voice was the first of what was to become a choir of voices.

Several months later, en route to Hawaii for a backpacking trip, I settled into my plane seat with Jonathan Schell's book, *The Fate of the Earth*.[43] I found it deeply disturbing and was relieved when I had to put it down until trip's end. But Schell's voice spoke to me. A week after I arrived home my friend Moira called to tell me I might not want her for my real estate agent because she was going to jail for her civil disobedience at the Pentagon. I responded, "Of course you'll be my agent; you're doing that work for all of us." I heard her voice. A few days later I picked up a copy of a writers' newsletter and read an article by writer Carol Bly about taking stands on the nuclear threat. She wrote, "Artists have taken a stand; psychotherapists, where are you?" Carol's voice spoke directly. I heard children in therapy say that they were afraid of growing up and, worse, that they would never reach adulthood. Their voices touched me. Then, as if I wasn't hearing enough, I met Helen Caldicott, spokeswoman for the antinuclear movement and author of *Missile Envy*. That did it! Her voice pierced my inner being.

All these voices now embraced me tightly; I no longer could avoid these calls to consciousness. Although I had been on the periphery of the antinuclear movement, I now realized I had to add my voice to nonviolent, proactive antinuclear resistance. I made the decision to join the protesters at a local nuclear guidance systems defense plant.

I didn't enter into this decision lightly. I thought about my adult children, my family, my friends. I wrote a letter to each of my children explaining why I was doing this. Then I thought about my professional reputation. What about my partners at Family Therapy Institute (F.T.I.), my "professional family"? What about my clients? Several clients had already seen me at the defense plant; others had recognized me on television news. I had to weigh my responsibility to act on my personal nonviolent values and the consequences for others.

I felt nervous at lunch the day I decided to tell my colleagues; they mattered to me. While I knew their values, I was not sure about their response to an action that could affect our fifteen-year-old business. Controlling the anxiety in my voice, I said, "I value very much what you think, and I have made my decision; I'm doing another action next week, and I'll be risking arrest this time." Then came the F.T.I. silence, an unconscious ritual of reflection. One by one, they affirmed my decision and asked how they could support me! Tears welled in my eyes, tears of relief. I carried their support with me.

I did get arrested. On the way to the workhouse I carried with me the support of my friends — the flannel gown from Pauline, the book

An Interrupted Life from Trish, the warm wishes of Debbie, Connie, Terry, and Norma.

After my arrest, I was allowed to make a few telephone calls. Toni, a suicidal client, had left a message on my answering machine. I returned the call to the Boston number where she was home visiting. As I listened to her describe her suicidal thinking and her despair, a male voice suddenly boomed out of nowhere: "All inmates return to your cells; time for bedchecks."

I gasped! I had not told Toni where I was calling from. Now what was I to do? The male voice boomed again: "I repeat, all inmates to their cells." Faltering at first, but then quietly and naturally I stated, "Toni, I'm calling from the workhouse; I'm in for civil disobedience and I'll be here a week. And I'm sorry but I have to hang up now." We ended the conversation hurriedly.

I worried that the abrupt ending would further trouble my disturbed client. Yet, when I saw Toni later in my office, she said, "By the way, I really appreciated your calling me when you were in jail. It really lifted my depression, and I was deeply touched that you cared enough to call me from there."

The jailer's voice of dominance epitomized male role power; it reminded me that we never can know when others' voices will influence us. Nor can we know the impact of our voices on others.

Oriana Fallaci's voice stays with me: "I have always looked on disobedience toward the oppressive as the only way to use the miracle of having been born. I have always looked on the silence of those who do not react or who indeed applaud as the real death of a woman or a man."[44]

The opposite of this "death" is life based on integrity. Expressing our voice is vital if we are to move from self-consciousness to conscientiousness. As we know our own truth and voice it, our relationship with the self grows and with it the self. We nourish and protect our spirit when we stay true to ourselves, thus this challenge is essential to our growth. As we dip down and touch our personal power, we also deepen our spiritual growth. Our spiritual growth is not a challenge in the same sense as the others, but our spirituality is the very essence of our being, the growing culmination of facing the challenges.

CHAPTER 7

DANCING WITH THE GODDESS AND THE WISE WOMAN: The Soul Shift of the Spirit

Guide my dance, that I may circle in completion.

MELANIE L. GENDRON

I felt "little" as my sister Sue and I walked past the twelve overpowering, tall, marble disciples into the high-ceilinged room. The warmth of the sunlight through the glass skylight contrasted sharply with the coolness of the pink marble vaults. It was closing time; we had pleaded with the guard to enter. We had buried our mother a month before and this was our first visit to the mausoleum where both our parents now rested.

I felt timid facing so much death. The two large marble vaults, or drawers, that held our parents' remains forbade us to come closer, giving a clear message: your parents are dead. Turning to Sue, I saw her eyes tear up. We hugged each other, cautiously at first, perhaps to ward off the rising wave of deep grief. We began to cry and soon were sobbing heavily with the anguish of being orphaned. We stepped closer to their drawers and slowly began to recount what we would miss: Mom and Dad's bridge table spats, Dad's riddles and limericks, the lively and sometimes chaotic dinner table, and Mom's sewing for us. Sue then turned directly to the vaults and said, "Look, Marilyn, Mom is on top!" "You're right," I smiled. "Say, Dad, what do you think of that?" we teased. We laughed, knowing in a flash of self-consciousness how ridiculous we sounded and how grateful we were for the relief our tears had brought us. We made other comments

185

almost as if to test whether they could hear us. "Can they hear us? Of course they can," I told myself. What an irony—standing before the drawers of the dead, yet feeling connected to the creative life spirit.

Feeling a little lighter, we recalled how our mother would time and again suggest that we show our latest tap-dancing routines to our aunts and uncles. We remembered how we dreaded those times; now, in looking back, we saw her requests as affirmations. Recalling how reluctant we had been, we began to talk teasingly to the "drawers." "Say, Mom, you always wanted us to dance; what would you like to see?" We glanced around the hall and, seeing no one, asked, "How about 'Take Me Out to the Ball Game'?" It all came back; we began tap dancing, haltingly at first, giggling and laughing at ourselves. Then, "How about 'I'm Alabamy Bound'?" Soon we were dancing freely—laughing, crying, and laughing some more. I began to feel a release; I felt free and light. This was no time to analyze; we kept dancing. Our spirits soared!

Totally present in the moment, we became exhausted in our joyful expression and fell into each other's arms, embracing in pure sister love. What had induced this change from tears to smiles? Something had impelled us to talk spontaneously to our parents. In the transformation from despair to joy, we felt the concurrent connection between ourselves, our parents, and our spirits. Chronological time had melted away; past and present had blended together. We felt a glowing radiant energy as we said goodbye to our parents.

Looking back, I recognize that my sister and I had shared a spiritual experience. Like any such incident, it is almost impossible to talk about. Putting words to an experience obviously removes me from it, yet I do remember my sense of wonder and awe. I thought of it as sacred, almost religious, but then wondered why. When I looked up the word "religious," I found its root to be *religare*, meaning to bind fast.[1] Well, that was certainly true! I have always separated religion from spirituality. Some religious experiences can be spiritual, but most spiritual experiences have the potential to be "religious" in the old sense of the word. I knew Sue and I never could have planned for such a gift; it just came. "We find it; we don't seek it," the old adage tells us. It is paradoxical that we search for the spirit outside when actually the spirit is searching to be known to us within. We search for the invisible; we naturally search for the spirit.

Recently I took a small group trekking in northern Tanzania. Thad Peterson, naturalist guide, had arranged for us to walk with our Maasai friend, Koieae. Koieae has status in his village because he is the village leader, is educated, and speaks English. Villagers hailed him as we passed through with our brightly colored backpacks and followed by donkeys carrying our excess gear and water. Koieae often stopped at the *bomas*, or circles of mud-straw dwellings, and spoke with the families. At times the women approached us, staring, and touched our jewelry and Western attire. We curiously examined them, too, our surreptitious glances changing to direct stares.

Koieae had returned from speaking with the old women who had hailed him while they were tending the babies. We asked, "What do they ask you?" Koieae replied, "They want to know what you're looking for." We smiled, knowing full well how ridiculous we must look to them. We certainly did look as if we were searching for some prized object. It was as if the Maasai women knew that we were indeed searching; their question had dual meanings. Why else would we fly all this distance to Tanzania, travel by vehicle up and over the rough trails to the Serengeti, and then trek on foot, carrying our essential belongings on our backs and sleeping on the ground?

Yet, what we were *really* looking for in our journey was spiritual growth, and the Maasai women gave voice to what we unconsciously knew. We had long ago outgrown our religious belief that "God" exists outside of us; here we were continuing our search to further heal our estrangement from the Goddess within and from Gaia, Mother Earth.

What had motivated us to backpack in Tanzania? Surely we wanted to see all the wondrous game on safari; surely we wanted to get in good condition for our climb on Mt. Kilimanjaro; and surely we wanted to return to the roots of civilization in Olduvai Gorge and the floor of the Rift Valley. Walking down to the cracked dry floor of the valley, we saw remnants of ancient times when people, animals, plants, and entire ecosystems worked cooperatively to achieve a balanced earth-spirit connection. Perhaps we were drawn here because we seek that balance and simplicity in ourselves and in our lives.

Somehow we found it easier here to recognize that we are part of the whole and to connect with the earth, experience the earth connection.

Playwright/poet Ntozake Shange states:

> i was cold/i was burning up/a child
> & endlessly weaving garments for the moon
> with my tears
> I found god in myself
> & i loved her/i loved her fiercely.[2]

You may prefer the word "God." I use the word "Goddess" because the God image has been a male image, reminding us of patriarchy; the Goddess concept has empowered women to connect with the ancient Goddess religions of Neolithic agrarian cultures. The Goddess also includes male; she is not dominant over males. Whether we call her Higher Power, Isis, or Sophia, we come together to connect with all that is. As Starhawk writes, "as birth-giver, weaver, earth and growing plant, wind and ocean, flame, web, moon and milk, all speak to me of the powers of connectedness, sustenance, healing, creating."[3]

Uniting ourselves in this natural relationship requires a journey. In my home hangs a favorite poster from an Ibsen play, the bold caption of which reminds me daily to "Come Take the Journey."

SPIRITUAL GROWTH:
THE TRANSFORMATION JOURNEY

We journey to prepare for the union of our separations. Many women use the word "recovery" to describe the process of growing spiritually. In fact, many find solace and a "plan" in following a Twelve-Step program, one of the "anonymous" groups that grew out of the Twelve Steps of Alcoholics Anonymous.[4] I often suggest to clients that they may want to join a Twelve-Step group to support their recovery process, reminding them it is hard to trust the invisible. We do move through a transformation journey. The first part of the transformation journey has six phases: facing emptiness, letting go, detaching, grieving, surrendering, and accepting.

Facing Emptiness

Florida Scott-Maxwell writes:

If we are bereft of all sense of a spiritual force arousing our awe,
granting us value, instilling us with fear of ourselves and our fate,
do we now seek some other greatness in which to lose ourselves?
Do we will to be contained, and protected from life's polarity?
Has the conception of oneness been projected onto the outside
world? If it is no longer centered in God giving us each a source
where we are greater than ourselves, are we empty, almost
meaningless?[5]

Many of us who have wandered away from ourselves and lost ourselves in other people, activities, and/or addictive relationships have
lost touch with our spiritual awe. We fear our emptiness. And many
of us do project our emptiness onto the outside world. And our emptiness crawls onto our laps, reminding us of its presence. Whether we
call it the dark night of the soul, the period of great doubt, or spiritual
barrenness, we all will face emptiness. We can't find solitude until we
have faced our emptiness. Facing our emptiness is lonely and can be
very frightening; yet it is the sacrifice that the true self demands. I
remember making the decision one night; something beckoned me. I
had cancelled my plans for the evening in order to be totally alone.
That meant no telephoning out, and no conversations if others called
me. I decided I needed to sit still and be, doing nothing.

Initially I felt frightened. I got up from the chair and walked
around, then told myself to go back and sit down. With my arms
and legs uncrossed and my hands opened, resting on my lap, I felt vulnerable. But I did not know about what. Then deeply buried feelings
rose in me; I wept. No sobs, I just wept. I then felt a cavernous place
within me. I felt terror. I wanted to walk away; what did this mean?
"Come back, self; experience it," I told myself. I soon did and found
myself sitting in the center of the raw nakedness of emptiness. This
was the first time in my life I had allowed myself to be with my emptiness. A deep calming began to rise within me; it wasn't peace as I now
know it to be, but it was still. Jacqueline's words come to me now:

189

"It only stays dark till midnight." I think I met the midnight of my soul that night.

Living in a culture that daily reminds us that we should "be happy" makes it difficult to accept the truth: suffering is a part of life. We only know joy because we know suffering. I remember ending that evening by dancing to Helen Reddy's record, "I Am Woman." I danced wildly and freely; I think it was an act of celebration. I had met another part of myself. I had not realized that night that I was giving permission to me to meet more of my self.

Letting Go

A friend has reminded me that letting go is essential to shift from doing to being. My new motto had become, "Do what you can and let go." My work with clay on the pottery wheel had taught me about life—if too much control and pressure are applied, a vase turns into a flat plate.

My friend once read a poem by a woman who said, "I remember those courses in school—when some took flute, others took band, and I took control." For most women in dysfunctional families control meant survival.

Letting go does not mean the opposite of control; nor does it mean defeat. Letting go does not mean sitting back passively and letting life happen to us; we have to show up for our part. We learn about letting go through our relationships.

Natalie had a concrete lesson in letting go when she stood near the cliff's edge. She and Rod, her life partner, had come on one of our couples' climbing trips; each had had several experiences belaying and climbing. Now Natalie was tightly anchored to both a rappel rope and a belay rope. The rappel rope, which is a double rope, remained fixed so she could lower herself down the face of the cliff. While on this rope, she was in charge of how fast or slow she moved. Her belay rope, the "umbilical" rope, connected her with her belayer, Rod, who was anchored securely to a tree.

Her anxiety had risen; she fidgeted with her carrabiners. When they were fixed, she stood still at the edge of the cliff. We talked to her; she remained frozen. Then she began to shake and cry. We knew that once she let go and allowed herself to go with the process and go over the edge, she would be fine. When Natalie heard her own voice and her own rationalizations—"I'm too old; I'm too fat; this is not an activity for women"—she started to laugh.

With a determined expression on her face, she lowered herself tentatively and slowly over the edge, leaning back and trusting, trusting, trusting. She then reached that point of knowing that the rope did hold, that her belayer had a secure hold on her, and that she was able to work the ropes with competence. When she reached the bottom of the cliff, she was beaming with delight and exhilaration. "The hardest part is facing the edge," Natalie said.

In facing our edges, we not only have to trust ourselves and our partners, we also have to trust in the process of life. (My climbing friend Annie and I used to laugh about life being an 800-foot rappel, a constant letting-go process.) It is the letting go to life that creates a spiritual "edge." You need only claim the events of your life to make yourself yours. Florida Scott-Maxwell writes: "When you truly possess all you have been and done, which may take some time, you are fierce with reality. When at last age has assembled you together, will it not be easy to let it all go, lived, balanced, over?"[6]

How do you let go to life if you don't have a sense of relatedness to the invisible? We can only have this relationship by risking the letting go. When we learn something through our body-self, we are able to release more of the unconscious material stored there. A useful tool in the process of letting go is the Serenity Prayer. "Letting go" are the words to describe the initial phase of the journey. To progress we must also detach.

Detaching

In our patriarchal, technological, shamebound culture we have been driven by our negative attachments to things, activities, and people. We attempt to fill our emptiness with things—cars, houses, furnishings, clothing. Compulsive eating, drinking, working, exercise, and shopping are negative attachments that disconnect us from ourself and others. Trapped by our need for perfectionism and control, we begin to believe the distorted perception that we can possess people, not just things.

Another negative attachment that is sometimes more constant because we have been socialized into it is our attachment to our strong, reactive feelings when we become overly involved in someone else's life. When our caring about another person extends far beyond our own boundaries and we attempt to control his or her behaviors and feelings, we have formed a reactive attachment.

Our attachment to our strong reactive feelings grew out of our undeveloped boundaries. As our boundaries develop, we can learn to detach from our insatiable hunger to be filled up and begin to feed our spirit-self. We begin to dissolve the emotional glue that keeps us captive to another. Detachment does not mean disconnection, shutting others out, or numbing our feelings. Detachment means ridding ourselves of the obsessive thoughts about someone else's behaviors that preoccupy us during the day and prevent us from sleeping at night. Have you ever felt that burning pit of codependency in your gut? When we are reactive or carrying heavy feelings for others, we are probably at most only 70 percent available to ourselves or to others. We block our spirit when we don't detach from our powerful feelings. When we can stay with ourselves through detachment, we are free to be fully present no matter what the situation. No more lying awake with obsessions about relationships or problems.

Detaching from reactive feelings is not detaching from acting on justice issues. When we react strongly to a justice issue, we must take a stand, with purpose and with passion. Through our detaching from negative attachments, more of our personal power is available to us for purposeful acts.

Detaching is also not passive; it is active. It comes from calm, not fear. In detaching we can feel our feelings, identify them, express them if we choose, and then let them go. We can separate the "you outside of me" from "my feeling that is in me." The Twelve-Step groups help here. Nonhierarchical and anonymous, they allow for mutual, honest sharing. Many women have found comfort in changing the male language and some of the concepts of the steps; yet they do know it is the wisdom of the steps, not the language, that really matters. We have to grieve the loss of the attachment.

Grieving

We must grieve our losses — our past self, lost childhood, and years of repression — to grow spiritually. When our relationship with the self is cut off by unresolved grief, we are cut off from our spirit. Also, our unresolved grief has often been converted into physical illness, anger, or depression. Our unconscious dammed-up energy is locked inside our body and needs to release itself. Perhaps you remember Judith from Chapter 2, whose buried grief released itself in a burst when she became so highly stressed in her rock climb. Judith learned graphically about spirit through grieving. It had been six years since the death of her father; she was stunned and overwhelmed at her delayed grieving.

In time we learn to recognize the quiet lapping waves of grief that wash over us in inconstant but continual patterns. Life brings loss, both necessary and unnecessary.[7] With some embarrassment, I remember my mistaken belief that after experiencing tidal waves of grief I was through with the grief process. What I now know is that if we're not grieving, we're not living at this point in life, so we may just as well surrender.

Surrendering

Surrendering to the invisible is difficult. Maggie was stuck in her climb. The dark, womblike overhang, which appeared to offer a secure tight corner to curl up in, had seduced her off her climbing route. Now she had jammed herself into the corner and couldn't get back to the open rockface. We had warned Maggie that many of us also had been lured over there but as usual our advice hadn't stopped her. Literally between a rock and a hard place, Maggie knew that if she slipped when traversing out onto the direct route, she would swing into the rockface and hurt herself. Maggie struggled, making several attempts to reach out and across the rock. Frustrated, she called down to her belayer, "Hey, throw me a concept!" We called up, "A concept will never get you up the rock, but you will!" I smiled, recognizing how Maggie's academic career had influenced her thinking. Maggie had learned to rely on concepts. Later, I recalled the words of Carl Jung, "A concept will always interrupt the experience."[8]

Maggie needed to trust herself, trust the invisible, and take a wide move across the rock to a solid foothold that would bring her back onto her climbing route. We reminded Maggie to surrender. Maggie asked, "What do you mean, surrender? Surrender to what, to whom? Haven't women's lives been all about surrendering?" I assured Maggie that I meant surrender to the Goddess, or Sophia, the Great Mother and spirit of female wisdom.[9] Sophia once represented God's female soul and was considered the source of his power.[10] Sophia is considered by many to be the archetype for spirit and matter, our collective Wisdom. Marion Woodman, Jungian psychologist, says "that continuous process within the eternal is what I think of as Sophia, Wisdom proper to the woman, the feminine Godhead."[11]

When Maggie prepared to move, her feelings flooded her—helplessness, anger, suspicion—so common in surrendering. She cried and then began to stretch her left arm and leg as far as she could stretch them. Taking a giant leap, she landed on a small rock ledge. She had found two miraculously placed "handholds"—two small rock nubbins on which to brace herself. There, she had made it! Maggie wept, and then beamed down to us; she was back on course.

Later that night Maggie said she realized that her move was truly surrendering and required a trust in "something," but she wasn't sure what. Maggie's will and control had served her well; surrendering was unknown to her. Maggie said it was easy to have faith in us, in me, and in her belayer, but it was difficult to have faith in herself or faith in the unknown. Much later she saw her climb as the initial phase of her spiritual growth.

Surrendering to the unknown in an addictive culture where control is primary is signing on for membership in a minority group. Surrendering does not mean giving up our will, it means giving up our willfulness. We need our will. When we surrender to whatever Higher

Power we choose, we begin to unite with our spirit. I do not mean the personification of a male god figure outside us, but rather the divine energy we feel within us. By allowing ourselves to surrender, we allow ourselves to be touched by grace.

Accepting

While working in Northern Ireland some years ago, I was struck by the high number of what I called coincidences. The Irish, to whom the spirit is not a stranger, grinned at me and said, "Why, Mar'lyn, what's for ya won't pass ya!" What's for us won't pass us—this was new and somehow very profound. I do not believe that there is some grand scheme that some should "have" and others should "not have." I do believe that many of our crises present new challenges that, if met, help us grow.

We are spiritually impatient; we try to force outcomes. During the trek in Africa, we noted all the men who would sit motionless for hours at the roadside. Members of one particular tribe say they wait to see what life will bring. Unfortunately, many women have learned about acceptance as conditional love, that is, that we are accepted as long as we are following the doctrines of our family and/or our church—"sinning" meant falling from grace and acceptance for many women. And many women still live with or meet the fragments of this conditional love.

When Jean entered therapy, I asked her, "How do you ask for help?" She stared at me with a blank expression on her face. I waited, then repeated, "How do you ask for help?" Jean spoke slowly as though she had heard new words. "I don't think I ever have before; I don't think I've ever needed to. I think I'm supposed to learn how to ask." Jean was beginning to learn that she could not do it alone. She acknowledged that she had been trying to push away a lot of flooding feelings that were surfacing. I talked with her about acceptance.

"Accept that you are accepted" are words of a theologian friend.[12] Eventually we have to accept this; we are accepted with our small sides, our pettiness, our humanness, and our mistakes. We are accepted in our shame; we are accepted in our deep self-respect. We are accepted by the Goddess; we are accepted by our companions. Acceptance marks the end of the first part of the journey. As we move through the five phases of the transformation journey, we ready ourselves for our spiritual pilgrimage to unite our estranged selves.

DEALING WITH OUR DUALISMS

We live with dualisms. "A dualism is like a dichotomy, the sense of two different elements which may live together in an uneasy truce and are frequently in conflict. They are essentially foreign to each other."[13] To develop our spirituality, we need to unite our separated parts: masculine/feminine; self/shadow (ego/intuition); and matter/spirit.

Masculine/Feminine + Socialization = Imbalance

"When one discovers the presence of the divine within, one experiences its presence as androgynous."[14] The word "androgynous" (from the Greek words *andro,* meaning male, and *gyne,* meaning female) refers to the balance of masculine and feminine within. Ignoring or dismissing androgyny keeps women in our stereotypic, devalued places, as objects. At conception all human beings are feminine; it is not until after the first five weeks in utero that the sex differentiation occurs. Immediately after birth, gender stereotyping begins; we are treated solely as boys or girls. Thus, boys are reinforced for being large, independent, and strong, whereas girls are rewarded for being dependent, sweet, and pretty. Even our choice of clothing, toys, and activities is dependent on gender. It is all right for a girl to be a tomboy until about age eleven or twelve, but a boy of almost any age who plays with "girl things" is called a sissy.

Socialized to accept limited cultural definitions of man and woman, we become unbalanced and often form negatively dependent relationships, seeking to complete ourselves by fusing with someone outside us. Yet, the natural and healthy dependency we yearn for is to be able to depend on *all* of who we are, not on someone outside us.

We naturally long for unity of all that is within us; we need it to be whole. Women can be strong, vulnerable, competent, sensitive, self-reliant, and connecting; none of these traits is biologically determined; they are all socially learned.

Allowing our true spirit to have the natural balance of the full range of our masculine and feminine within requires a shift in consciousness. When we allow our true spirit to manifest itself, we are acting on all that we *know* that lies within us. We cannot allow gender stereotyping to prevent us from becoming who we can be. Isak Dinesen writes that "Women . . . when they are old enough to have done with the business of being women, and can let loose their strength, must be the most powerful creatures in the world."[15]

Self/Shadow

When I was a child, one of my favorite radio shows was "The Shadow." The program began with "Only the Shadow knows . . ." followed by a deliberate and knowing laugh, "Heh, heh, heh, heh." On hearing that laugh, I *knew* the Shadow knew; I'd sit glued to my chair. I was both frightened of and very drawn to the mystery program; it was exciting to be scared.

Back then I was afraid of the mystery program; years later I discovered I was afraid of mystery itself. To look back I see that the Shadow, Lamont Cranston, was a truly good character. Back then I knew nothing about the "shadow of the soul." At one time I thought my "shadow" was the same as my "dark side," referring to my limitations, my negative attributes. As Florida Scott-Maxwell writes:

> There seems a widespread need of living and learning the dark side of our nature. Perhaps we are almost on the point of saying that evil is normal, in each of us, an integral part of our being. This age may be witnessing the assimilation of evil, thereby finding a new wisdom. We have been insisting for centuries that evil should not be, that it can be eliminated, is only the absence of good, resides in others; if others are evil we are not, or so little

that it hardly matters. . . . Are we learning that without the tension between good and evil there would be no dynamism in life? . . . Then what seems our decadence may be the stirring of a new reality, even a new morality, God willing and man able.[16]

The shadow is separate and different from the dark side of our nature. The shadow is simply the unconscious, that which is unknown, that which contains both pain and potential. Of course we are never without our shadow; it's just that it isn't always visible to us. Indeed, seeing my reflected image on a sunny day visibly reminds me that my shadow is not my conscious self.

The growing self has both a conscious mind, the aware ego self, and an unconscious mind, the undiscovered self. Together, they are the "me and my shadow" as the song title suggests. The Goddess, the unconscious, and intuition are all invisible, having no formal language and dwelling. The ego, the rational and reasoning self, is the other sphere.

Ego.   Writing about women's ego is complex because of the disunity that exists for women. From birth on, virtually all of us were socialized to hang on others' perceptions and decisions (especially men's) rather than our own. Indeed, we were taught to placate and massage the "male ego" at the expense of our own. We were not accorded the full entitlement to represent ourselves in our patriarchal culture.[17] In addition, many of us were raised in dysfunctional families where our boundaries were constantly invaded or ignored. To survive in our shamebound family, we developed a strong, false self.

This substitute self, our hungry false self, is vulnerable to our ego, which, when fed with titles, degrees, self-importance, and designer labels, seduces us off our path—just as the dark overhang enticed Maggie off her climbing route. Puffed up with externals, our false self crowds out the true self that holds our unconscious, our shadow, thus flattening our spirit.

Jean had been meditating in a silent retreat for almost a week; it had taken almost five days for her mind to slow down. She said her mind felt like JFK Airport with something taking off and landing every few minutes. On the sixth day she felt quiet inside. Her retreat teacher had warned her that she might face some pain, but Jean had not been prepared for it. Jean felt deep pain under her ribs; it was as though her ribs were cemented together with concrete. Tears came. She recalled the teacher's words, "Stay with it." Gradually, she felt the concrete breaking away; she continued to breathe deeply. Then tears came again, only this time tears of compassion, the compassion for her own spirit. Her spirit forced her way through the thick concrete and held her own; Jean realized her spirit was going to make it. Finally her spirit fully broke free; with the concrete falling away, her spirit emerged. Jean embraced her true self and felt warmth and compassion. Jean wanted to sing and dance; she made a commitment to nurture and guard her spirit. When I saw Jean after her return, I asked her what her "concrete" was. She said, "Why, my ego, of course, and it almost took over!" Then, she puzzled, "Why did I use a psychological term for something so embedded in me?" I reassured her that she did not have to analyze it but trust what she knew.

Huston Smith, a theologian, says, "The only time you're aware of the eye is when there is something wrong with it."[18] Our "I" does remind us of its presence when we feel hurt or pride is wounded. It signals that we need to dip into our past and work through the pain, trusting we will receive more information from the unconscious.

The ego, however, is frightened to receive from the unconscious; the ego has to be strong enough to let go of its unyielding perfectionism and "doing it alone." And when the unconscious releases its knowledge, the ego has the awesome responsibility of deciding what to do to integrate the material; it doesn't just happen. The ego must contemplate the energy released from the unconscious in order to transform this energy into spiritual power.

Letting go, or nonattachment, is imperative if we are to unite with our natural "other"—the unconscious, or the shadow self—knowing this is never completed in a lifetime.

Jean asked, "Is this the Goddess's great joke? I've worked so hard to get a self and now you say I should let it go? Why work on developing a self at all?" "Because we cannot let go of it until we *have* it," I reminded her. I continued, "And this is not a matter of letting go of the self. Rather, this is a matter of expanding the real self."

Yet we cannot strive for this nonattachment to our ego. Buddhists warn us that *striving* for nonattachment itself becomes a severe attachment and can result in spiritual narcissism. "If you haven't experienced it, it simply isn't true," is an old Sufi saying. As we experience letting go, our body, the storehouse of our unconscious, releases more awareness and energy through our feelings, and we become more conscious of our selves. We then can grow from self-consciousness to conscientiousness, no longer burdened by the vigilant critical "eye" of the shameful self. As we move from our false self to "I," our shadow and our self (our "I") gradually merge, and we move from object to subject. We do a balancing act on a spiritual teeter-totter as our ego balances and our shadow becomes spirit. We need our ego, yet we offer our ego to the "gift of Grace," that nourishing connection between our unconsciousness and our consciousness. Sophia, with her great wisdom, supports the ego in making energy-transforming decisions to achieve this union. The catalyst for this merger is our intuition.

Intuition.   When I speak of "intuition," I do not mean a quick, flashing hunch. Rather, intuition is based on the expression of our highest knowing that surpasses all reason. This ancient way of knowing, another way of seeing present that which was present before the days of symbolic thought, cannot be measured.[19] Our intuition is so highly developed today that it operates automatically below any level of consciousness. Consequently, our everyday perceptions are riddled with intuition. Definitely not mystical, intuition allows for the most direct examination of the human mind possible. Intuition is the catalytic channel for uniting our newly surfaced unconscious material with the conscious mind. As more of our unconscious becomes known, our intuition deepens. We can absorb and reflect experientially, affectively, and unconsciously. This, in turn, allows the formation of energy, thus expanding our spiritual potential.[20]

Spirit/Matter

Virginia Satir had strongly urged me to go to Findhorn, a spiritual community on the north coast of Scotland. She called it the spiritual center of the universe and commented, "They play Bach for the flowers." My friend and I had read in *The Saturday Review of Literature* that Findhorn's residents grew 35-pound cabbages in rock-sand soil—cabbages they said grew in response to love. Friends and family teased us before we left for Findhorn, asking us to bring home a 35-pound cabbage. At the airport, my friend's husband teasingly asked, "Say, bring me some of that magical soil, will you?"

On the flight home my friend and I chatted about the Findhorn principles: to work with love and to never work alone. In our workshop there we had practiced focusing loving thoughts onto our work, much of which had been grueling. Curious, we had taken some soil from the center of the richly blooming herb garden.

On return home I took the soil to the University of Minnesota's testing laboratory for chemical analysis. I didn't keep the report (I wish I had!) but I can paraphrase it. "Such and such percent sodium chloride, such and such percent other chemicals . . . absolutely nothing can grow or could be expected to grow in this highly alkaline soil."

Somehow we weren't too surprised, and my friend's husband had little to say. The test results reinforced the Findhorn philosophy that there is spirit in all matter.

This spirit, known as energy, can be transformed. There are two kinds of energy: *tangential energy* (physical, atomic energy), which we see for instance in steam rising from the teapot's boiling water, and *radial energy*, or energy within. Radial energy is our spiritual energy, the energy of consciousness.[21] A lump of coal is merely a piece of carbon until it is ignited and gives off its tangential energy, warmth.

We have both tangential and radial energy, physical and spiritual. Our physical energy converts into spiritual energy as we evolve on our journey along the spiral. Conversion begins with respect for the spirit within all matter. Community members at Findhorn aspire to treat all matter and all people with respect; gardeners handle their tools carefully and oil them well after using them.

Although "New Age" proponents focus on reformed energy, matter becoming spirit is certainly not a new idea. Vipassana Buddhism, Christian mysticism, and the philosophy of East Indian yogis and Native Americans reflect this principle. Hindus greet one another with "*Namaste*," meaning "Hello," which is said while pressing their palms together and bowing. In doing so, they acknowledge the divine within.

Any form of energy can be converted to another form of energy. For example, anger can be converted into compulsive work or random motor behavior (finger tapping or rapid foot movements), and deep hate can be converted into deep love.[22] Pain is energy; psychotherapy involves energy conversion whereby dammed-up energy is released and balance is restored. Most of this energy, whatever its form, is available for growth. I often tell new clients that psychotherapy is like Drano; we are going to dredge the stuck stuff up to clear their spiritual drains. Transforming our energies can unite our estranged selves. We seek experiences to aid us in this transformation process.

Many women adopt a spiritual practice to help them remain balanced. This spiritual practice may or may not be religious. Some women want to acknowledge the history in them and may choose prayer. Women are learning that prayer is diverse; we can experience gratitude as prayer, and we can experience petitionary prayer (asking so our God, Goddess, or Creative Spirit can say no). For example, Jean didn't think she prayed. And then one day she read Henri Nouwen, who stated that gratitude is prayer.[23] Jean was surprised: "Why, I pray every day then, because I give thanks every day." Many women practice a daily form of meditation or sitting in silence. Women choose a public (or exoteric) identification or a private (or esoteric) identification to attain spiritual-religious balance.

THE EXOTERIC AND THE ESOTERIC

"How on earth do you do it?" Jean asked. "Do what?" I asked. She went on, "Here I am with all my religious inheritance, and now I am finding such deep satisfaction in my new Eastern philosophies and religions. I do feel a bit schizy at times." "Well," I replied, "there is one way that has helped a lot of us. We can identify both parts within us with language that reflects the old and the new. The *exoteric* is my public, known religion that I either inherited from my parents and/or took as my own; the *esoteric* is my personal, intimate, private practice."[24] Jean nodded and smiled, "Well, that certainly helps me pull my polarity together. I feel relieved, and that makes sense; I'm not who I was, my past is in me, and I have a new spiritual connection."

Jean talked with me about her religious upbringing. She had turned away from her church. She was angry because although she knew that all religions grew out of spiritual experiences, Jean saw that most seemed to have lost much of their spiritual base, making it difficult to derive meaning in them.

Jean acknowledged that leaving the church was an act of personal power. "Climbing out of the conformity and self-protection levels into her self-awareness levels" was a real risk.[25] Joining others who have been deeply pained and angry about her church's exclusion of women, Jean deeply grieved her church and its rituals. She had said goodbye to her church dogma and had met her "individual experience of becoming one with the Source of Creation." [26]

Many religious settings have been spiritually inadequate; at a time when church attendance is down, the number of women in spirituality groups has increased. Women find it extremely difficult to make peace with an institution that excludes women so blatantly. Many groups of Christian and Jewish women have changed their liturgy. Today a scattering of women have key roles in a few churches and synagogues. Women today live in an environment of religious pluralism. Some choose a traditional religion, translating or expanding its hierarchical language into inclusive language. Many women find community, social support, social gospel, and a moral guidance system in their religions. Some women found it was the place where their families did their very best. As Karen said, "I always knew I was loved there."

Others choose no formal structured religious affiliation and turn to esoteric spiritual practices, Eastern philosophy, Native American religion, and spiritual healing.

Theologians have warned us about attempting to integrate psychology and spirituality because psychology deals with the difficulties in living and spirituality "deepens the question of life itself."[27] Many women find that ancient practices bridge "life's difficulties" with the "deepening questions." It is natural for women to seek more time alone. Some learn to develop an aura of silence as they grow spiritually so they can "tune in" to their Higher Power at all times.

To take up the practices of ancient cultures that celebrate nature, many women have turned to the Goddess. Through the Goddess cultures, as well as through modern physics, we have learned that matter and energy are not separate energies, but are the same thing in different forms. Shamans and witches have always known this, but our traditional literature has taught us to see witches as evil, dark, and frightening. The word "witch" comes from the word *witan*, meaning "to see, to know."[28] Today women choose this ancient word because it does not negate our darkness; it is inclusive, like Native American spirituality, and considers Nature, Gaia (Mother Earth), to be sacred.

Witchcraft involves using our personal power, our within-power, to direct our energies by choosing and by using will. Women can know acceptance through very concrete ways. Witchcraft invites the use of magic, "the art of changing consciousness at will."[29] It is hands-on; experiencing this energy means being connected with our being, our true self.

Jean asked, "How on earth do I get connected to this Goddess? How do I connect with the spirit in me?" I suggested that one very practical way is to breathe, since our very existence depends upon breath. In fact, the word "spirit" means breath; it comes from the Latin word *spiritus*, meaning "breathing." Daily we breathe 23,000 times and take in 3,000 gallons of air; if we exercise, we take in 25 times as much.[30] As we breathe deeply we can regulate our breathing and our thoughts and feelings stabilize, allowing us to become more relaxed. We can synchronize our physical movements with our breath; our movement influences our breath. As our emotions stabilize with our breathing, we can be in touch with our body. We have many stories of the body-self releasing the unconscious in the form of repressed or stuck feelings, thoughts, and events, but this release and working through also bring us closer to our true self. It is the resurrection of the Wise Woman.

RESURRECTING THE WISE WOMAN

It is not the "resurrection *of* the body; it is the resurrection *within*."
Jean had heard a French analyst say these words and puzzled over
them. Jean thought deeply about her friend Allie's comment to her—
"Your body doesn't fit who you are." Jean had struggled with being
overweight and was beginning to know that she *is* her body, both body
and mind, and they are united. Writer Vicki Noble states, "In every
culture where the goddess is revered, women dance in ecstatic celebration of the sacred energy that can be felt and enjoyed in the
body."[31]

It takes many years for most of us to accept our body-self and
recognize our body as a concrete expression of our spirit within.
Often our visibly "disabled" friends (with spinal cord injuries, polio, or
congenital "disabilities") have reminded us that the rest of us are only
"TABS," that is, "temporarily able bodied" persons. Eventually we all
will have physical limitations. It is our internal "able-bodiedness" that
is the crucial issue. Many of us, with our distorted perceptions, have
held negative body images and felt sexual shame. The obese and the
anorexic are fighting their battles for consciousness through food—
the acceptance or rejection of it.[32] In doing so, they trap their spirit.
At some time we learn we must go deep within to face the underlying issues.

Our cultural messages about what women are to be—hungry
consumers of beauty/love products—contributes greatly to the struggles with the underlying issues. Eventually we learn that we can
transform our energies through a resurrection process that will take
us to our own place, the home of the Wise Woman. William Johnston
writes:

> I believe that in this psychological turmoil, grace is working
> gently, if painfully, in the unconscious, inviting our number-two
> personality, our true selves, to emerge from the womb into full-
> ness of life. Quite often the whole process of middle-age crisis is
> nothing less than a mystical experience of death and resurrection
> to a new life which is filled with true joy.[33]

In working with women in therapy on "adult children" issues, I often use guided imagery to aid them in reclaiming buried childhood stories and feelings. As they find the voice of their "inner child" and develop more defined boundaries, their false self dissolves and their true self emerges. It is at this point that women realize they have choices. I suggested one day to a client that she go to the Wise Woman within her to hear her knowing truth. Using guided imagery to go deep within her *present*, not past, self, we learned paradoxically that in embracing the "inner child," she experienced the resurrection of the Wise Woman. Some women had no difficulty finding their Wise Woman. You may want to read this into a cassette tape and then listen to it and do the exercise, so that you can meet your own Wise Woman.

With your eyes open and seated comfortably, breathe deeply and let all tensions fall from your shoulders. Be aware of all that your senses bring to you. Pay attention to what you see, what you hear, what you taste, what you smell, what you are touching. Now, paying careful attention to your breathing, pay careful attention to your feelings as you close your eyes and let go. Pay attention to all the details of your breathing. Now, gently open your eyes and take in all that your senses bring to you. Slowly, slowly, breathe in . . . breathe out . . . Now picture yourself at the edge of a clearing; the dark woods are behind you. Be aware of what you are feeling as you go forth. As you continue your journey, all you need is in you. As you stand in this place, know this as your place. And now, continuing to breathe, go down, down, deep into yourself, for you are about to meet your true self. She knows all she needs to know; listen to her and you will stay true to you. She has been there all along, waiting for you, guiding you often back on your path. Her name is the Wise Woman, your spiritual connection to the universe. Now picture her; pay attention to all the details of your breathing and continue to let go while I talk. Picture your Wise Woman; what does she look like? Is she standing or sitting? What is she wearing? Sit before her; sit with her. Just look into her face; allow yourself the freedom to just *be* with her. Be aware of what you're feeling now. And now you can ask any question you like or tell her anything you like. Listen to her voice. When you are through with your meeting, say goodbye to the Wise Woman and know that she is always going to have this place. Know that she is with you, to be visited any time you choose. She will not betray you; she is your true self. She is your Eternal Wisdom. And now, leaving this sacred place, say goodbye to your Wise Woman, knowing she will always be there for you to return to.

Jean smiled as she opened her eyes after the above guided imagery. "I feel so peaceful," she said. "Do you want to tell me about your experience?" I asked. I was aware of how much more risky it was for me to ask about spirituality; discussing sexuality was much easier for me. I was aware of how deeply intimate my question was. Jean described her Wise Woman as a very elderly, soft woman with kind eyes, who wore a long robe and was seated on a grassy knoll. She said the woman offered her hand to Jean. Jean said she felt tentative only for a moment; they sat in silence for a few minutes. "Then," Jean continued, "I asked her several questions about several new relationships. She told me that I was on the right path, and I was smart to take my time and learn about each of these people." Jean said, "This is amazing, and yet I feel very comfortable; she truly felt familiar to me."

What would have seemed to some New Age hocus-pocus some time ago now appeared to Jean as a vital, true aspect of her true self. She had truly given birth to her self. Her Wise Woman, the voice of her spirit, was her connection with Sophia, the Goddess of Wisdom, who allows the energy to live and connects us with all women of all times.[34] It takes a long time to find our connection to Sophia. We surrender.

This new birth, this second birth, is rich with new values. We realize that "a sense of self-worth and a sense of self-creation are fundamental to spiritual maturity" and can get on with our lives.[35] We begin to participate in the being of the world; we take responsibility for our world being. This means that we grow a deep respect for not only ourselves, but for others. And as we see the sacred being in each of us, we see that when we injure a relationship, we are injuring the human order of being.[36] With the rebirth come with new ways of being.

INTIMACY: WE DON'T SEEK IT, WE FIND IT

I had lost my billfold. I looked for it in the usual place in my handbag. When couldn't find it, I scurried throughout my home and returned to my bag. I told myself, "It must be here; I keep it here." Discouraged, I again looked about my place and again returned to my bag, even more insistently telling myself, "It's got to be here; I always keep it here." After another thorough search around my home, I returned for a final look at my now-emptied handbag and finally admitted, "The billfold is not here."

I had such a strong belief about where my billfold was that it was difficult to look elsewhere or to accept that it wasn't where I believed it to be. I had been reluctant to look elsewhere for it; in clinging to my beliefs, I was stuck.

We still get caught, often unknowingly, in what intimacy means, despite our moving away from old meanings of sexual as sensual or lustful. Our media reinforces romantic myths that imply intimacy is an outcome, something we get or master. Intimacy has been marketed like any other commodity; advertisers have inundated us with a "Polaroid" mentality about intimacy—no delayed gratification. Despite our growth and awareness, we find ourselves with a belief system telling us to look outward for intimacy. Seeking is inherent in this belief system. Our popular culture's outcome orientation regarding intimacy reinforces our seeking; my billfold story reminds me of how strong a hold this is. Socialized into linear thinking, we get stuck in "if-then" thinking.

In our desire for intimacy, we have often lived in *"ifness."* Our "if this, then that . . ." is an inherent link with our desire for closure and completion in relationships. The "if" is half a phrase; on the other side of "if" is "then," symbolic of linear, outcome-oriented thinking. For example, "If I am in a relationship, then I can have happiness and intimacy."

When I was newly single, I walked into new places and situations with my "if" antenna turned on "high," wondering "if"—*if* I meet someone special, *if* I am liked—*if, if, if.* I recall hearing Jacqueline's statement, "If stands stiff in the corner," and then pretending my "if" antenna wasn't there.

"Ifness" is passive and goes nowhere, except in fantasy, day-dreams, and romantic novels. This assumption implies closure; it would all be wrapped up—as neatly as a magazine advertisement promises. One day I realized my "ifness" antenna had fallen limp. Freedom! Freedom from seeking closure and an end to looking "out there."

Eventually we must finally accept that "ifness" is a setup for a downfall; we can complete anything—end a relationship, end jobs, turn in book manuscripts—but life continues to bring more beginnings. We need to say farewell to closure and to "ifness" so we can get on with the process of intimacy. Carolyn Heilbrun states, "When the hope for closure is abandoned, when there is an end to fantasy, adventure for women will begin."[37]

This adventure, following the challenges of our "inventure," is based on letting go of closure and intimacy as an outcome; it is a relearning of intimacy.[38] We experienced contact and we called it connection; we experienced unhealthy fusion and we called it oneness; and we experienced intensity and we called it intimacy. Intimacy is the co-creation of an experience with shared closeness and connection in a variety of activities that are deep and personal. To know connection, oneness, and intimacy as a process requires new ways of being.

NEW WAYS OF BEING

Empathy, not power, is the rich soil from which intimacy grows as we shift from doing to being. Empathy is a healthy joining, a healthy dependency we work *with*, not against. Often we heard about empathy as our ability to *feel* with one another. We now understand the *cognitive* aspect of empathy—the abililty to maintain one's integral sense of self and make decisions and act from that place.[39] We all need to be able to count on others to help us cognitively and emotionally with our experiences and tasks.[40] Certainly we will have power, but it is power-as-linking; we don't have to do it alone.[41]

With power-as-linking, we move away from the dominance we have all lived with for so long and return to ancient feminine principles.

In adopting this new way of being, women and men enter "a new consciousness in which competition will be balanced with cooperation and individualism will be balanced with love."[42] We can begin to live in *partnership*, a state where the roles of both women and men are far less rigid, allowing the entire human species a maximum of developmental flexibility.[43] Author Riane Eisler states:

> In this sense, our reconnection with the earlier spiritual tradition of Goddess worship linked to the partnership model of society is more than a reaffirmation of the dignity and worth of half of humanity. Nor is it only a far more comforting and reassuring way of imaging the powers that rule the universe. It also offers us a positive replacement for the myths and images that have for long blatantly falsified the most elementary principles of human relations by valuing killing and exploiting more than giving birth and nurturing.[44]

This reconnection with the Goddess marks a spiritual transformation wherein we respect and act on the higher goals of humanity that have been in existence from time immemorial.[45] We can continue to become more conscious.

While studying in a group in India we met with spiritual leader Jiddu Krishnamurti shortly before he died. Krishnamurti spoke of "choiceless awareness" in describing how consciously present we can be. He described this kind of presence as the sun breaking through a cloud. This choiceless awareness is within each of us and can be available to us in any number of ways. We can join men and women—old and young—in egalitarian relationships, with a full range of intimacy possible.

As we change our behaviors, unlearn our beliefs, and connect with the self, we dance with the Wise Woman and consequently dance with the Goddess. This becomes the soul shift of the spirit. We are available to intimate illuminating experiences; we begin to know the divine within.

Jean and Gil were very drawn to each other and had decided to pursue their relationship seriously. Knowing how long it takes to "see each other," they decided to not become sexually involved until they were ready to enter a committed relationship. At this point they had a solid, intimate, and affectionate friendship.

One night after they had been out to dinner, Jean and Gil lay on Jean's bed, holding each other, sometimes talking, sometimes remaining silent. They enjoyed their long silences together. Suddenly Jean felt warmth coming over her, almost like some light fabric was wrapping itself around her. She immediately ruled out a hot flash; this warmth was very different. Then a wide band, a gossamer band of love, began encircling both of them, wrapping around them and between them, steadily and gently. In awe, they remained motionless. Jean whispered to Gil, "Are you experiencing what I am? He replied softly, "Yes." The band continued to flow around and between them, and then Jean experienced a white core of light within her, from head to toe. This core of light then moved toward another core of light, the one within Gil. Jean experienced both cores of light meeting each other, entering into each other, and then separating. The light centers danced back and forth, uniting and then separating. The rhythmic movement lasted for some time, then gradually disappeared. Gil whispered, "This was a primitive union." Jean felt through her clothing to touch her bones. They were soft and pliable; she had never known such malleability. Gil whispered that he too felt the suppleness. In wonder, they lay motionless, lingering with the mystery they had just experienced. It was totally beyond any experience either had ever known.

Later, Jean began to analyze it. She recalled what she had eaten and drank. Surely one glass of wine with dinner couldn't have triggered this experience; and Gil had only had tea with dinner. Then Jean turned to spirituality books, seeking an explanation, a name, a concept. She shyly checked with a few trusted friends to see whether they had experienced anything similar. She could find no way to understand it and wanted to make some "if-then" meaning from it. Finally she realized that she had experienced something not to be named, something that would forever remain a mystery. Jean and Gil had opened their hearts and the divine love of the Goddess had graced them both with wonder. Moving through all of her challenges, Jean now trusted more deeply her creative spirit, dancing with the

Wise Woman and the Goddess. She no longer needed to believe; she *knew*. Toni Morrison writes:

> When she realized what her situation in the world was and would probably always be she threw away every assumption she had learned and began at zero. First off, she cut her hair. That was one thing she didn't want to think about anymore. Then she tackled the problem of trying to decide how she wanted to live and what was valuable to her. When am I happy and when am I sad and what is the difference? What do I need to know to stay alive? What is true in the world? Her mind traveled crooked streets and aimless goat paths, arriving sometimes at profundity, other times at the revelations of a three year old. Throughout this fresh, if common, pursuit of knowledge, one conviction crowned her efforts: since death held no terrors for her (she spoke often to the dead), she knew there was nothing to fear.[46]

This comes to a stopping place, not a true ending, in gathering the threads of women's experiences and knowledge, weaving another section on our own tapestry of women's lives, women's psychology, and women's adult growth.

Let there be beauty and strength, power and compassion, honor and humility, mirth and reverence within you.

NOTES

EPIGRAPH

Emily Dickinson, *The Complete Poems of Emily Dickinson*, ed. Thomas H. Johnson (Boston: Little, Brown, 1960), 247.

INTRODUCTION

1. The work of Erik Erikson, the pioneer of adult development (*The Eight Stages of Man*), literally set the "stage" for a model of life in eight stages with specific psychological tasks to accomplish in each chronologically segmented stage. For further reading see Erik H. Erikson, "Identity and the Life Cycle: Selected Papers" in *Psychological Issues*, 1 (1): 5–165. Erikson did caution not to take these too literally. In fact his wife, Joan Erikson, speaks of a tapestry to illustrate the interweaving of all the different threads of development. Also see Erik Erikson, "On Generativity and Identity: From a Conversation with Erik and Joan Erikson," *Harvard Educational Review*, 51(2): 249–69 and *Childhood and Society*, 2d ed. (New York: Norton, 1963), 270–71.

2. Erik Erikson, "From This Point of View," in *Identity: Youth and Crisis* (New York: Norton, 1968), 267. The full quotation is in a discussion of woman's "inner space," the psychoanalytic perspective on female psychology. The statement appeared in a discussion of an adaptive point of view that pointed out the limitations of focusing on what is not there.

3. Daniel Levinson, in his studies of the "seasons" of a man's life, focused on individuation and achievement in his perspective on "life structures" in adult development. George Vaillant stated that adult adjustment was related to occupation, based on his longitudinal study on Harvard males. He concluded that "a man's capacity to remain happily married over time" is the strongest indicator of mental health. Of course no one interviewed the wives in the study; we wonder what their responses would look like. Roger Gould was the first to include women in his studies, writing about "adult consciousness" as an evolving process. Gail Sheehy included the work of Gould and Levinson as support for her interviews; in writing the interviews of both men and women she wrote about the exclusion of women. For

further reading here see Daniel Levinson in collaboration with D. N. Darrow, E. B. Klein, M. H. Levinson, and B. McKee, *The Seasons of a Man's Life* (New York: Knopf, 1978); George Vaillant, *Adaptation to Life* (Boston: Little, Brown, 1977); and Roger Gould, *Transformations: Growth and Change in Adult Life* (New York: Simon & Schuster, 1978).

4. Vaillant, *Adaptation to Life,* 320.

5. Erikson, *Identity: Youth and Crisis,* 292.

6. Bernice L. Neugarten, "Time, Age, and the Life Cycle," *American Journal of Psychiatry,* 136 (1979): 887–94.

7. Elsa Frenkel-Brunswik studied under Charlotte Buhler, a prominent developmental psychologist and credited her teacher. For further study see Elsa Frenkel-Brunswik, "Studies in Biographical Psychology," in *Character and Personality,* 5 (1936): 1–35.

8. Beauvoir, Simone de, *The Second Sex,* trans. and ed. H. M. Parshley (New York: Knopf, 1953).

9. The original *Ms.* became financially strapped and faced women's complaints and subscription cancellations due to offensive advertising messages. As I write this, *Ms.* has had its welcome rebirth with Robin Morgan and Gloria Steinem and without advertising!

10. Rachel T. Hare-Mustin, "A Feminist Approach to Family Therapy," *Family Process,* 17, no. 2 (1978): 181–94.

11. Marianne Walters, Betty Carter, Peggy Papp, and Olga Silverstein, *The Invisible Web* (New York: Guilford, 1988).

12. Gilligan asserts women's sense of morality arises from being connected. She has continued her studies on the lives of girls and women. For further study see Carol Gilligan, *In a Different Voice: Psychological Theory and Women's Development* (Cambridge, MA: Harvard University Press, 1982). For reading on the work at the Center for the Study of Gender Education and Human Development at Harvard, see Carol Gilligan, Janie Victoria Ward, Jill McLean Taylor, eds., with Betty Bardige, *Mapping the Moral Domain* (Cambridge, MA: Harvard University Press, 1988).

13. Their ongoing work is entitled *Work in Progress* and is published at the Stone Center for Developmental Services and Studies at Wellesley College. For further reading see Mary F. Belenky, Blythe Clinchy, Nancy Goldberger, and Jill Tarule, *Women's Way of Knowing: Development of Self, Voice and Mind* (New York: Basic, 1986). For women in therapy see Thelma J. Goodrich, Cheryl Rampage, Barbara Ellman, and Kris Halstead, *Feminist Family Therapy: A Casebook* (New York: Norton, 1988).

14. Rachel Hare-Mustin continually examines the psychology and construction of gender. For further reading see Rachel T. Hare-Mustin and Jeanne Maracek, eds., *Making a Difference* (New Haven, CT: Yale University Press, 1990).

15. Hare-Mustin, "A Feminist Approach to Family Therapy."

16. Merle A. Fossum and Marilyn J. Mason, *Facing Shame: Families in Recovery* (New York: Norton, 1986).
17. Lorie Dwinell referred to this as she described the "adult children" movement and Claudia Black, Claudia Bepko, and Jo-Ann Krestan addressed the dysfunctional and alcoholic family at the annual meeting of the American Family Therapy Association, Colorado Springs, Colorado, June 1989.

Chapter 1
I'M AN ADULT WOMAN:
Why Don't I Feel Grown Up?

1. *Oxford Dictionary of English Etymology* (New York: Oxford University Press, 1966), s.v. "crisis."
2. Chungliang Al Huang, *Quantum Soup* (New York: Dutton, 1983), 5.
3. Florida Scott-Maxwell, *The Measure of My Days* (New York: Penguin, 1968), 65.
4. Simone de Beauvoir, *The Second Sex* (New York: Bantam, 1961).
5. Anne Wilson Schaef, *Women's Reality* (Minneapolis, MN: Winston, 1981).
6. Rachel Hare-Mustin, "Family Change and Gender Differences: Implications for Theory and Practice," *Family Relations* 37 (1988): 36–41.
7. Ibid., 36.
8. Claudia Bepko and Jo-Ann Krestan, *Too Good for Her Own Good* (New York: Harper & Row, 1990).
9. Betty Carter and Monica McGoldrick, eds., *The Changing Family Life Cycle: A Framework for Family Therapy* (New York: Gardner, 1988), 53. Many women, including Bernice Neugarten and Jessie Bernard, have found this in their studies.
10. Lillian Rubin, *Intimate Strangers* (New York: Harper & Row, 1983), 52. Here is an excellent description of the British object relations school. Melanie Klein pioneered in going beyond Freud by focusing not just childhood experience but the interplay between the individual and society. For further reading see Melanie Klein, *Contributions to Psycho-analysis, 1921–1945* (London: Hogarth, 1948).
11. Beth Erickson and Charme Davidson, "Grief Issues in Therapy" (paper delivered at the annual meeting of the American Association of Marriage and Family Therapy, San Francisco, California, October 1989).
12. Harriet Goldhor Lerner, "Problems for Profit," *The Women's Review of Books*, 7, no. 7 (April 1990): 15–16.
13. Marianne Walters, "The Codependent Cinderella Who Loves Too Much . . . Fights Back," *The Family Therapy Networker* (July/August 1990): 52–55.

14. Erik Erikson, *Childhood and Society,* 2d ed. (New York: Norton, 1963). Erik Erikson designated eight major tasks that must be met in the "stages" of development. While presented in orderly "steps," Erikson warns against making this too neat a picture. (It is noteworthy that Daniel Goleman in 1988 explained that although Erik Erikson and Joan Erikson did the life-cycle theory jointly, it is his name alone that appears in the literature.)

15. Carol Gilligan, *In a Different Voice: Psychological Theory and Women's Development* (Cambridge, MA: Harvard University Press, 1982), 155.

16. Mary Baird Carlsen, *Meaning Making* (New York: Norton, 1988), 35.

17. *Minneapolis Star-Tribune,* 4 October 1988.

18. Robert C. Aylmer, "The Launching of the Single Young Adult", in Betty Carter and Monica McGoldrick, eds., *The Changing Family Life Cycle,* 2d ed. (New York: Gardner, 1988), 191–208.

19. Gilligan, *In a Different Voice.*

20. Rachel Hare-Mustin and Jeanne Maracek, eds., *Making a Difference* (New Haven, CT: Yale University Press, 1990), 22–64. Hare-Mustin states that it can be dangerous to focus on sex differences with women viewed as relational and men as rational, the Parsonian "instrumental" males and "expressive" females. She challenges Gilligan and Chodorow and the cultural feminists by stating that when we praise women's caring we may be praising women's subordination.

21. Marianne Walters has stated this privately and publicly in June 1990, saying we may recognize that "the social is political."

22. Bepko and Krestan, *Too Good for Her Own Good,* 36. These authors caution women against buying into the "overresponsibility trap" and remaining caught in the "superwoman syndrome."

23. *Oxford Dictionary of English Etymology* (New York: Oxford University Press, 1966), s.v. "compete."

24. *American Heritage Encyclopedic Dictionary* (Boston: Houghton Mifflin, 1987), s.v. "season." For further reading on the "seasons" concept in adult development, see Daniel Levinson, *The Seasons of a Man's Life* (New York: Knopf, 1978).

25. It is noteworthy that the very word "season" comes from the Middle English "sesoun," which came from the Latin for "sowing time."

26. Scott-Maxwell, *The Measure of My Days,* 65.

27. Barbara Walker, *The Woman's Encyclopedia of Myths and Secrets* (San Francisco: Harper & Row, 1983), 344–45.

28. Marion Woodman, *The Pregnant Virgin* (Toronto: Inner City, 1985), 168.

29. Susanne Langer, *Philosophy in a New Key: A Study in the Symbolism of Reason, Rite, and Art* (Cambridge, MA: Harvard University Press, 1942).

30. Bepko and Krestan, *Too Good for Her Own Good. Newsweek* (16 July 1990,

48) in a cover story reported that the average American woman spends seventeen years raising children and eighteen years helping aging parents.

31. Woodman, *The Pregnant Virgin*, 154.

32. When adults seem to be on "automatic pilot" in blind loyalty to the family's unconscious, I often suggest they work toward making the unconscious conscious. One valuable resource is by Claudia Black, *Repeat After Me* (Denver, CO: M.A.C. Printing, 1985).

33. There are several references stating that an old nurse, "alte Maria," was the source for approximately one-third of the original Grimm collection. For in-depth reading about the fairy tales and their influence see Madonna Kolbenschlag, *Kiss Sleeping Beauty Goodbye*, 2d ed. (San Francisco: Harper & Row, 1988), 4. Other writers revealed that Wilhelm Grimm's wife, Dortchen, gave them the legend "Rumpelstiltzken" and young Marie Hassenpflug gave them "Snow White and the Seven Dwarfs." For further information see Robert Zinti, "A Celebration of Enchantment," in *Time*, 21 January 1985, 41.

34. Jack Zipes, "Child Abuse and Happy Endings," *New York Times Book Review*, 13 November 1988. For further information see Kim Ode, "Between Bathtime and Bedtime," *Star Tribune*, 25 February 1989, Variety. Zipes points out that perhaps these stories were written and told to expose the shame adults feel about their cruel behaviors toward children. He points out that expert Bruno Bettelheim's work is so well received because we want to prevent ourselves from seeing our contradictory attitudes toward children. Zipes points out that the Grimm brothers consciously changed mothers into stepmothers to protect "mothers."

35. Mary K. Richards, *Centering* (Middletown, CT: Wesleyan University Press, 1964), 92.

36. This term was used by Janet Hagberg and Dick Leider to describe their work in life and career renewal. See Janet Hagberg and Richard Leider, *The Inventurers* (Reading, MA: Addison-Wesley, 1987).

37. Jill Purce, *The Mystic Spiral* (London: Thames and Hudson, 1974), 7.

38. Joan Gould, *Spirals* (New York: Penguin, 1988), 7.

39. Carlsen, *Meaning Making*, 79.

40. Bernice Neugarten, "Time, Age, and the Life Cycle," *American Journal of Psychiatry* 136 (1979): 887–894. For further reading see *The Changing Family Life Cycle*, eds. Betty Carter and Monica McGoldrick (New York: Gardner Press, 1988).

41. Gail Sheehy, *Passages* (New York: Dutton, 1976). Several writers have continued the argument against linear developmental formulas about adult development, recognizing that crises are not "predictable" as Gail Sheehy implied in *Passages*. In *Grown-Ups* (New York: Putnam, 1987) Cheryl Merser, writing about those born after World War II, points out that the forms adulthood is taking are less limited than they were in previous generations.

42. Francine Klagsbrun, review of *Grown-Ups* by Cheryl Merser, *The New York Times Book Review*, 18 October 1987, 11.

43. Gilligan, *In a Different Voice*, 129.

Chapter 2
MOVING OUT IS NOT LEAVING HOME:
The Challenge of Leaving Home

1. Carl Whitaker has often said there is no such thing as an individual; we are all "family fragments." He has said this in personal conversations as well as in the Master Class series he presented in St. Paul, Minnesota, at the Family Therapy Institute during 1979.

2. Rene Schwartz, "Family of Origin: A Journey Home Again" (paper presented at the Family Therapy Institute's fifteenth anniversary conference in June 1985).

3. See Ivan Boszormenyi-Nagy, *Invisible Loyalties* (New York: Harper & Row, 1973). In his book he states that our loyalties to parents and grandparents keep us "stuck" in limiting relationship patterns as parents and spouses. He refers to this as the "original loyalty."

4. Virginia Satir, *The New Peoplemaking* (Mountain View, CA: Science and Behavior Books, 1988), 53.

5. It is essential that we recognize that fusion and distance are opposite sides of the same coin. "Fusion" or "enmeshment" has typically been misused in therapy to refer to closeness in relationships, especially by females. Women who are concerned with the "connecting" in their relationships are therefore devalued, blamed by themselves and their therapists. The Women's Project in Family Therapy has forced the family therapy profession to examine gender patterns in families and in therapy. For a thorough discussion of this see Marianne Walters, Betty Carter, Peggy Papp, and Olga Silverstein, "Redefinitions," *The Invisible Web* (New York: Guilford, 1988), 20–21.

6. I want to point out that I am not talking about the natural flow of love between parent and child; I am referring to the desperate neediness of the parent whose energy is focused vertically instead of horizontally (with one's own generation).

7. Jessie Bernard writes about "his marriage" and "her marriage." In 1973 Jessie Bernard wrote about the very different satisfaction levels of men and women in marriage. See Jessie Bernard, *The Future of Marriage* (New York: Bantam, 1973), 209.

8. Gus Napier, *The Fragile Bond* (New York: Harper & Row, 1988). Gus Napier wrote about the changes in his own marriage to his wife, Margaret. In addition, he has given major addresses and workshops on this subject and has

been a major voice in discussing mutuality in marriage. Perhaps he is the only male on the lecture circuit addressing male narcissism. For further reading on men and therapy read *Men in Therapy* by Rob Pasick and Richard Meth (New York: Guilford, 1990).

9. Marianne Walters has said this many times. One of the recent occasions was a workshop in Minneapolis, Minnesota, for the Social Workers Conference "Mothers and Daughters" (co-led with her daughter Suzanna Walters), June 1989.

10. Anne Richardson Roiphe, "Up the Sandbox," in Sharan B. Merriam, ed., *Themes of Adulthood Through Literature* (New York: Columbia University Press, 1983), 114–15.

11. Several writers have stated this; it reflects object relations theory, describing how our early life internalizations go with us into our adult lives.

12. Different terms are used to describe what I refer to as "intrafamily marriage." For further reading about "pathological interdependences" that result from enmeshment see Robert Aylmer, "The Launching of the Single Young Adult," in Betty Carter and Monica McGoldrick, eds., *The Changing Family Life Cycle: A Framework for Family Therapy* (New York: Gardner, 1988), 203.

13. In writing about the politics of talk, several writers are discussing the incidence of clinical depression and learned helplessness among women. See Mary Belenky, Blythe Clinchy, Nancy Goldberger, and Jill Tarule, *Women's Way of Knowing: Development of Self, Voice and Mind* (New York: Basic, 1986), 167.

14. While role loss is associated with depression (many homemaker women are out of "jobs" at mid-life), the reason Jewish women experience higher rates of depression is due to the very important mother-children relationship, the most important tie in the traditional Jewish family. For in-depth reading, see Vivian Gornick and Barbara Moran, eds., *Women in Sexist Society* (New York: New American Library, 1971), 178.

15. Depression in women has often been linked to women's socialization to be helpless and dependent. But Lillian Rubin points out it is much more than the stereotype in that interpretation. In *Women of a Certain Age* (New York: Harper & Row, 1979), she states that even though the research shows that most women do not grieve and despair the departure of children and are in fact often relieved, the myth prevails (228). In *The Changing Family Life Cycle* (New York: Gardner, 1988), editors Betty Carter and Monica McGoldrick also state that women are often thankful for the new opportunities in work and social life that become available. Lillian Rubin found that most women were looking forward to their own time in life. Grace Baruch, Rosalind Barnett, and Caryl Rivers differ with Maggie Scarf's premise about depression and women—that it stems from relationship problems. These writers state that depression is closely related to work life and that the best

preventive is for women to develop their sense of mastery. See Baruch, Barnett, and Rivers *Lifeprints* (New York: Signet, 1983). For Maggie Scarf's perspective, read *Unfinished Business* (New York: Knopf, 1978).

16. I chose the term "desperate dependency" to denote the negative aspect of dependency. Too often "dependency" has been viewed as negative and womanly. I refer here to the dependency continuum with desperate dependency at one end, interdependence in the mid range, and exaggerated independence at the opposite end.

17. Here I have taken from the work of D. Nevill in Irene H. Frieze, Jacquelynne E. Parsons, Paula B. Johnson, Diane N. Ruble, and Gail L. Zellman, *Women and Sex Roles* (New York: Norton, 1978), 54. We currently seem stuck with a no-win meaning for the word "dependency" due to the overvaluing of men's "apparent" independence. Women have learned to take care of men's need for nurturing with little in return.

18. E. E. Maccoby and C. N. Jacklin, "The Psychology of Sex Differences," in Frieze et al., *Women and Sex Roles*, 55.

19. The dependency, however, is not always apparent. We frequently see women who are "apparently independent" or what we call "aggressive victims," who have survived by acting totally independent, masking the needy child within.

20. Rene Schwartz, "Family of Origin."

21. Don Williamson talks about "peerhood" as becoming more equal with our parents. He writes about giving up the need to be parented and that when we do we can go deeper into the self and can "transcend the boundaries of the self." This comes from "Thirty Something: Falling in Love (Again) with One's Own Former Parents" (plenary address at the American Family Therapy Association in Montreal, June 1987).

Chapter 3
HOW DO I LOVE ~~THEE~~ ME:
The Challenge of Facing Shame and Finding the Self

1. Rene Daumal, *Mt. Analogue: A Non-Euclidian Adventure in Mountain Climbing* (Baltimore, MD: Penguin, 1974), 42.

2. Thomas Patrick Malone and Patrick Thomas Malone, "Selficide," *Pilgrimage* 15, no. 1 (January/February 1989).

3. Jean Paul Sartre, *Being and Nothingness*, trans. H. E. Barnes (New York: Philosophical Library, 1956), 222.

4. Daniel Goleman, "Shame Steps Out of Hiding and into Sharper Focus," *New York Times*, 15 September 1987, 23.

5. Merle A. Fossum and Marilyn J. Mason, *Facing Shame: Families in Recovery* (New York: Norton, 1986), 5.

6. Research on shame is being conducted by David Cook at the University of Wisconsin–Stout. He has developed the Internalized Shame Scale (ISS). In his unpublished manuscript, "Internalized Shame Scale" (February 1989), Dr. Cook states (p. 3) his research shows that women experience more shame than men.

7. The shame affect is built in, before language. Shame itself is not pathological; it is seen as a developmental ability greatly affected by a family's response to a child. Many writers state that in infancy shame is a primal energy. See Louis H. Stewart, "Affect and Archetype in Analysis," *Archetypal Processes in Psychotherapy*, eds. Nathan Schwartz-Salant and Murray Stein (Pittsburgh, PA: Chiron, 1987), 132.

8. Cook, "Internalized Shame Scale."

9. In a telephone conversation with David Cook in spring 1989, he stated that since women tend to be much more sensitive to relationships and since shame is experienced in relationship, women feel responsible when relationships end. Cook suggested that perhaps this is why women's alienation scores are higher than men's.

10. Merle Fossum often stated this in our shame workshops at Family Therapy Institute; I added "ageist."

11. Stephanie Brown at Stanford Alcohol Clinic, who did the earliest work with children of alcoholics and their intimacy struggles, reported this quotation from a member of the group who was describing her family's rules.

12. Fossum and Mason, *Facing Shame*, 86.

13. Ibid.

14. Gloria Steinem said this at the Chart-Wedco Conference in Minneapolis, Minnesota, 14 August 1990.

15. Often I ask clients to write their "family rules" as a way to understand the silent grip they hold on us. These rules, which also apply to overresponsible males, were adapted from the list of a generous client who gave me permission to use them here.

16. Fossum and Mason, *Facing Shame*, 71.

17. David Finkelhor, *Sexually Victimized Children* (New York: Free Press, 1979). One out of three girls is abused by age eighteen. See Ellen Bass and Laura Davis, *Courage to Heal* (New York: Harper & Row, 1988), 20.

18. Carol Gilligan quoted Toni Morrison's writing about "love" as the hiding place for violence at the Family Therapy Networker Conference, February 1989.

19. Richard Gelles, *The Violent Home* (Beverly Hills, CA: Sage, 1974). See Charlotte Kasl, *Women, Sex and Addiction* (New York: Ticknor and Fields, 1989), 200.

20. Ntozake Shange, *For Colored Girls Who Have Considered Suicide When the Rainbow Is Enuf* (New York: Bantam, 1980), 52–54.

21. Virginia Satir, *The New Peoplemaking* (Mountain View, CA: Science and Behavior Books, 1988), 118.

22. Nell Noddings, *Caring: A Feminine Approach to Ethics and Moral Education* (Berkeley and Los Angeles: University of California Press, 1984), 73. Here she discusses Buber's concept of "one caring" and "one cared for" and reciprocity in relationships. David Berenson also writes and speaks about Buber in his articles and lectures on spirituality.

23. The concept of "received knowledge" refers to listening to the voices of others and attributing their knowledge to outside "authorities" as sources of the truth. To read further about the different ways in which women view their reality and interpret "truth, knowledge and authority" see Mary F. Belenky, Blythe M. Clinchy, Nancy R. Goldberger, and Jill M. Tarule, *Women's Way of Knowing: Development of Self, Voice and Mind* (New York: Basic, 1986), 35–51.

24. Belenky et al., *Women's Way of Knowing*, 36. Many women report struggle with accepting their own trauma response when they have witnessed a sibling's sexual abuse. They therefore often have difficulty in acknowledging their own buried feelings and pain.

25. This is the phrase to describe "self-in-relation" theory. Since women's sense of self is organized around connecting and relationships, it is necessary to develop new language to reflect different ways of thinking. For further study see Janet L. Surrey, "Self-in-Relation: A Theory of Women's Development," *Work in Progress No. 13* (Wellesley, MA: Stone Center for Developmental Services and Studies, Wellesley College, 1985), 2.

26. Ibid.

27. Noddings, *Caring*.

28. The language of "false self" and "ideal self" comes from object relations theory. The defensive false self protects the painful past and the "real self" consists of all our self-images. Here I have used the word "ideal" self to refer to the ethical standards we set for our "selves." These are the standards that, when violated, can induce shame. For further reading see James F. Masterson, *The Search for the Real Self* (New York: Free Press, 1988).

29. Fossum and Mason, *Facing Shame*.

30. Surrey, "Self-in-Relation."

Chapter 4
FROM ANONYMOUS SELF TO TRUE SELF:
The Challenge of Forging an Identity

1. Jane Middleton-Moz and Lorie Dwinell, *After the Tears* (Deerfield Beach, FL: Health Communications, 1985). For specific issues concerning those who have grown up in alcoholic families (Adult Children of Alcoholics) in

addition to other issues such as eating disorders and sexual abuse, see Claudia Black, *Double Duty* (New York: Ballantine, 1990).

2. Carol Gilligan, Family Therapy Network Conference, Feb. 1989. Also see Carol Gilligan, Janie Victoria Ward, Jill McLean Taylor, eds. with Betty Bardige, *Mapping the Moral Domain* (Cambridge, MA: Harvard University Press, 1988), 290.

3. Dick Gregory, *No More Lies* (New York: Harper & Row, 1971).

4. Empathy is primary in working therapeutically with women who were emotionally orphaned in the parent-child relationship. Empathy can be learned and transferred to other relationships. For thorough discussion see Judith V. Jordan, Janet L. Surrey, and Alexandra G. Kaplan, "Women and Empathy," *Work in Progress No. 82–02* (Wellesley, MA: Stone Center for Developmental Services and Studies, Wellesley College, 1983), 15.

5. Marianne and Suzanna presented their material on "Mothers and Daughters" in a workshop in Minneapolis, Minnesota, in 1989.

6. For full discussion see Marianne Walters, Betty Carter, Peggy Papp, and Olga Silverstein, *The Invisible Web* (New York: Guilford, 1988).

7. Brunetta R. Wolfman, "Women and Their Many Roles," in *Work in Progress No. 83–03* (Wellesley, MA: Stone Center for Developmental Services and Studies, Wellesley College, 1984), 3.

8. Ibid.

9. Janet L. Surrey, "Self-in-Relation: A Theory of Women's Development," *Work in Progress No. 13* (Wellesley, MA: Stone Center for Developmental Services and Studies, Wellesley College, 1985).

10. This was stated in a talk I heard in Minneapolis by Meridel LeSueur at the Minnesota Worldwide Women Gala, September 1989.

11. This entry into men's world was symbolic of women's other-directedness and attempting to join the white, male system in order to gain status.

12. Carole J. Chandler, "ACAs: The Paradox and the Dilemma," *EAP Digest* (November/December 1987), 3.

13. Surrey, "The Self-in-Relation."

14. Carol Gilligan (plenary lecture, Family Networker Conference, Washington, D. C., February 1989).

15. Gilligan, *In a Different Voice*, 168.

16. The concept of self has received much attention, especially since it is so prevalent in Western thinking. Yet the notion of "self" doesn't match women's experience. As mentioned in Chapter 1, current models have not worked for men either. See Jean Baker Miller, *Toward a New Psychology of Women* (Boston: Beacon, 1976). Dr. Miller headed up the Stone Center at Wellesley and in her early writings joined others in addressing the question, "Can women have a self?" Since the adult development writers all wrote about development as separating ourselves out from others, we grew up with

a model for men that did not fit women or include their experiences. Many writers tried to fit women into the models; the models told us where we should be. As women we have had to remind ourselves that these are literally man-made "mental representations."

17. Rachel Hare-Mustin has stated this in several personal and public discussions from 1978 to the present.

18. This was stated in David Berenson's lecture, "Spirituality" at the Family Networker Conference, Washington, D. C., February 1989.

19. Gilligan, *In a Different Voice.*

20. This information came from the research of Dr. Josette Mandanaro at Wingspread (women's health care center) in Santa Cruz, California, 1981. It has long been known that women receive a disproportionate amount of drug prescriptions for both physical and mental conditions. See L. S. Fidell, "Put Her on Drugs: Prescribed Drug Usage in Women" (paper presented at the meeting of the Eastern Psychological Association, May 1973), in "The Meaning of Care: Reframing Treatment Models," *Work in Progress No. 20* (Wellesley, MA: Stone Center for Developmental Services and Studies, Wellesley College, 1985), 9.

21. Harriet Goldhor Lerner, *The Dance of Anger* (New York: Harper & Row, 1989).

22. Henrik Ibsen, *A Doll's House,* in Sharan Merriam, ed., *Themes of Adulthood Through Literature* (New York: Teachers College Press, 1983).

23. Carl Whitaker in private discussion and consultation, 1981.

Chapter 5
EMBODYING OUR BEING:
The Challenge of Sexual-Spiritual Integration

1. This definition was one we used in the Program in Human Sexuality, Department of Family Practice, University of Minnesota, in the Sexual Attitude Reassessment Program from 1974 to 1984.

2. Thelma Jean Goodrich, Cheryl Rampage, Barbara Ellman, and Kris Halstead, *Feminist Family Therapy: A Casebook* (New York: Norton, 1988).

3. Dorothy Tennov, *Love and Limerence* (New York: Stein and Day, 1979).

4. Ibid., 23–24.

5. Ibid., 74.

6. Harvey Milkman and Stanley Sunderwirth, *Craving for Ecstasy* (Lexington, MA: Lexington, 1987).

7. Dorothy Parker, "Symptom Recital," *Enough Rope: Poems* (New York: Liveright, 1926).

8. Antoine Saint Exupery, *The Little Prince* (San Diego, CA: Harcourt Brace Jovanovich, 1943), 87.

9. Tennov, *Love and Limerence*, 214.

10. Ibid., 210.

11. Goodrich et al., *Feminist Family Therapy*.

12. Ibid.

13. Sociologist Jesse Bernard writes about the difference between "his" marriage and "her" marriage in *The Future of Marriage* (New Haven, CT: Yale University Press, 1982). Bernard's research highlights women's dilemma: while marriage matters more to women than to men and therefore they make more adjustments and sacrifices for marriage, they are still less happy with their marriages. To review more on this read Monica McGoldrick, "Women and the Family Life Cycle," in Betty Carter and Monica McGoldrick, eds., *The Changing Family Life Cycle: A Framework for Family Therapy* (New York: Gardner, 1988).

14. Goodrich et al., *Feminist Family Therapy*, 72.

15. Diane Barthel, *Putting on Appearances: Gender and Advertising* (Philadephia: Temple University Press, 1988). Quoted by Judith Goldstein in "Z," May 1989.

16. David Finkelhor, *Sexually Victimized Children* (New York: Free Press, 1979). For further reading see Charlotte Kasl, *Women, Sex, and Addiction* (New York: Ticknor and Fields, 1989), 39.

17. Carol Gilligan (plenary lecture, Family Networker Conference, Washington, D. C., February 1989).

18. Meridel LeSueur (Minnesota Worldwide Women Fund-raiser, Fine Line Cafe, Minneapolis, Minnesota, April 1988).

19. B. Volicer, "Variation in Length of Time to Development of Alcoholism by Family History of Problem Drinking," *Drug and Alcohol Dependence* 12, no. 1 (1983): 69–83.

20. Charlotte Kasl, *Women, Sex and Addictions* (New York: Ticknor and Fields, 1989).

21. Ellen Bass and Laura Davis, *The Courage to Heal* (New York: Harper & Row, 1988).

22. Jo-Ann Krestan said this in her talk on addicted families at the American Family Therapy Association Conference, Colorado Springs, Colorado, June 1989.

23. Many women have stated they felt more comfortable with Women for Sobriety groups in which the language used is inclusive. These groups are available in all major cities throughout the country.

24. Milkman and Sundwirth, *Craving for Ecstasy*, 44–49.

25. Ibid.

26. Ibid.

27. Eli Coleman, "Family Intimacy and Chemical Abuse: The Connection," *Journal of Psychoactive Drugs* 14 (1–2): 153–157.

28. Ibid.

29. Lois Braverman spoke about women's friendships in the Women's Institute at American Family Therapy Conference, Colorado Springs, Colorado, June 1989.

30. Simone de Beauvoir, *The Second Sex* (New York: Bantam, 1961), 382.

31. Jessie Potter speaks often about the clitoris as a forgotten word. "Clitoris: Still a Forbidden Word," in *Contemporary Sexuality*, vol. 21, no. 10, Nov. 1989. Also, see Harriet Goldhor Lerner's "Vulva Consciousness," 1989.

32. Stephanie S. Covington, "Physical, Emotional and Sexual Abuse," in *Focus on Family and Chemical Dependency* 9, no. 3 (May/June 1986), 42.

33. Ibid.

34. Judith Herman, cited in Covington, "Physical, Emotional and Sexual Abuse," p. 43.

35. Ibid.

36. Bass and Davis, *Courage to Heal*, 96.

37. Covington, "Physical, Emotional and Sexual Abuse," 11.

38. Ibid.

39. Ibid.

40. Ibid.

41. For further reading see Gilligan, *In a Different Voice*, 59.

42. Deborah Anna Luepnitz, *The Family Interpreted* (New York: Basic, 1989), 130.

43. Ibid.

44. Frederick Humphrey, "Treating Extramarital Sexual Relationships in Sex and Couples Therapy," in Gerald Weeks and Larry Hof, eds., *Integrating Sex and Marital Therapy* (New York: Brunner/Mazel, 1987).

45. This notion was the foundation for several articles that appeared in women's magazines, including *Ms*.

46. Pauline Boss, "A Clarification of the Concept of Psychological Father Presence in Families Experiencing Ambiguity of Boundary," *Journal of Marriage and the Family* 39, no. 1 (Feb. 1977): 141–51. For further reading see Pauline Boss and J. Pamela Weiner, "Rethinking Assumptions About Women's Development and Family Therapy," in C. J. Falicov, ed., *Family Interactions: Continuity and Change Over the Life Cycle* (New York: Guilford, 1988), 235–52.

47. Thompson, K., *Esalen Catalog* (Big Sur, CA: Esalen, 1985).

48. William Masters, Virginia Johnson, and Robert Kolodny, *On Sex and Human Loving* (Boston: Little, Brown, 1986), 536.

49. Ibid., 554–55.

50. This statement is common sense, yet many women need to be reminded that this does not mean there is something wrong with them; the statistics are against them.

51. Carol Connolly, "Last Resort," *Payments Due* (Minneapolis, MN: Midwest Villages and Voices, 1985), 22.
52. This was quoted by James B. Nelson in a talk on "Family Sexuality" at the International Family Sexuality Conference in Minneapolis, Minnesota, June 1982.
53. David Olson and Mark T. Schaefer at the University of Minnesota were the first to define the differences (1978).
54. James B. Nelson, *Between Two Gardens* (New York: Pilgrim, 1983), 84.
55. Joanie Gustafson, *Celibate Passion* (New York: Harper & Row, 1978).
56. Pepper Schwartz and Phillip Blumstein, *American Couples* (New York: Pocket, 1985).
57. Many countries have referred to clitoridectomies as "female circumcision" rather than genital mutilation.

Chapter 6
STANDING UP AND SPEAKING OUT:
The Challenge of Expressing Personal Power

1. Betty Friedan, *The Feminine Mystique* (New York: Dell, 1963); Jean Baker Miller, *Toward a New Psychology of Women* (Boston: Beacon, 1976).
2. Carol Gilligan, *In a Different Voice* (Cambridge, MA: Harvard University Press, 1982).
3. *Oxford Dictionary of English Etymology* (New York: Oxford University Press, 1966), s.v. "power."
4. Janet Hagberg, *Real Power* (Minneapolis, MN: Winston, 1984), 19.
5. Mary F. Belenky, Blythe M. Clinchy, Nancy R. Goldberger, and Jill M. Tarule, *Women's Way of Knowing: Development of Self, Voice and Mind* (New York: Basic, 1986), 53.
6. Riane Eisler, *The Chalice and the Blade* (San Francisco: Harper & Row, 1988), 28.
7. Hagberg, *Real Power*, 201.
8. Bell Hooks, *Talking Back* (Boston: South End, 1989), 9.
9. Eisler, *The Chalice and the Blade*, 20.
10. Crystos, quoted in *A Woman's Journal* (Philadelphia, Running Press, 1985).
11. Hooks, *Talking Back*.
12. Gilligan, *In a Different Voice*.
13. The Serenity Prayer is published in *Fifty Years with Gratitude* (New York: Alcoholics Anonymous World Service, 1985).
14. Simone de Beauvoir, *The Second Sex* (New York: Bantam, 1961).
15. Marguerite Ickes, quoted in *A Woman's Journal* (Philadelphia: Running Press, 1985).

16. Rhoda Levin, author of *Heartmates: A Survival Guide for Cardiac Spouses* (New York: Prentice Hall, 1987), was the first person I heard use this word.

17. Constance Ahrons, divorce researcher, in personal conversation, 1989. Also, see *Demography Journal*, where the National Center for Health Statistics publishes its findings. In the *Capitol Bulletin #390*, 22 March 1989, research cited that the marriage rate in the United States is about double the divorce rate.

18. "Mirror: Divorce Rate Nearly Doubled in 10 Years" *Minneapolis Tribune*, 2 May 1989.

19. This term was coined by Constance Ahrons, whose divorce research was published in several articles. For further reading see Constance Ahrons and Roy Rodgers, *Divorced Families: A Multi-Disciplinary Developmental View* (New York: Norton, 1987).

20. "Mirror," *Minneapolis Tribune*.

21. Personal conversation with Constance Ahrons, 1989.

22. I first heard the term "family of affiliation" in graduate work at the University of Minnesota in courses taught by Richard Hey.

23. Florida Scott-Maxwell, *The Measure of My Days* (New York: Penguin, 1979), 66.

24. Carl Whitaker has stated this in several lectures.

25. Lenore Weitzman, *The Divorce Revolution: The Unexpected Social and Economic Consequences for Women and Children in America* (New York: Free Press, 1985). For further discussion on divorce, economics, and women see Sharon Hicks and Carol M. Anderson, "Women on Their Own," in Monica McGoldrick, Carol M. Anderson, and Froma Walsh, eds., *Women in Families* (New York: Norton, 1989).

26. Judith Stern Peck and Jennifer R. Manocherian, "Divorce in the Changing Family Life Cycle," in Betty Carter and Monica McGoldrick, eds., *The Changing Family Life Cycle*, 2d ed. (New York: Gardner, 1988), 342.

27. Eisler, *The Chalice and the Blade*, 197.

28. "Worker, Mother, Wife," *Women, Public Policy and Development Project* pamphlet (Minneapolis, MN: Hubert H. Humphrey Institute of Public Affairs, University of Minnesota, August 1984), 1.

29. Ibid.

30. Ibid.

31. Cynthia Crossen, "The Working Woman's Nightmare," *Wall Street Journal*, 21 June 1989.

32. Ibid.

33. "The Job Market Opens Up for the 68-Cent Woman," *New York Times*, 12 January 1989, 1.

34. Pepper Schwartz and Phillip Blumstein, *American Couples* (New York, Pocket, 1985).

35. Monica McGoldrick (plenary address, American Association for Marriage and Family Therapy Conference, Washington, D. C., 1988).
36. Betty Carter and Monica McGoldrick have both stated this in public and private conversations.
37. Susan Griffin, *Woman and Nature* (New York: Harper & Row, 1978), 53–54.
38. Eisler, *The Chalice and the Blade*, 28.
39. Ibid., 203.
40. Platon, quoted in Eisler, 39
41. Gilligan, *In a Different Voice*, 23–24.
42. Gilligan, *In a Different Voice*, 23
43. Jonathan Schell, *The Fate of the Earth* (New York: Avon, 1982).
44. Oriana Fallaci, *Interview with History* (New York: Houghton Mifflin, 1976), 13.

Chapter 7
DANCING WITH THE GODDESS AND THE WISE WOMAN:
The Soul Shift of the Spirit

1. *Oxford Dictionary of English Etymology* (Oxford, England: Clarendon, 1966), s.v. "religious."
2. Ntozake Shange, *For Colored Girls Who Have Considered Suicide When the Rainbow Is Enuf* (New York: Bantam, 1977), 67.
3. Starhawk, *Dreaming the Dark* (Boston: Beacon, 1988), 4.
4. "The Twelve Steps of AA" are taken from *Alcoholics Anonymous,* 3d ed. (New York: Alcoholics Anonymous World Services, 1976), 59–60.
5. Florida Scott-Maxwell, *The Measure of My Days* (New York: Knopf, 1968), 17.
6. Scott-Maxwell, *The Measure of My Days,* 12.
7. Lorie Dwinell said this in personal communication, August 1990.
8. Carl Jung, quoted in lecture at Lloret de Mer, American Humanistic Psychology Conference, 1978.
9. Barbara G. Walker, *The Woman's Dictionary of Symbols and Sacred Objects* (San Francisco: Harper & Row, 1988), 198.
10. Marion Woodman, *Addiction to Perfection* (Toronto: Inner City, 1982), 74.
11. Ibid.
12. James B. Nelson (Week of Enrichment, University of Minnesota, January 1979).
13. Ibid.
14. This was discussed at Sexuality and Spirituality Workshop in Forres, Scotland, at the Findhorn Foundation, 1978.
15. Isak Dinesen, quoted in Carolyn Heilbrun, "Women Writers: Coming of Age at 50," *New York Times Review of Books,* 4 September 1988, 128.

16. Scott-Maxwell, *The Measure of My Days*, 9–10.
17. Deborah Luepnitz, *The Family Interpreted* (New York: Basic, 1988).
18. Huston Smith said this in our "Philosophy and Art of India" class discussion–study group in Mahabalapuram, India, January 1986.
19. Gerald May, *Will and Spirit* (New York: Harper & Row, 1982), 25.
20. Marion Woodman, *The Pregnant Virgin* (Toronto: Inner City, 1985) 62–65.
21. From lectures on Teilhard de Chardin held in Minneapolis, Minnesota, 1980.
22. Carl Whitaker has stated this in his telephone case consultations during 1976–78 at the Family Therapy Institute in Minneapolis, Minnesota.
23. Henri Nouwen, *Reaching Out* (New York: Doubleday, 1966).
24. Huston Smith, personal conversation, 1986.
25. Heilbrun, "Coming of Age at 50."
26. Starhawk, *The Spiral Dance* (San Francisco: Harper & Row, 1989), 10.
27. Gerald May, *Will and Spirit*, 26–27.
28. *Oxford Dictionary of English Etymology* (Oxford: Clarendon, 1966), s.v. "witch."
29. Ibid., 13.
30. Jack Engler, *Yoga Journal* (September–October 1989), 19.
31. Vicki Noble, quoted in *A Woman's Journal* (Philadelphia: Running Press, 1985).
32. Woodman, *Pregnant Virgin*, 82–85.
33. William Johnston, quoted in Janice Brewi and Anne Brennan, *Midlife: Psychological and Spiritual Perspectives* (New York: Continuum, 1985), 36.
34. Woodman, *Pregnant Virgin*.
35. Maria Kolbenschlag, *Kiss Sleeping Beauty Goodbye*, 2d ed. (San Francisco: Harper & Row, 1988), 193.
36. Ibid.
37. Heilbrun, "Women Writers: Coming of Age at 50," 25.
38. Dick Leider, *The Inventurers* (Reading, MA: Addison-Wesley, 1987), 3.
39. Judith V. Jordan, "Empathy and Self Boundaries," *Work in Progress No. 16* (Wellesley, MA: Stone Center for Developmental Services and Studies, Wellesley College, 1984).
40. Ibid.
41. Eisler, *The Chalice and the Blade*, 193.
42. Willis Harman in Eisler, *The Chalice and the Blade*, 195. From Willis Harman, "The Coming Transformation," *The Futurist* (February 1977): 5–11.
43. Eisler, *The Chalice and the Blade*, 195.
44. Ibid.
45. Starhawk, *Dreaming the Dark*.
46. Toni Morrison, *Song of Solomon* (New York: New American Library, 1977), 149.

SELECTED READINGS

Bass, Ellen, and Laura Davis. *The Courage to Heal.* New York: Harper & Row, 1988.

Beauvoir, Simone de. *The Second Sex.* Translated and edited by H. M. Parshley. New York: Knopf, 1953.

Belenky, Mary F., Blythe M. Clinchy, Nancy R. Goldberger, and Jill M. Tarule. *Women's Way of Knowing: Development of Self, Voice and Mind.* New York: Basic, 1986.

Bepko, Claudia, and Jo-Ann Krestan. *Too Good for Her Own Good.* New York: Harper & Row, 1990.

Black, Claudia. *Double Duty.* New York: Ballantine, 1990.

Carter, Betty, and Monica McGoldrick, eds. *The Changing Family Life Cycle: A Framework for Family Therapy.* New York: Gardner, 1988.

Dickinson, Emily. *The Complete Poems of Emily Dickinson.* Edited by Thomas H. Johnson. Boston: Little, Brown, 1960.

Eisler, Riane. *The Chalice and the Blade.* New York: Harper & Row, 1988.

Fossum, Merle, and Marilyn J. Mason. *Facing Shame: Families in Recovery.* New York: Norton, 1986.

Friedan, Betty. *The Feminine Mystique.* New York: Dell, 1963.

Gilligan, Carol. *In A Different Voice: Psychological Theory and Women's Development.* Cambridge, MA: Harvard University Press, 1982.

Goodrich, Thelma Jean, Cheryl Rampage, Barbara Ellman, and Kris Halstead. *Feminist Family Therapy: A Casebook.* New York: Norton, 1988.

Griffin, Susan. *Woman and Nature.* New York: Harper & Row, 1978.

Gustafson, Joanie. *Celibate Passion.* New York: Harper & Row, 1978.

Hare-Mustin, Rachel T., and Jeanne Maracek, eds., *Making a Difference.* New Haven, CT: Yale University Press, 1990.

Hooks, Bell. *Talking Back.* Boston: South End, 1989.

Jordan, Judith V. "Empathy and Self Boundaries." *Work in Progress No. 16.* Wellesley, MA: Stone Center for Developmental Services and Studies, Wellesley College, 1984.

Kasl, Charlotte Davis. *Women, Sex and Addictions.* New York: Ticknor and Fields, 1989.

Kolbenschlag, Maria. *Kiss Sleeping Beauty Goodbye.* 2d ed. San Francisco: Harper & Row, 1988.

Lerner, Harriet Goldhor. *The Dance of Anger.* New York: Harper & Row, 1989.

Luepnitz, Deborah Anna. *The Family Interpreted.* New York: Basic, 1988.

SELECTED READINGS

Masters, William, Virginia Johnson, and Robert Kolodny. *On Sex and Human Loving*. Boston: Little, Brown, 1986.

McGoldrick, Monica, Carol M. Anderson, and Froma Walsh. *Women in Families*. New York: Norton, 1989.

Milkman, Harvey, and Stanley Sunderwirth. *Craving for Ecstasy*. Lexington, MA: Lexington, 1987.

Miller, Jean Baker. *Toward a New Psychology of Women*. Boston: Beacon, 1976.

Napier, Gus. *The Fragile Bond*. New York: Harper and Row, 1988.

Nelson, James B. *Between Two Gardens*. New York: Pilgrim, 1983.

Noddings, Nell. *Caring: A Feminine Approach to Ethics and Moral Education*. Berkeley and Los Angeles: University of California Press, 1984.

Scott-Maxwell, Florida. *The Measure of My Days*. New York: Penguin, 1968.

Starhawk. *Dreaming the Dark*. Boston: Beacon, 1988.

Surrey, Janet. "The Self-in-Relation: A Theory of Women's Development." *Work in Progress No. 13*, Wellesley, MA: Stone Center for Developmental Services and Studies, Wellesley College, 1985.

Walters, Marianne, Betty Carter, Peggy Papp, and Olga Silverstein. *The Invisible Web*. New York: Guilford, 1988.

Woodman, Marion. *Addiction to Perfection*. Toronto: Inner City, 1982.

———. *The Pregnant Virgin*. Toronto: Inner City, 1985.

INDEX